RON
ON THE

Ronald Eyre, born in 1929 in Staincross, Yorkshire, went to the Queen Elizabeth Grammar School, Wakefield, and read English at University College, Oxford. He was Secretary of the Oxford University Dramatic Society, acted and directed.

From 1952 to 1956 he taught. He joined B.B.C. Television as one of the original quartet of School Television producers and for eight years directed television drama. Most of his writing has been for T.V.

Since 1964 he has worked mainly as a free-lance theatre director in London: at the Royal Court, for the National Theatre, in the West End and for the Royal Shakespeare Company, to which he returns for his first theatre project in four years.

From late 1974 to mid 1978, when he completed this book, he was engaged on the making of *The Long Search*.

RONALD EYRE
ON
THE LONG SEARCH

*Ronald Eyre's own account of a
three-year journey*

COLLINS
Fount Paperbacks

First published in Great Britain by Fount
Paperbacks in 1979 with a larger
hardback edition published by the British
Broadcasting Corporation.

© Text Ronald Eyre 1979

© Illustrations Peter Montagnon, Mischa
Scorer, Paul Godfrey, Jonathan Stedall,
Brian Lewis and Caroline Mackersey, 1979

Made and printed in Great Britain by
William Collins Sons & Co Ltd, Glasgow

Contents

List of Illustrations

Introduction

The easiest answer to the question 'What is *The Long Search* about?' is: 'It's about religion'; though that was an answer I never liked to give. It was conceived as a film series for B.B.C. Television somewhere around 1973, took most of four years to make and was first transmitted between September and December 1977 in thirteen parts. Week by week the *Radio Times* received from *The Long Search* office what was called the billing—the title of the programme, the names of a few of those who had helped it to happen, a short paragraph of enticement and description meant to waylay an audience. Few, I should imagine, noticed certain tell-tale modifications in wording in the course of those three months. For the first eight films, the announcement began: '*The Long Search*—a thirteen-part worldwide film series on man's religious quest.' The next three went: '*The Long Search*—a thirteen-part worldwide series on man's quest for meaning.' The last two read: '*The Long Search*—a thirteen-part worldwide series.' The rest was silence.

There are various explanations for the changes, all of which carry some weight. The first is that the word 'religion' appears to alarm, depress and send to sleep a large section of the British public. If we were to duck under their guard with films that we hoped were neither depressing nor soporific, it became necessary to drop the lethal word. The second is that a change in wording was needed to indicate a change in the feel of the films. The first few made dogged attempts to reflect off small surfaces some of the grandeur of the great religious traditions, whereas most of the later films were not quite so formal. The third is that the work itself changed. To raise money, win support, it had been necessary at the start to make claims which, though made in good faith, did not hold up. If we had had the foresight to describe right at the start the sort of films we would be making by the end, I very much doubt if the series would have gone ahead. Money, time and facilities were made available for a great survey of the religions of the world—encyclopedic, informative, clarificatory, authoritative. The films themselves are exploratory, paradoxical, open-ended. They may not get very far but they get far enough to show that the vision of all the Great Religions of the World laid out like allotments for strangers to poke about in is a great lying mirage.

In many radical ways, *The Long Search* differed from the other grand series that the B.B.C. had attempted. In every other case the writer and guide could properly be rated an authority: Kenneth Clark on painting and architecture, Jacob Bronowski on scientific man, Alistair Cooke on America. It was inevitable that, in the parade of worthy subjects for new series, 'religion' should appear. It was equally inevitable that, whoever was chosen to appear in front of the camera would turn out to be the wrong man. If he professed a faith, he would offend all who professed a different faith. If he professed no faith, he would be dismissed as an all-round outsider. If he were a great authority on religious matters—say, an academic in the field—he would fall victim to those who say that religion is the private concern of ordinary people. If he were no authority, why should anyone give him a hearing? In choosing me, I should say that the B.B.C. were seeking out a certain vacancy, a hole in the middle, a perambulant question mark. For me, it really was a long search—a long search, for a start, for a way of doing *The Long Search*. But it also and secretly happened to coincide with matters on which in some messy way I was already engaged. Which meant that when the

B.B.C. asked me to undertake this particular strange assignment, I could hardly believe my luck.

I was Peter Montagnon's idea. So, in the form in which it finally appeared, was *The Long Search*. He begot it, nursed it, fought off its enemies, taught it to walk, only once nearly lost heart and then only for a moment. Before he produced *The Long Search*, he was the B.B.C.'s Head of the Open University; before his B.B.C. days, a soldier and a spy. He is light-footed and of a gentle demeanour. He is also the toughest, most tenacious man I have ever met. It is characteristic of him that, as I write this, he is packing a light-framed rucksack with three pairs of socks and a minimum of clothing to take a camera team to one of the last uncharted valleys on the borders of Tibet. He has a taste for narrow ledges, heady heights and assignments that are next to impossible.

Out of early consultation came a suggested list of subjects and locations. Out of painful trial and error emerged two highly talented collaborators, Mischa Scorer and Jonathan Stedall, who shared the direction of the films, the kick-back from the inevitable disasters, the credit for the thirteen productions that, after four or so years of doubts and queries, did really emerge at the other end.

Out on location we were rarely more than six people: a director, a director's assistant, a cameraman, a camera assistant, a sound recordist, often an electrician, always myself. But the spread of consultation that went on beforehand and the extent of labour that followed involved a small army. Their names will not appear in the text that follows, as it was decided to let this report float free of the series so that it might have a meaning for those who did not see the films. They are listed under Film Acknowledgements at the back of the book. They know that I know that they know the high esteem in which they are held.

As the months and years went on, a certain pattern of work started to evolve, lumpy and agonized at first, more elegant as time went on. Take, as an example of the pattern working smoothly and well, the sequence of events that led to the making of the film *A Question of Balance* in Taiwan. The decision to make a film on what we could find of the religions of China had been taken years ahead in discussions at home. The decision that the film should not be set in mainland China was taken, without consultation with us, by the Government of the People's Republic of China who refused permission. The adviser for the film was Dr Joseph Needham of Cambridge. He was lured to an italianate dive near the Tottenham Court Road and, as part of a series of such meetings, heard what we were hoping to do and offered advice and further names—one of which was that of Dr K. M. Schipper, a Taoist priest who teaches at the Sorbonne. In the meantime, arm's-length arrangements going only so far, two *Long Search* directors who happened to be finishing work in the Far East stayed over at the end of their assignments to visit, one of them, Hong Kong, the other, Taiwan, as a way of assessing the merits of each as the site for the on-coming search. As it turned out, the report from Taiwan was more enthusiastic than that from Hong Kong. Once he was free to take off, Jonathan Stedall, the film's director, following the notes and maps of his pre-decessor, flew to Taiwan to meet people and to collect material for a story-line.

During most of this I was engaged on other films and innocent of all but the sketchiest knowledge of the religions of China. My own homework began with a course of rapid relevant reading, further conversation with Dr Needham and a flight to Paris, where Dr Schipper nailed me to the floor with the depth and enthusiasm of his scholarship and his high hopes for the film which we could eventually bring home. By the time filming began, I had read what I could, including the director's summary of possible places and people to film. He had found, as the *Question of Balance* chapter makes clear, a clutch of outstanding Taiwanese helpers. My own question of balance, both in this film and in all the others, was how to know a little but not too much, how to be open and receptive and not simply vacant, how to know enough to ask the first question but not quite enough to think I knew the answer. In these early days I really did think that goodwill, a mind resolutely open and a painstaking determination to take in whatever lay before me would lead through to the truth. I had yet to understand my own blinkers—North of England, Dissenting, a bit Puritanical, convinced of the virtues of Honesty and Hard Work—and the blinkers of the whole *Long Search* series—Western European, scientific, intrusive, lordly. By what right do I presume to tread on someone else's territory? What makes me imagine that I have it in me to be fair? Shouldn't I know a great deal more about where I stand before I presume to take readings on anybody else? But these were matters for later.

It was always the intention that there should be two *Long Search* books. One was to give a framework of reference in the field of religious studies and was to appear as the films appeared. This was Professor Ninian Smart's *Background to the Long Search*. Inevitably it contains little reference to the films, as the text had to be completed ahead of the journeys. Any detailed account of what shifts, what blockages and what little enlightenments occurred during the search itself had to wait until it was all over and there was time, as now, to sit down and write. The order of the following chapters is not exactly the order in which the *Long Search* films were made or the order in which they have usually been transmitted. Since there is little cross-reference between chapters, the reader who wishes to rearrange them yet again should feel free to do so—except that *Loose Ends* is meant to come last.

For their invaluable help, advice and constant encouragement I should like to thank Nina Coltart, Elsie Herron, John Hosier and Colette King.

1

Protestant Spirit U.S.A.

To emerge from a line of Protestants and go in search of Protestantism is very like a dog chasing its tail. Whenever we went in search of the alien, the exotic, we sought out ways of making it less alien, less exotic. In this case, where the search was for the familiar, the home product, there had to be ways of making it less familiar, less like home. The first precaution was to look for the world's greatest agglomeration of Protestants outside Europe and go there. The U.S.A. offers itself immediately: close on one hundred million practising Protestants in a population of two hundred and sixteen million, and by 'practising' something more energetic and engaged is meant than the nominal Protestantism of large sections of the Protestant population of Europe. Perhaps the biggest shock for anyone from Europe approaching American religion is how centrally it sits in the whole of American life. The religion of America really does seem to be Religion itself, no matter what the denomination. Once inside America, any European knows how far and deep the secularization of Europe has gone. The American picture is not all reassuring. Churches run like big businesses, manipulate the newspapers and the television stations, range in their opinions from utterly conservative red-hunting Fundamentalism to experimental, progressive, risk-taking Liberality. But battles that, in Europe, would be fought entirely secularly, with churchmen looking on and lending a hand where they could, seem in America to be church concerns.

To bring the search into sharp focus it was decided to

pitch it almost entirely in one place and the chosen place was Indianapolis, Indiana, roughly where two lines bisecting the U.S.A. north-south and east-west might cross. The time chosen for the search was the period between Thanksgiving and Christmas; to put it crudely—between the thought that God so loved America and the thought that God so loved the World. Throughout, the shops in the commercial centre of the city advertised their commercial Christmas and in the dead centre, known as the Circle, there were display-boards with Christmas scenes, one showing a wooden New England church with a slender spire and set in a pine forest. Its windows shone warm and bright, and towards it walked a well-heeled church-going family in danger of nothing more lethal than a snowball— he in top hat and frock coat, she in bonnet and crinoline, with diminutive replica children to match. One of the radiating cross-roads that shoot through the Circle and out of town is called Meridian. We stayed there in a rambling, faded, generously proportioned hotel where the windows opened, in preference to the tighter, better appointed air-capsule across the road where they didn't. Once I walked twenty blocks in the out-of-town direction to see a friend. I met one other pedestrian. He was black and, like me, looking sheepish. The tension between the bleak abandonment of the streets by walkers and the message peeling out from the amplifiers at the Circle ('O, hush the noise, ye men of strife, and hear the angels sing') tears the gut apart.

Every Saturday, the Indianapolis papers carry two or three pages of clamorous, tightly-packed church advertisements. They would nearly all be rated Protestant. Sedate Episcopalian and Methodist announcements of times of services are elbowed aside by star-spangled variety ads for independent enterprises. These often carry a photograph of the preacher, the promise of treats, and threats of hell-fire. In the two Fundamentalist churches we chose to explore we became treats ourselves, and the arrival of a B.B.C. camera team was carried by each in their Saturday advertisements. European Christianity, to its cost perhaps, has often found itself the guardian of good taste. Here it is possible to buy a Jesus T.V. and night-light which is a head of the Saviour in frosted glass, a car-sticker reading 'Honk if you love Jesus', small rubber adhesive patches that carry finalities like: 'God said it. I believe it. That settles it.' This pushy advertising style knows exactly what it is doing. It is offering certainty, upwardness and comfort where the pain of their opposites is felt to be too overwhelming and too near.

Two pieces of anchor-work seemed necessary right at the start of the search for Protestantism. One was to bring to the surface a few of the assumptions I was making without knowing that I was making assumptions—what did Protestantism mean to me? The other was to seek the advice of someone who was not merely passing through but had long been observing the American scene. In this way there would be more of a chance of avoiding unconscious doctoring on my part and more of a chance of rising above the area of the search and keeping it in some perspective.

My own Yorkshire, coal-mining, Methodist background was one of endless dissent. We dissented, as Methodists, from the Anglican establishment that held what seemed very like a colonial outpost in the village in which I was born. Seven sturdy Dissenting chapels served a labouring population of, at the most, five thousand. Four had joined together in the Methodist Union, though they did not mix— one Bethel, one Wesleyan, one New Connexion, one Primitive Methodist. Twenty yards from the chapel I attended—called Providence New Connexion—and a hundred yards from Bethel stood the independent Wesleyan Reform. Ostracism reserved in other societies for Roman Catholics or Jews began, in our society, with ostracism of the Wesleyan Reform. Further out lay the Church of Christ and the Mount Zion Pentecostalists. Once a year, on Whit Tuesday, the Sunday Schools of these seven chapels processed round the village behind weighty banners, each needing the muscle of six men to carry it. On Whit Tuesday, the year's new clothes came out. The order of the procession went in strict rotation so that no seniority could be established, no prior right to march first. The Anglican Church, a building frailer than any of the grand chapels, crouched at the top of the hill as if in fear of attack. In the spirit of ecumenism, an approach was once made by the Methodists to the Vicar to invite the Anglicans to join the yearly procession of witness. Talks broke down on the Methodist refusal to let the Anglicans parade first by right. Now, thirty years later, the chapel that meant most to me is a shirt factory and its nearest rival is a light engineering works. Formal Methodism appears to be on the retreat, not so much from an enemy with any special intention to harm, as from creeping indifference, a feeling that the snobberies, disputes, life-style and piety of yesterday have little to do with today. The danger in a proprietorial attitude to Jesus, in too much confidence that 'we' have His ear in a way that 'they' do not, is that as the structures die the Jesus who is too closely identified with the structures dies too. To reclaim those parts of Yorkshire to which I belong it almost seems as though He is going to have to change His name; or, at least, wait until His name and reputation have been forgotten, and His Gospel can once again be preached as something strange.

The gifts that Methodist religion would seem to have left with a largely post-religious society are a feeling that individuality and personhood must be protected at all costs; that no hierarchy or system of government shall presume to interpret my life to me; that, if there is a God, He wishes me to deal with Him direct; if there is no God, I should parley with no substitute authority. The Bible enjoins us to bear one another's burdens and this a Dissenting society of the sort that did much to form me is willing to do. At the same time, we should bear our own burdens. Bunyan's pilgrim figure, 'standing in a certain place, with his face from his own house, a book in his hand and great burden on his back', knows that there is no carrier on earth on whom he can off-load the weight of being himself. Grace Abounding may loosen the straps and let the burden fall, but it is safe to assume that, once it has rested firmly on your shoulders, the marks will stay there the rest of your life.

A few months before the journey to Indianapolis, one of my aunts died. She had wanted, from her earliest years, to be a missionary, a deaconess, an evangelist, but the family was poor and she went into domestic service. Though thwarted of her main ambition, she fought out a rear-guard action ever after, running prayer groups and teaching Bible classes. When, towards the end of her life, she started to go blind and one day alarmed herself by knocking a kettle off a hissing, unlit gas-ring while she scrabbled on the floor for dropped matches, she consulted none of us, sold her house and set herself up in an Old People's Home. From there the mission continued. After she died a carrier bag containing her diaries and her Bible came my way and I took her Bible with me on the search for Protestantism. She had won it in 1906 for learning and repeating seven psalms. For a lifetime she had made notes in the margins and on the fly-leaves: texts of sermons, names of preachers, notes in transit. Before Psalm 126 she had written 'If you are depressed, read—'. Beside the words in Psalm 81, 'But my people would not hearken to my voice; and Israel would none of me', she wrote 'God save England'. Beside the words in St. John's Gospel Chapter 4 verse 24, 'God is a spirit and they that worship him must worship him in spirit and in truth', she wrote 'Worship anywhere'. In verse 18 of Chapter 9 of St. Luke's Gospel, 'And it came to pass, as he was alone praying . . .', she underlined the word 'alone' and wrote alongside '19–9–54 Alone. Prayer changes things'. In a specially Protestant way she lived dangerously. Though some of the things she wrote would give comfort to those who say that once saved, God will look after the rest, the evidence of her life is that her religion and her Bible study kept her on the move, at risk, not closing but opening. Because her death came so near the journey to the U.S.A., she came to exemplify what I thought to be Protestant essentials: a personal relationship with God, unmediated by a priesthood; the centrality of the Bible as God's Word; an obligation to use energy, wit, new insight to challenge all complacency, all torpid settlement, especially your own.

To build a bridge between the expectations I brought with me from England and the Protestantism I should meet in America, I sought help from an indefatigable adviser— Martin Marty, Professor of Church History in the University of Chicago and a Lutheran Pastor. What adjustments, I asked him, would be necessary, to relate what I brought with me to what lay ahead? The start of his answer threw up three main characteristics of the Protestantism we would be looking at.

The first he described as 'the Sense of Mission'. The early American pioneers are often identified with the Children of Israel in the Old Testament. They have the same frailty on a vast and unwelcoming landscape, the same assurance of God's support, the same unquestioned obligation to do what is necessary to see the chosen people survive. Secondly, he spoke of 'the Politics of Voluntarism', by which I took him to mean the right of individuals to seize and enjoy their freedom irrespective of the log jams and traffic jams to which such freedom must inevitably lead. The third was 'the Action of Busy-ness' or, as he caught it in a neat phrase, 'Grace, obscured by Activity'. There is no time when it would seem utterly right to do nothing. The works of Satan must fall, if they fall at all, before a God-backed thrust.

Within these useful abstractions, Dr Marty pictured American Protestants addressing the question: 'What does your love for Jesus lead you to do for somebody else?' They would group themselves according to their answers. All might agree that the purpose of a church is its ministry. But some would say the ministry works to save people *in* society as it now exists. Others would say the ministry works to save people *from* society as it now exists. Those Protestant Churches in America that Dr Marty called Mainstream or Mainline have a tradition of outreach into society; indeed they bear a strong responsibility for the making of that society in the first place. They are the Methodists, the Lutherans, the Episcopalians, what would be the established Church of America if America ran to such a thing. Against them are ranged those for whom the world is irreclaimable and diabolic. Their ministry, using the Church as an Ark in time of a flood, is one of drawing floaters to safety, having them 'saved'. They are usually called, because of the literalism of their approach to Holy Scripture, 'Fundamentalists'. The scene that awaited me in Indianapolis, he warned, was temporarily one of Mainline decline and Fundamentalist advance. As he put it, in a nice disposition of adverbs, the Mainliners use the language of 'still' ('We *still* have two thousand members,' 'We *still* do well in this area or that'), whereas the Fundamentalists speak the language of 'already' ('Our budget is *already* a million and will be a million and a half by next year', 'We *already* have thirty buses bringing our members to church'). But, on a longer view than a flying visit, it would be possible to see the situation as temporary. Unease or defeat (the Red Peril, the Yellow Peril, Vietnam) generally produces an upsurge in conservative Fundamentalism. The restoration of confidence tends to feed the Mainline.

Alongside both these groups are the Black Churches.

Black interests, said Dr Marty, represent the 'scandal', in the Greek sense of the 'stumbling block', in American society. Blacks are somewhere in the middle of the American drama. If the spirit of Protestantism is seen as a temporary investment of a particular fringe of society with particular responsibility and particular meaning, then the spirit of Protestantism could surely be seen to be winging its way towards the American Blacks and other pressured, emergent groups, who are living out the ironies of trying to work out God's purpose, in a society that is also working out God's purpose but is working it out with different results.

Before I had even taken the first step in the search for the Protestants of Indianapolis, Dr Marty, surveying with foreknowledge what lay ahead, was wondering ruefully where we were going to find in our search what he called 'tragic sense', the weight of real complexity, the ironic mind that Abraham Lincoln showed when he observed that, though both sides in the Civil War may claim God's backing, God was hardly likely to fight on both sides and against Himself. At the time he spoke I was too anxious about the run-up to Indianapolis to take much notice, but the words lodged themselves in the corner of my jaw to be chewed later.

Three sites in Indianapolis were chosen to stand for the three main groups that made up Dr Marty's design of American Protestantism. The Mainline was represented by North Methodist Church, built in 1930s' Gothic with a quadrangle of support buildings that give it the air of a prosperous monastery. The Baptist Temple represented the Fundamentalists. Its main preaching space was a congress hall to seat three thousand, fronted by a line of flag-poles. It worked at that time to a budget of two million dollars, had seven thousand members, a total staff of one hundred and fifty with two hundred and five Sunday School classes, and it ran its own hospital and day school. The Black representative was Mount Vernon Baptist Church, a plain preaching hall with auxiliary meeting rooms in one of the poorer quarters of the city. Sunday service was hot and crowded, and many of the swaying women flicked paper fans that carried, sometimes, family portraits of Martin Luther King, sometimes, pictures of the Last Supper.

Each of these groups belonged to a society that is saturated by newspaper and television coverage and each had a characteristic reaction to us as aliens making films. The Black Baptists were amiable but detached. They did not see how anything we might be doing could concern them, though their pastor does a daily broadcast. The Fundamentalists were great showmen. At the sight of a camera or a bank of lights they stirred and projected in the best tradition of show business. Rejecting the world outside, they recreated the shape of it—advertising, commercial buoyancy, the distractions of entertainment—within their own context and for their own purposes, which is, in brief, the saving of souls. The Mainliners had doubts. They were warm towards us as visitors, guarded towards us as men with cameras. They knew the danger of celluloid, how a statement made with one intention could be cut to mean another. Their particular line of sensing the ambiguities in any situation, resisting too much generalization, suspending judgement—which made them natural searchers—also made them cautious.

The Methodism I knew from birth was the Methodism of Dissent. 'Does your Methodism', I asked Dr Richard Hamilton, Minister of North Methodist Church, 'dissent or does it consent to the society you live in?' 'I would say', he answered, 'that Methodism consents. It is part of our society. The whole tone of dissent that was in the beginning is distant from most of us here.' If, as Richard Hamilton implies, there is no division between his society and his Methodism, then its failures must be felt as the failures of Methodism too. If it is dangerous to walk the Indianapolis streets at night, if there is bad Indianapolis housing, if there is social injustice and racial discrimination, Methodism has to carry its part of the reproach. If Methodism tried, as the Fundamentalists do, to draw its skirt aside to avoid contamination from society and the world, it would discover, like someone who starts pulling at the wrong bit of wool in an old jumper, that it was unravelling the whole garment. This understanding of the indivisibility of religious meaning and social process tends to cover a church like the North Methodists in sly camouflage. Its architecture may be bold and Gothic. Its marbled pulpit may jut up through the centre of the sanctuary apse like a megalith. Its choir may sing, against all my Methodist expectations, a version of the Magnificat in Latin. Its Christmas decorations may include a life-size crib tended by a delicate cardboard sculpture of the Blessed Virgin, known, by the devout Methodist sculptress who made her, as Our Lady. But, as far as I can sense it from talks with its Minister, the purpose of this Methodist church is less to summon in the saved and pull up its drawbridge, than to reach out beyond its apparent boundaries and try to meet outside society along a frayed edge of personal relationships and unjudging attempts to understand and help.

'What is the most important thing you do?' I asked the minister. The reply came deliberately: 'The most important thing I do, I think, is to try to relate my understanding of the life and work of Jesus Christ to individual persons. It isn't a matter of trying to rescue either myself or other people from a burning fire. It's a matter of trying to release me and other people to be what we were really intended to be.' He does not speak of 'releasing' but of '*trying* to release'. He does not speak of 'relating the life and work of Jesus Christ to individual persons' but of 'relating *my understanding* of the life and work of Jesus Christ to individual persons'. You need to understand, he points out with no attempt to overwhelm, truss up and save me, that 'your mind is limited, your understanding is limited, your heritage is narrow. There is truth a lot bigger than you know and understand; and you have to leave that edge open.' When I watch, in the film we eventually made, the high definition certainties of the Fundamentalists and the high dramatic sweep of the Blacks alongside the low-key ambiguities of the North Methodists, the effect is to make me despair, not of the Methodists but of the adequacy of celluloid and recording tape to pick up and present the most courageous attempts to be true to a complex situation.

In a corridor behind what the North Methodists call the sanctuary (what I would call the church) is a hefty notice-board giving details of the week's activities. Some relate directly to church: the Membership Seminar, Getting Straight about the Bible and, boldly named, the Stuffers Club, which is a group of ladies who enjoy being together and stuffing church circulars into the buff envelopes. For others, the North Methodist Church plays host: the Korean Congregation, or Common Cause, a citizens' lobby group. The Committee for Community Concern meets regularly in the house of one or other of its members. I watched them one evening start to negotiate their way through some uneasy straits on the matter of support for a group of wild youngsters who had opted to change their ways and now needed backing.

The committee itself, about twenty strong at the meeting at which I saw them in action, toned well with the un-ostentatious, quite spacious sitting-room of the chairman, Dick Fredland, who lectures in political science at the University of Indiana. They were unostentatious too, at a guess comfortably but not flamboyantly well off, good listeners all, and, though whites predominated, there were one or two blacks. I went on to meet them from a Funda-mentalist gathering at which the name Jesus came down on the heads of the congregation again and again like a great relentless hammer. Jesus was not named once in the Committee for Community Concern. When I mused aloud on why this should be so in a gathering of Christians, a troubled ripple of surmise pursued the question round the room. My outsider's guess would be that, for many to whom the North Methodists' style might appeal, Jesus exists strongly, but in solution. He is invoked not directly but by implication. He does not make dramatic entrances to save souls, but working through the prayerful actions of concerned people, He leaves a modest imprint. To name Him among friends in a business meeting of the Committee for Community Concern might be seen as preacher's cant. To name Him too readily to strangers might seem like pious hustling. 'What', I asked, 'would you do if someone came to you and said: "Teach me to be a Christian"?' The chairwoman-elect of the committee, whose doubts about our motives for attending the meeting at all were a long time dying, answered, very much to the point: 'Well, I guess I would have to develop a relationship with that person and go from there.'

There had been little time for the Committee for Community Concern to develop a relationship with the slender, assured young man who sprawled in the hot seat in Dick Fredland's parlour and answered questions about his scheme called 'Youth Illustrates'. His sponsor was a black downtown pastor who introduced him and vouched for his soundness. The boy himself was open about his record. He was on parole. 'I've spent time in prison and I've been into the Indiana Youth Centre and several other places of captivity.' His scheme, 'Youth Illustrates', is that young people, many of whom have known trouble, should dramatize crime instead of committing it. In this way they might themselves learn how crime is geared into a whole set of attitudes and ways of life; would-be criminals might learn that crime, except momentarily, does not pay; and a jittery public might learn that crime has a context, part of which their own fearfulness and lack of understanding does something to maintain. When he had spoken at length he and his sponsor left, and the Committee set about discussing what they should do to help. What they played out was a session of 'North Methodists Illustrate'.

One of Richard Hamilton's assistant ministers, who is a committee member, had done some quiet exploration on his own about the persuasive young impresario: 'I think he is everything he says he is.' Perhaps the scheme needs a little more refinement and they should be encouraged to confine their endeavours to manageable topics instead of straining to offer blanket solutions to all the crime problems of the inner city. But the Juvenile Delinquency organizations are thrilled that this form of self-help should have arisen among the young themselves. Who, queried one committee member wryly, is a performance by 'Youth Illustrates' designed to help? Not, he thought, the members of North Methodist Church. 'I would doubt very much if one tenth of one per cent of the people in North Church are involved in active crime'. Those who might benefit are likely to be on the streets already and what can a steady well-heeled church do to convince them that, when 'Youth Illustrates' speaks, they should listen? This, thought another, was not quite the point. If 'Youth Illustrates' performs for the congregation at North Methodist, they help themselves, and part of helping themselves is being taken seriously by those they would expect to reject them. 'It becomes a positive stroke in a Transactional Analysis sense, it seems to me—to let them come to this congregation. They are bound to get a favourable response, even from the most restrained church members. Here are kids gone bad who have turned good, and you cannot help but be appealed to by that.'

Members of Mainline Protestant churches admit that

their membership has declined in recent years. There was a Mainline boom after the Second World War but, as one of their number phrased it, 'They took great risks in society, they were very Protestant in that they were also very self-critical and today they are suffering for this.' But it is Protestant to take risks. Without risks there is no growth. 'Protestantism renews itself by getting to its sources. This means that in the Mainline churches there is more attention again to inner spiritual life, to the life of meditation and prayer, to the recovery of the impetus that people get from the Bible.'

After the meeting of the Committee for Community Concern I raised with Dick Fredland the subject of the decline in the membership of his shade of church and the boom in fast-talking Fundamentalism. Should he not think of changing his tack? His reply, which flung aside caution and won the next best thing to applause from the rest of the committee, went as follows: '*Despite* the mongers of fear having full pews and *despite* the large armies marching behind them, history, as far as I observe it, does not bear out the wisdom of their course of action. Love,' (delivered with unusual weight as if to make sure I did not leave Mainline Protestantism with nothing more substantial than a wilting posy of ambiguities) '*Love* is the modifying force that will overcome the problems we confront ourselves with.' And that, though he still did not say the name itself, is what I take to be the general Mainline understanding of Jesus.

The Fundamentalists at the Baptist Temple left me in no doubt that towards me they had one intention and one intention only: to win my soul for Jesus. If I happened to be standing in front of a film camera when I made my submission, so much the better. After a morning session of the Sunday School for the Deaf, that he had conducted with verve and patience, Sonny Snell, one of the assistant ministers, agreed to be interviewed. Each was after his bit of soul: mine was his caught as the camera turned; his was mine caught as Jesus brought me down with a flying tackle. What, I asked him, was the purpose in all this effort, the deaf Sunday School, the bus ministry? Evangelism, came the answer. Our world is burning and going to hell. Those already saved are manning the lifeboats. Hands shoot over the sides down to the dark sea where millions who do not have to drown are drowning.

So long as the questions revealed nothing of me ('What work do you do?' 'What does "saved" mean?'), Sonny Snell supplied straight answers. Changing gear, I asked him how he would deal with someone who said he didn't think he was too bad and he didn't see why all this paraphernalia of being saved should be necessary.

The someone I was talking about must surely be me. With a deft tweak of the carpet, he had me lying on the floor and was breathing down at me: 'Can I ask you a question, Ron? Your name is Ron, isn't it? Are you saved?' 'I don't think so', I managed, after what I experienced as a gap of an age, though no doubt the answer followed smartly on the question, for I truly knew I meant it. Pressing his advantage, he whipped from his inside pocket a small red Bible, found the appropriate text and asked me to choose between Heaven and Hell. 'I don't want to be frightened into a decision', I wrestled feebly. 'I'm not trying to frighten you', came back the reply. 'You're too intelligent for that: unless a man's holding a gun on you.' On consideration and casting aside all the other possible replies as chickening out, I opted for eternal life. If I really meant it, he said, really meant to accept Jesus as my personal saviour, we could both kneel down together, say a short prayer and, from then on, I would enjoy the same salvation as he had. If the Baptist Temple and Sonny Snell had had their way, *The Long Search* would have been very much shorter.

Sonny Snell's father had been 'a moonshiner and a

bouncer in three or four bars in Cincinnati'. Dr Greg
Dixon, chief minister and star preacher at the Baptist
Temple, did not know his father till he was about 27. At the
age of four he had been given away by his mother to a
barber whom he affectionately calls 'one-legged Luke'. He
stayed with Luke and Mrs Lucas for several years. When he
was fourteen, his benefactors took him to an old-fashioned
tent revival meeting. 'On 5 May 1932,' as he puts it, 'Greg
Dixon was born physically. The third Thursday night of
August, 1946, Greg Dixon was born spiritually.' He now
preaches salvation. Part of that salvation is safety, but there
was nothing safe or cushioned about the world Greg Dixon
or Sonny Snell knew before Jesus hooked them out of it.

Greg Dixon spends an hour each day studying the works
of Charles Darwin in order to refute them. Darwin he rates
as one of the great incarnations of Satan in the history of the
world. At the mention of Evolution (not my mention but his
—for I imagined that most people had by now accommo-
dated themselves to some version of what Darwin wrote
about) he seems to hunch and swell, suggesting that, with
all the other gifts, God gave Adam a bristling animal
mechanism that comes into play in the presence of real
danger and real Evil. Other diabolic incarnations who stalk
the world in its last days are Karl Marx and Sigmund
Freud, one preaching evolutionary economics, the other
suggesting the possibility of a downward spiral into the
shadowy region of the Unconscious, both of which can
produce, in those of a Fundamentalist turn of mind, a
sickening vertigo.

The Fundamentalist world-view, to the extent that I can
catch a glimpse of it, is fixed and crystalline. The Bible is the
Word of God literally inspired and to be understood
literally. The timetable of Salvation is pegged out in a
sequence of unambiguous divine actions: the Creation of the
World and of Man, the Election of the Children of Israel,

the Birth, Death and Resurrection of Jesus, the prospect of the Second Coming. The Baptist Temple, with its wish to draw its membership through its doors and seal all the cracks, to satisfy the needs of its people within its walls so that they need have no dealings with Satan's world outside, acts like a gigantic rescue ship. It awaits the Rapture, the seizure from the Earth of all saved souls living and dead, the reign of the Anti-Christ, the world-dictator, three and a half years of illusory prosperity, three and a half years of troubles, then the End of the World. 'Heaven', preached Greg Dixon in a forceful sermon, 'is a real place, a ready place, a reserved place. It is as real as Chicago, as London, even as Indianapolis.' Its gates have real pearl. Hell-fire is real fire. There is a picture of Heaven on the wall of the deaf Sunday school. Grey-green pines rise in the morning mist. Wide stairs wind upwards and through them. The mansions are towers. The mind that sees winding stairs as potentially wearisome and tall buildings as too reminiscent of urban tower blocks is not the same mind as can see here a picture of Heaven. After my last meeting with Dr Dixon I think I may have moved unusually fast down the steps of his head-quarters and stood by the car waiting for someone to come and open the door. Puny manoeuvre! The preacher came to see us off and got down to the urgent business of the meeting. If I had not accepted Jesus as my personal Saviour, I should do so and fast. There is no time like the present.

Is there any respect, I found myself wondering, in which I am a Fundamentalist? There is no Biblical Fundamentalism in my background. The Bible, though regarded as a uniquely precious document, is not free of the flaws of all other documents and I was raised, in a Protestant way, to quiz it critically. But I suppose I knew from childhood that, fundamentally, I had the goodwill of a family; fundamentally, I lived in a small society that knew me and I it; fundamentally, I knew circumstances where it was at least possible to go to school, on to a university and out into a world where it seemed fundamentally possible to alert others to my particular needs and presence. Buoyed up by this hidden Fundamentalism, I have been free so far to enjoy complexity, ambiguity and danger. But what if I had been fundamentally denied these secret fundamental securities?

At the end of one of the services at the Baptist Temple, curtains behind the preacher parted to reveal an extensive wall painting of the River Jordan flooded with sunset. In front of it stood a wide and narrow glass-fronted tank entered by flights of steps at either end and carrying about five feet of water. Ten or so people, while I was there, came down for baptism. They raised their hands, made a Profession of Faith and, held by a preacher who covered their nose and mouth with a protective pad, were lowered into the water and out again. 'Buried in the likeness of His death; raised in the likeness of His resurrection.' Later, their hair still wet, I talked to one or two of them. None presented that dauntless front that seems to be both the public and the private style of Fundamentalist preachers. The streets alarmed them, the lurking threat that watches you along the sidewalks of the city where nobody will dare to intervene as you go down. In state and national capitals, politicians argue and cannot agree. Radio and television fill the homes of the innocent with wars and rumours of wars. Fear rides on the backs of the powerless like a juddering ape. What can you do to loosen its grip? In his moment of last-reel extremity, the Man of God shoots off the locks of your jailhouse and enters your life. He offers the Bible as certainty, Salvation as security, the Community of the Saved for companionship, the Assurance of Heaven as hope. It is easy to say, as you leave the cinema, that you have only been watching a film. It is hard to deny, when you are part of the action, that you are glad things can work out this way.

Protestant Spirit U.S.A.

Though there were few blacks in South Yorkshire thirty years ago and none of us had been to the U.S.A., there was a story then current in Methodist circles about a black Christian in New York. Having been told that a church was the House of God, he picked one of the grandest and tried to get in. Each time he tried, he was ejected. Woeful and confused he sat on the church steps and wept. Feeling some-one alongside him, he looked up expecting to be told to clear the steps too, and there was Jesus who stooped, patted him on the head and said: 'Don't worry. I've been trying to get into that church ever since they built it.'

Mount Vernon Baptist Church stands, and looks as though it may need help if it is to stand much longer, in one of the poorer quarters of Indianapolis. Its congregation, when I saw it, was all black. Over seventeen years the minister, Mozel Sanders, taciturn except when he is sweating out one of his great, jazz-singer sermons, has built up his membership from twenty to nearly fifteen hundred. Few are well off; few would feel comfortable even if they found their way to one of the great preaching stadia of Indiana-polis. Even so, the minister talks to his congregation as if they are on the *inside* and those whom Jesus came to save and care for are still on the *outside*. The Church, he said in one of his Sunday morning talks, including his own modest establishment, is like the cemetery. It takes in everything and gives out nothing. 'We'll take the General Offering . . . the Benevolent Offering . . . and all the other Offerings. Somebody next door can be starving; and two dollars may be the difference between feeding a family . . . and we want to know: what church do you belong to? We want to know: what did you do with your money?'—Then a sudden furious cry—'What difference does it make when a person's hungry?' At our first meeting I asked him: 'Is the Gospel about doing things for people?' 'That's *all* the Gospel is about', he replied. 'I don't think you can talk to me about

Christ if I'm hungry.'

It was Thanksgiving when we reached Mount Vernon for the first time—and snowing. In the sanctuary, the choir and a small backing group were limbering up for one of the minister's regular broadcasts on a local radio station. In the school room, church members and neighbourhood people were serving up turkey dinners in travel packs. In a side office, a volunteer telephonist, calling everybody on the phone and off 'sweetheart', was taking dinner orders from any, white or black, who cared to ring in. Small gangs of boys were carrying cardboard cases of packed dinners down to waiting vans and distributing them round the town. Mount Vernon, joining forces with two other churches, had been organizing this annual treat for the past four years. On the day I watched, two thousand dinners went out. More continuously, Mozel Sanders runs the Indianapolis O.I.C. (Opportunities Industrialization Centre). It is housed in a disused school building which is rented for a dollar a year and teaches Typing, Key-punch, English, Mathematics, Minority History and Urban Relations to any who qualify as disadvantaged. To anyone who recommends that the disadvantaged should pull themselves up by their bootstraps, Mozel Sanders points out that many of them do not have boots. He draws no sharp line between what happens at church services and what happens the rest of the week: 'O.I.C. is church to a great extent and church is O.I.C. I don't think you can separate them because we're talking about blood—human beings.' He had a racy figure of speech to put the church building in its proper place: 'You know, I often say that church is kinda like the Sanitation Department. That is, you don't take the garbage cans away. You take the garbage away and leave the cans because next week there'll be some more.'

The most exhilarating hours in Indianapolis were spent at Mount Vernon during the weekly identifying, bundling up and disposal of garbage. The senior and the junior choirs had their own distinct uniform. The younger girls wore caftans monogrammed with the initials of the church. The older women wore plain white smocks. The men wore white shirts and bow ties. A small jazz-combo stood in support. Stewards patrolling the aisles wore badges: 'Master-at-arms', 'Vice-president', 'Member'. A small nursing staff in hospital uniforms with starched bonnets stood by to help anyone overcome by heat or the Spirit. The service moved through prayer, singing, Bible reading, preaching, in a sequence of well-scored emotional peaks and troughs which reached their sustained height at the end of the minister's sermon when his broken phrases were pushed aloft by anti-phonal blasts on the organ. 'Jesus . . . my elder brother . . . Jesus . . . friend of the friendless . . . Jesus . . . the rainmaker out of nowhere . . . Jesus . . . the lily of the valley . . . Jesus . . . the bright morning star . . . Jesus . . . the hot towel . . . Jesus . . . Jesus . . . Jesus . . .' At that point he flung his microphone down on his desk and mopped his brow while motherly attendants 'there-there'd' weeping people back into their usual minds. He had listed in his sermon the things he liked about Jesus. Through them it was possible to read a submerged catalogue of a certain kind of modern, urban ache. Jesus never gets above Himself. The only qualification necessary to become a friend of Jesus is that a person has to be bad. With Jesus you always have adequate representation. You can see Jesus without an appointment. Jesus doesn't send His secretary out to see what you want. Jesus doesn't set up a recording machine to take a message. Jesus makes Himself available.

It was never the idea that each of these journeys should end with a manifesto laying down a definition of the -ism that had been the subject of the search. Yet from time to time there was a need to try to be Olympian for a second or two, to rise above it, see the broad shape. This was never possible in Indianapolis for the sights and sounds contradicted each other and there was no nearby hillock from which to take a distant view. It was only later that I was able to draw one or two interim conclusions. And it was then I realized that, throughout, I had been thinking of Protestantism in two different senses and that the time had come to set them apart. 'Protestantism' is the name of the impulse to keep things moving, to be free, to walk all over God's Heaven by right, to challenge any system, to change. 'Protestantism' is also the name of a certain style in Western Christianity, developed since Martin Luther. It is a firm, historical label. It would seem to be as true and as useful to draw a parallel elsewhere and say that 'Catholicism' is the name of the impulse to preserve, to hand on, to stabilize. 'Catholicism' is also the common name of a certain type of Western Christianity. But not all the churches that are Protestant in the second sense are Protestant in the first. They are subject to the swings of a pendulum. Sometimes they move; sometimes they settle down. Sometimes they are Protestant; sometimes they are Catholic. I wonder if Catholics are sometimes Protestant too?

2
INDIA
330 Million Gods

We took a rowing-boat, while it was still dark on the second day of the search for Hinduism, and pushed it out into the River Ganges. Dawn was, of course, expected, but to behave as if it might never arrive and to allow oneself a moment of surprise as it did, is a more grateful way of starting the day. Behind us to the west was the Holy City of Benares like a crenellated observation platform. Ahead were the mud flats and the darkest part of the sky. When light struck, it was a pink shaft, sharp at its extremities, with knuckles of light in the centre, like a clenched fist. The boatman shipped his oars for a second or two and mumbled a prayer. Bathers on the shore-line bobbed their devotions in a series of total immersions. Platforms of marigolds were pushed out over the water. Throughout, as it does night and day, the public address system in one of the riverside temples transmitted the same unbroken formula—*Sri Ram, Jai Ram, Jai, Jai Ram*, meant to be monotonous, meant to lodge in the ear and keep itself turning, meant to be the pivot of the day: the wheeling repetition of a Name of God.

About an hour later we paid off the rowing-boat, took a power-driven launch like a regatta barge, and started up-river, past the cremation steps, where the woodyards supply raw materials for funeral pyres and corpses burn, and beyond the town. Most of my companions were above on the observation deck. Two of us were below with the boatman. His assistant, a boy in his twenties, wore a long white scarf. Couldn't somebody, I asked, do something about the percussive floorboard that rattled in time with the engine just by my foot? The boy, who was treading lithely along the outer lip of the boat, swung in, dropped down and bent to settle it. He raised the floorboard. His scarf tumbled down to the propeller-shaft that ran the length of the boat, caught on it, whipped his head downwards and broke his neck. In long seconds the possibilities—stop the engine, throw it into reverse, cut his scarf, pull him off—paraded slowly before our eyes but nobody moved. When regular time came back, the engine was killed, the prow turned shorewards, a handful of people jumped out to look for help, and the subsiding boy, with bloody eyes and a swollen tongue held by his teeth, was laid on a bench. I took my sweater and scarf off and put them over him, just in case. It was certainly too late when our people left the boat to search for a hospital; far, far too late when a doctor and a nurse ran down and pronounced the boy dead. The boatman at the wheel, looking ahead without focus, letting out spasmodic screams, then looking ahead again, got the boat round facing the city and the journey back began. Along the tops of the river-steps were people, running. Near the mooring-stage howling women tumbled from the houses and the crowd moved in.

This happened on the second day of three years' worth of travelling (for the Hindu journey was the start of *The Long Search*). I had volunteered to take instruction in matters of life and death—why, according to the world's pundits, we were born, what happens to us when we die, what we do in the meantime—but I never expected the lessons to come so close. Not surprisingly, a bleakness settled on the whole *Long Search* enterprise once that boy died. We wanted to pack up and go home. Was there much point in handling the fissionable material of life and death as if it lay outside us when it lay within and around us? Who cares what the books say when the rattling floorboards say sudden death? The same afternoon we went to a potter's yard and watched him making pots—flinging the clay on the wheel, moulding it, stacking it, baking it, if need be—breaking it; creating, preserving, destroying. Hindu lessons were crowding in on us whether we chose to hear them or not.

Only twenty-four hours earlier we had been congratulating ourselves on our good luck. We had happened to pick, as the starting day of all our journeys, the birthday of the elephant-headed god, Ganesha. He is the god of Good Beginnings. His squat, red image sits over doorways of Hindu houses. He is invoked by authors at the start of books, composers at the head of scores, brahmin priests on the way into their prayers. He has many shrines in Benares. The one we chose to linger by was shaped, as so many Hindu temples are, like a cluster of mountain peaks. From dawn till dusk, a steady crowd pushed in and out, as if it were polling day. Devotees rather than voters cast their devotions rather than their votes and emerged with the air of duty done. They brought flowers for the god, sweets for the children, little bright, clay Ganesha effigies for themselves. Enough to make Judaic, Islamic and much Christian blood boil. But I never met a Hindu who did not understand that the clay image was no more than a pointer to a truth. In itself it is clay or metal or stone. 'If I want you to see an object,' said one of my Benares gurus, 'how long must I point to it?' He answered for me: 'So long as you have not seen the object. Once you have seen the object, I remove my finger.' 'But,' I moved in, 'aren't there some people who spend the whole of a life-time gazing at your finger and never see what you are pointing at?' 'Of course,' he replied, 'and, for them, God is not in a hurry.'

A few weeks later, in a remote village in North Bihar, I was to see hundreds of school children bring flowers and sweets and saris and lay them at the feet of clay images of Saraswati, Patroness of Learning, one image for each school. For three days they sang to her, acted for her, prayed to her. On the third day they took her in an ox-cart and threw her in the temple pond where, presumably, she dissolved. People in glass houses, in constant danger of idolizing Jesus, the Qur'an, the Mosaic Law, God, the Bible, Promotion Prospects or Motor Cars, should not throw stones.

Nor should they expect their own form of clarity. It is the Judaeo-Christian-Islamic style to look for regularity of belief, worked out in nicely articulated creeds, a close-shave of theological endeavour mowing down all the stubble of alien gods and practices and leaving one whisker standing—call Him God, Jehovah, Allah. There are many Hindu incarnations of divinity, but no recurrence of Hindu prophets to call the wayward into line. There is a great tradition of Hindu scripture, but no one Bible or Qur'an on which a Hindu in court can lay his hand and swear. There are Hindu eras but no Moses on Sinai, no Jesus in Bethlehem, no Muhammad and the Angel to usher them in. There is, for all I know, as much mystery in the story of the Creation of the World and the Garden of Eden in the Book of Genesis as there is in the classic Hindu account of the start of things; but, where Genesis asserts, the Rig-Veda, oldest of Hindu scriptures, shrugs:

Whence all Creation had its origin,
He, whether He fashioned it or whether He did not,
He who surveys it all from the highest heaven,
He knows—or maybe even He does not know.

If nothing else can, the idea of an omni-ignorant God should be enough to throw the mind off its habitual Judaeo-Christian tracks.

In at least two clear senses, as far as I can discover, Hindus

of a devout turn of mind may be said to acknowledge One
God, and are as monotheistic as those who have claimed a
monotheistic monopoly. No Hindu devotee of Rama or
Krishna, I should imagine, puts into his prayer the mental
reservation that he is praying to a segment of divinity. They
dive into their God as swimmers into the sea, and they
swim. Muslims give God ninety-nine Beautiful Names;
Hindus give him three hundred and thirty million varie-
gated faces. The common word for devotion to a god is
bhakti and it implies not servility, abjection, partiality but
passion, fusion. Secondly, there is an understanding, not
perhaps among all Hindus, but among all who can or care
to handle the mightiness of the idea, of a universal World-
Soul, an All-Pervading Essence, which is given the name
Brahman. It is without gender, personality, features. Those
who are most keenly aware of the danger of positives resort
to negatives. It is not this, not this. Three attributes, however, this Brahman, this World-Soul, does claim: existence
(*sat*), consciousness (*cit*) and bliss (*ananda*).

The same claim can be made for each individual soul
(called *Atman*). It too is characterized by existence, consciousness and bliss. Why then are we not consciously and
blissfully boundless? It is to this mighty teaser that the
monks, the swamis, of the Ramakrishna Mission, with its
house in Benares, apply themselves. But they do it not by
lapsing into a state of cosmic de-focus but a disciplined life
of prayer, meditation, study and conspicuously by running
a fine hospital, out-patients' department, homoeopathic
dispensary, a home for the old and disabled, a centre for
outdoor relief work and a dairy.

Brahmachari Ashok is a novice monk and a doctor. His
day starts at 4 a.m. with reading, meditation and worship,
either by himself or with the rest of the swamis. At eight
o'clock he goes round the hospital wards or to his surgery, a
small room in a clamorous courtyard already under siege

with patients. Some of them have arrived on the backs of fathers and sons; some, travelling for hundreds of miles, in bullock carts. His main woe is that they arrive too neglected and too late. He is passionate on the need for health education. His day ends at ten o'clock in the evening. Between times he has had to find time for further study, meditation, community worship and his laundry.

On his desk, beneath a sheet of glass so that every time he writes a prescription and sweeps it across to a patient he uncovers his saint, is a photograph of Sri Ramakrishna sitting cross-legged in his loin cloth and looking frankly into the camera. Ramakrishna died in 1886 and seems to have belonged to that rare company of men and women for whom the visible world is porous to divinity. As a young man he had little schooling and served in the temples in Calcutta, experienced ecstatic states, saw visions of Kali, the Great Mother, and married, and although he never consummated his marriage his wife stayed with him all his life. Both were regarded as Divine Incarnations. To taste God in all His forms, he became, for a time a Muslim, then a Christian. He saw visions of the Buddha and of Christ. His verdict was that 'all religions are one' and there is no need to squabble. The aim should be to make a Christian a better Christian; a Muslim a better Muslim; a Hindu a better Hindu; and to recognize that in every creature there is a spark of divinity which calls for respect and worship. There is in existence a 'Gospel of Ramakrishna', in English too, the record of a God-drenched man.

His disciple, Swami Vivekananda, was of very different disposition, well-schooled, forceful, missionary, zealous, a speaker of English, a world-traveller. The parallel (exclusive claims apart) between Sri Ramakrishna and Swami Vivekananda on one side, and Jesus of Nazareth and St Paul on the other is irresistible. Till the end of the nineteenth century the missionary tide had been flooding steadily from West to East; Muslim in the Mogul Empire, Christian in the European descent on India. Vivekananda was one of the first and most effective of those who did something to turn the tide, claiming that, though Hinduism had badly frayed at the edges, it still contained the profoundest and most elevated religious thinking in the world. His missionary journeys to Europe and America roused the West and the news of the rousing of the West roused the East. He dominated the Parliament of Religions that happened in Chicago in 1893 and on his return to India he founded, in 1897, the Ramakrishna Mission, a movement of social action and reformed and refined Hinduism that deliberately rebuffed the slur that Hindu spirituality is an impregnable tangle, that Hindu ritual is buffoonery and a mask for tyranny and sharp practice, that Hindu self-absorption is so total that the story of the Good Samaritan, shifted to a Hindu context, would become a tale of the wise man who passed by and the idiot who wasted his time helping a stranger. The mission is given the name Ramakrishna following the Hindu custom that a disciple honours his guru. The energy and founding vision belong to Vivekananda.

'What', I asked Brahmachari Ashok at the end of a day, when the last shirt had been pulled down over the last wheezing bared chest and the last wailing infant with the earache had been nudged calm and syruped to sleep, 'is the difference between working in a mission hospital and working in some state concern?' 'As far as medical practice is concerned,' came the reply, 'possibly very little, I can be useful to humanity anywhere'. The difference is in what lies behind the practice. 'In the mission I am reminded every moment of the ideal of my life.' Which is? 'Which is—shall we say?—God-Realization.' The Vivekananda missionary zeal remains; he took time to explain. 'You know, identity between one person and another person or between one person and God can never be produced on the level of body. Two bodies are entirely different. Nor can an identity be produced on the level of mind. My mind and your mind are working entirely differently. Our intake of impressions is different. Our deep-rooted conditionings are different. But an identity can be produced on the level of Self. I think I make myself clear.' He did if, by the Big Self, he meant Brahman, the all essential, all conscious, all blissful World-Self, and if, by the Other Self, he meant Atman, the all essential, all conscious, all blissful Individual Self which, properly understood, is identical with the World-Self. Yet it is all still painfully abstract. 'Yes. It is a very, very abstract thing. Difficult to grasp. So we try to put it in the form of a god, a personal god. And what is a god? Something that is most dear to us, isn't it? This is a very simple concept. Now, if a patient comes to me and let us say I put aside the word "Atman", I can say "God". A patient comes to me as God. And, if I really consider him as God, I will worship him.' Worship him? 'Yes. Actually that is what we say. We worship him.' He left space for a glimmer of Hindu enlightenment to break through. 'Have you met the swami who does the dressings? The old swami?' The man he referred to was a deft, pacific, unshockable man with an apron over his ochre swami's gear, who spent the surgical part of his day uncovering, cleaning and dressing ugly wounds and angrily septic sores. 'He does not care whether you are looking at him, whether you praise him, blame him; nothing. He is doing his worship. That's all.' For long hours I had seen Brahmachari Ashok tapping chests, peering down throats, into ears, under bandages, up nostrils, working leg-joints, kneading bellies, scanning spots, writing prescriptions, covering and uncovering his desktop to reveal the steady gaze of Sri Ramakrishna warily photographed nearly a century ago. 'How', I asked, 'does your work in this consulting room tie up with worship in a temple, where gods are more regularly reckoned to be?' His answer was classically simple. 'The devotee in the temple puts flowers in front of an image. I put medicine in front of a patient. But the idea is the same. The devotee is trying to realize the Reality behind the image. I am trying to realize the Reality behind the patient. The difference is that in the temple the devotee is worshipping at an image made of stone. But here I have a living image,' (and here he also threw down a gauntlet) 'so I think that the sort of worship we are doing here is much superior.'

A day in the life of the Universe, on the Hindu count, lasts 4,320 million ordinary years. This is followed, presumably, by a night of equivalent grandeur and another day. Each of these 'days' or kalpas consists of a thousand inner rotations or mahayugas. Each mahayuga consists of four yugas of irregular duration, the earliest longest, the latest shortest. Since 3101 or 3102 B.C. (calculations vary) we have been in the fourth yuga or Kali-yuga of the current cycle. The Kali-yuga spans the period from the departure of the gods from the earth, leaving scraps of wisdom for the human race to scan as the light fades, to the onset of night. The Kali-yuga still has 38,120 years to run, give or take a year or two. The idea of the Kali-yuga can account for, though it need not make more tolerable, what is felt to be the universal retreat from godliness, the collapse of civility, the rising thirst for possessions, the upsurge of devils, the disappearance from the earth of its primal gleam, though on that time scale no one human being could possibly notice a change except as the Kali-yuga reflects itself in the universal experience of beginning a life, believing oneself to be immortal, and sooner or later facing the fact of death.

The Kali-yuga was the theme of a number of troubled Hindu conversations. At the Ramakrishna Mission, though, I befriended an old man who seemed to come near to cracking its gloom. He was a retired professor of mathematics, frail, shrunken and garrulous, who spent his days sitting on the arcaded walkway that runs round the old men's section of the Ramakrishna home for the aged and waiting, like a fly-catcher, for someone to talk to. One lens of his spectacles had cracked and was held in place by adhesive plaster. He was hard of hearing and without teeth. He had know better days. As he put it rotundly, 'I have had the privilege of knowing directly the disciples of Sri Ramakrishna. I have brought very much inspiration from them. Such inspirations naturally I cannot get now. This aspect has diminished.' A blast at his eardrums: 'Which aspect?' 'The spiritual.' Alongside was a busy hospital. Not a hundred yards away a young novice monk was tending his patients and the dressing-room swami was swabbing away infection. 'The hospital too?' But he would not relent: 'Everything has, by course of time, deteriorated. I have been watching the movement for seventy years.' We seemed set for a rapid replay of the Kali-yuga when I asked, bracing myself for the question: 'Are you afraid to die?' At first he misheard me. I shouted it louder: 'ARE YOU AFRAID TO DIE?' He answered without hesitation: 'Yes. I am afraid to die. Still.' Still? Then he stirred, turned himself in his chair and gripped what he had to say like a handrail: 'But I think . . . that when death will come . . . I shall not be afraid. Just before death, when death is immediate and certain.' 'What do you think happens when you die?' I ventured. The question worked like a tonic. 'I think . . . I was an Individual; I am an Individual; I shall be Universal. That is my idea. That is, I shall not know death particularly. The body will go of course, but I shall not die.' 'And of course,' I ventured, 'when you are Universal, you cannot know fear.' 'When I am Universal what need I fear? Everything is myself. Whom should I fear? Fear will go away absolutely.' The one word in the whole encounter which recalled how his voice must have sounded before it

46

dried up was the word 'absolutely'. Then he added a postscript. 'Krishna-Consciousness is what I desire. Krishna is Universal. Everything is included in him. That is my idea.'

Krishna in some accounts is one of the incarnations of the god Vishnu. Another incarnation is Rama. Another, unexpectedly, for he was hard on the brahmin pundits, is the Buddha. One more incarnation is expected before the end of the Kali-yuga. Vishnu, in the same account, is one of a trinity of gods who work to underpin the universe: Brahma (without an 'n') is the Creator; Vishnu, the Maintainer; Shiva, the Destroyer. But when my venerable friend at the Mission spoke of Krishna and Krishna-Consciousness, he did not seem to me to be shuffling the Hindu pantheon in a game of Favourites. He was talking about the Everlasting Arms—the Existence—the Consciousness—the Bliss. *Sat-cit-ananda.* Ramakrishna himself might have added: Jesus, Jehovah, Allah, God.

If the whole of the search for Hinduism could have been confined to the Ramakrishna Mission, this report could be shapely, regular, well-flexed and elevated. It would also have been notable for its display of social conscience. But the Hindus have never known—or at least, never listened to—the prophetic frenzy which needs the Oneness of God to be confirmed by oneness of practice, oneness of creed, oneness of face. What they lose in push they gain in variegation. And a search for Hinduism that does not, at some point, sit like a chameleon on a flowery table-cloth, sweating fit to burst at the variety he is trying to reflect, is no true search. It had to take to the road somehow, however gingerly.

Compared with the hippy trail, my further journey was sedate. After some preliminary clarifications—like the discovery that a head rocked from side to side means 'yes' and not 'no', that a roll of cloth strapped to a bicycle and wheeled down to the cremation steps at Benares is certainly

47

a corpse, that a naked man on a bicycle with ashes in his hair is not a public nuisance but an exceedingly private ascetic—I laid myself open to unstinting advice from one or two of the people who happened to be nearest to hand: the Manager of the Benares hotel we stayed at, the Director of Tourism, the District Magistrate, the translators who saw us through some of the hazards of a babel of languages, the Maharaja of Benares, all of whom had ideas on the right move to make next. But first, with the exception of the Maharaja to whom such a question would have been the height of impertinence, I asked them all where *they* stood in the matter.

Mr Das, Manager of Miss Clark's Hotel, Benares (at the time I met him, having labour troubles, which meant that the waiters wore armbands reading 'We Want Bonus' and meals were punctuated by concerted cries of militancy from the kitchen) is a devotee of Rama. Regularly he bathes in the Ganges and practises Hatha Yoga, sits on the river bank in meditation, and daily a brahmin priest comes to his house to conduct a *puja*, a worship ceremony at the family altar. He is himself a *Vaisya*: that is, he belongs to the third traditional class of Hindus and may not himself do priestly work. Nor may he cook in his own kitchen. His cook comes from a brahmin family and a low wall keeps her and the fire separate from Mr Das and his family. The family altar, behind closed doors which are opened daily for the family worship, is a tiered arrangement of god-images, banked up with flowers and lit with concealed lighting. In the place of honour are Rama, his consort Sita and his henchman Lakshmana, represented by indistinguishable, smiling, ornately-festooned dolls. In the morning they are roused; in the evening put to bed. Rama, hero of the great Hindu epic, *The Ramayana*, and sixth incarnation of the god Vishnu, is a model of good faith in friendship, constancy in marriage and kindness to all creatures, the cherished ideals of the Das household, as of many others. Where it seems right to speak of God choosing the Jews and the Christians, Hindu gods are themselves chosen. Framed pictures form a backing to the altar: one of them the great goddess Kali, with the same face as Rama and Sita but happening to be standing on the chest of her consort, Shiva, and carrying in her fists bunches of severed heads. Though her eyes smile, her tongue drips blood. Near her is a photograph of Sai Baba, one of the most popular Holy Men and Miracle Workers currently alive in India. In Mr Das's sitting room, sent by a (presumably) Christian brewery, was a calendar bearing a picture, in the style used for the god Rama, of John the Baptist. In sheds fronting his garden, he has one or two sacred cows. Whether Mr Das is orthodox I have no way of knowing, as I never discovered how Hindus settle these matters, but he is certainly orthoprax: he *does* the right things. He is strictly vegetarian, drinks no alcohol, pays respect to his god, honours his guests, supports his cow, bathes in the Sacred River. He cannot, in one incarnation, slip the intervening stages. But orthopraxy now may lead him to a rebirth higher up the spiral—as a *kshatriya* (the warrior or king class) and eventually as a brahmin (the class of the priests).

The Director of Tourism claimed at first to leave religion to his wife who tends the family altar, but admitted later a respect for two living masters: one he called the Deoria Baba, an ascetic who lives, virtually on air, on a small platform built over water. He has prescience, knows the needs of visitors before they speak them. The other is Sai Baba, the Master who can materialize objects out of thin air. One evening devotees of Sai Baba gathered in Clark's Hotel to watch a film in which Sai Baba, dressed in a red silk gown with cherubic grin and an Afro haircut, walked through a large congregation of devotees to a platform where he stood, thrust his arm elbow-deep into an upturned vessel and materialized, I think, grain. It could have been salt. The eye darted for signs of a concealed vacuum pump but, to all appearance, we were witnessing a miracle. How, I asked, can a Master do these marvels? Because, came the answer, he is nearer to Nature.

The District Magistrate saw religion as mainly the concern of the elderly, and the elderly as that part of society that gathers most respect from the younger. The word *puja*, used for the ceremony of worshipping a god, is also used for the reverence which younger people pay to their elders. For himself, he acknowledged the working of Karma, which means literally 'action'; but, beyond the letter, means all that propels each of us through this life and on to the next incarnation, the ineluctable law of cause and effect—in Christian terms, 'As ye sow, so shall ye reap'; for the District Magistrate, 'As you do, so shall you be'.

The most mysterious of these unofficial Benares advisers was Mr N. K. Sharma, nominated by the Tourist Office to accompany and translate for us. He is a devotee of Kali, the Great Mother. Is she not, I asked, the Presence with the bloody tongue and the severed heads? (The picture of the dead boatboy never went away.) 'She is powerful to punish wrong,' said Mr Sharma. The boy, in his view, lived an incomplete life and will finish it in another form. In just what form is beyond our understanding. I hope that the fact that he died doing me a kindness counts in his favour in his next cycle. There is not a mosquito, not a plant, in the Hindu account, which does not participate in the karmic process. Could you, said someone in Benares, bow to a flower? I said (and meant) that I could. 'Then you could be a Hindu.'

Mr. Sharma's assistant was a fierce Rajput in a dark turban, a red slit-mark down his forehead. He held himself like a sentry. One of his forebears had won the Victoria Cross. The mark on his forehead, to anyone who knew, showed him, he said, to be a Shakta, a devotee of Shakti, the

Female Force. Was Shakti the same as the Kali that Mr
Sharma worshipped? Yes and no. Shakti power is the
animating power of the goddess. Without her, the god lies
inert. Shakti is Kali. Shakti is also the power that propels
the universe. Shaktipat is the bestowal of power on a
devotee. To all appearances, a master, a guru may bestow
it. In reality, the power bestows itself and the guru is the
channel, the means, the bridge.

One of the film's advisers, Shivesh Thakur, was in Benares
preparing to take us to his home village in North Bihar. He
is Professor of Philosophy in the University of Surrey,
England. Appropriately he keeps a certain distance. There
is, he said, a long tradition of scepticism in Hinduism. It is
not heretical. It is accepted.

The Maharaja of Benares is regarded as an incarnation
of the god Shiva, for Benares is Shiva's adopted city. He
received us in a balcony chamber in his palace over the
Ganges. He dressed simply in a white dhoti, plain cap,
slippers. A venerable retainer served tea and sweet cakes.
Birds flew in and out to pick up the crumbs. In his ante-
chamber were photographs of visiting royalty—including
Queen Elizabeth and Prince Philip, Archduke Franz
Ferdinand, Nicholas II and the Empress Alexandra. 'How',
he asked, (the British Government was having trouble at
the time) 'is the Mother of Parliaments?' Governments
now, he said (speaking of his own too) rarely understand
the aspirations of the people. Below his balcony was moored
a modest white barge. In this he proposed to sail to
Allahabad to join his people for the Mela, the great Ganges
bathe that takes place in one of four riverside sites every
seven years. He suggested that, to see Hinduism at its basest,
at its silliest, at its mightiest, at its most sublime, we should
go there. It meant a detour (we had planned to make
straight from Benaresto North Bihar) but, yielding to hints
from the river, we meandered.

The gathering, the Mela, at Allahabad lasted a month in the form of a non-stop outdoor Hindu ecumenical congress down on the mudflats where the Ganges flows into the Yamuna and the mythical Saraswati tumbles from the sky to join the confluence. An Allahabad newspaper regularly reported the number of bathers 'at the junction of the three rivers', as it might report the cricket scores. At the height of the Mela, two million worshippers entered the water to greet the same dawn. We would have been there too except that a wily police launch, fearing trouble at the sight of strangers, steered us expostulating in the opposite direction and brought us back well after sun-up. One of our number had more success at Hardwar, another of the four specially privileged Ganges bathing places, on an even grander occasion. This was the Khumba Mela, a twelve-yearly event. He managed to catch sight of the fringe of a colony of bathers numbering seven million.

By an impressive feat of planning, the camp site had spacious main roads flanked by enclosures and tents in which teachers taught, singers sang, police co-ordinated and the hungry ate. In the equivalent of a Mela suburb, small plots of land were marked out for use by holy men, some in simple tents, some lying in the open. Whether they wear ochre robes, have shaven heads, have hair matted with ash, go naked, carry a staff, a trident or even, as in one case, a trailing live python, they are reckoned to have undergone some act of renunciation. The classical Sanskrit name of one who renounces is *sannyasi*. Traditionally it meant a brahmin, a Hindu of the priestly class, who has gone through the stages of student, householder, 'forest dweller', and at the end of his life reaches the stage of renouncer or religious beggar. Since the days of the great Shankara, the 8th-9th-century philosopher who for rapid Western placing is sometimes called the Thomas Aquinas of Hinduism, it has been thought regular to proceed straight from the stage of brahmachari or learner to that of sannyasi or renouncer. Dr Ashok, the tireless young doctor at the Ramakrishna Mission, is now brahmachari and, when he takes his full vows, will be a sannyasi. The yogi ascetic at Allahabad who spent large parts of his day in a sweltering meditation sitting within inches of a cow-dung fire is a sannyasi. The ex-professor at the Massachusetts Institute of Technology who now wears an ochre robe and teaches Vedanta, the most elevated Hindu philosophy, is a sannyasi. All sannyasis are reckoned to teach by example. Some of them formally teach.

It is the Hindu tradition for a learner to have a particular teacher, a guru. 'Guru' is a composite of two words meaning 'darkness' and 'light'. This is a role more intimate than that of classroom instructor to pupils. It is more a form of spiritual parenthood in the course of which the teacher alerts the learner to his true situation either by leading him to an understanding of the scriptures or by providing a psychic charge to the marrow which, metaphorically, blows the head off and lets in the light. In Allahabad there were traces of both kinds of gurudom: scholars on platforms expounding scripture, disciples attending their masters with a radiant devotion that I on the outside would have to call love. By chance I lit upon a chain of devotion: an American ex-marine had a guru who was a notable holy man and singer of epic poetry; and the singer's guru was a leathery old sadhu, all but toothless and wearing, when I met him, banana leaves for a loin-cloth and a scarf round his head. To the extent that Ramdas, the marine, spun me round the camp-site on his moped and explained what he thought I should know, he was my guru. So the chain could be numbered loosely at three and a bit. Gurus learn from their gurus. I wonder if gurus also learn from their learners.

The Mela dispersed and, no doubt, the Ganges flood-waters rose to clear the site. When we arrived in North Bihar, in the remote village of Bhith Bhagwanpur, thirty miles from the border of Nepal, rain was awaited, the earth was cracked, spindly bullocks dragged rattling ploughs across fields of stones. We camped in a mango grove uprooted by floods. Grain stocks were low, though everyone at the time had something to eat. The next village was eating three days a week. It was heroic of one of the village schoolmasters to boast: 'We are disaster-proof men'. Bhith Bhagwanpur is so very nearly self-supporting that it would seem a pity if wit cannot devise the small apparatus, whatever it is, that would raise it just over the margin and render it safe; not with the safety of a great Western city that is safe until the petrol runs out, the drains seize up, the power fails, but with a more modest borderline safety of having enough and no more.

Shivesh Thakur had two concerns in taking us to his birth-place. He wanted to forge a link between Surrey University (where he teaches Philosophy) and a few leading spirits of Bhith Bhagwanpur. To this end, intrepid Audrey Perkins, a representative of the Surrey University Engineering Department, joined the search. Shivesh Thakur also wanted to show how, in a village setting, certain ritual practices that, taken solo, would seem merely decorative or excessive, have a community meaning.

As a brahmin child, Shivesh had himself undergone initiation as a brahmachari. A Sacred Thread had been placed round his neck. He had joined the Twice-Born. Traditionally initiation would have been followed by years of instruction with a brahmin guru, learning the scriptures. At the three Thread Ceremonies I saw at Bhith Bhagwanpur the young initiates, in sets of three, had their heads shaved, their nails pared, their threads invested; and, in one case, the boys then spent a few minutes standing on home-made wooden skate-boards as if on diminutive chariots, wearing a replica of travelling robes and carrying parasols while a scratch jazz-band played them away. The journey to the guru must once have been a considerable wrench.

In explanation rather than defence of the Hindu class system (I am instructed by those who know to use the word 'class' rather than 'caste'), Shivesh quoted Plato, who had envisaged a healthy society in similar layers and pointed out that, in its original intention, class was connected with aptitude. A brahmin was one with an aptitude for study. A *kshatriya* was one with an aptitude for government and war. A *vaisya* was one with an aptitude for trade. The *shudra* was one with an aptitude for service, though in his case it was probably left to brahmins to decide. The Untouchables, Gandhi's Children of God, were outclassed entirely. Their association with certain defiling trades rendered them isolate. Two thousand years ago, the Teaching of the Buddha undermined the Class System, gave hope to the classless, roused the ire of the brahmins, opened the way for the exile from India of Buddhism, now leaking back. Class mirroring aptitude could have been flexible. Class passed on by birthright had to be tyrannous. Sooner or later the gifted son of the classless is going to break a system which keeps him from the wells and temples used by the wastrel son of the brahmin; and the gifted son of the brahmin is going to give him support.

It was not the demarcation of class that Shivesh Thakur held up for approval in Bhith Bhagwanpur, but the demarcation of one stage of life from another, a part of the Hindu tradition, he thought, with much to recommend it. The cycle of one traditional brahminic life moves through four stages or ashramas, to use the local word. Before initiation, a child (a boy, in fact, for like nearly every other religious tradition, the boys have it) is not considered to be brahminically born. At about ten, with the induction into pupilhood, the imposition of the Thread, and the new status, he enters the first of the ashramas. At marriage, he enters the second and becomes a Householder. Shivesh himself, though it scarcely shows in Surrey, is at this stage. So is his elder brother, farmer of Bhith Bhagwanpur and head of the Thakur household. Until the marriage of his son, he carries the family on his back, decides where to advance, where to pull back and controls the economy. At about the time he can become a grandfather, he will, without ceremony, enter the third ashrama which goes under the name 'Forest dweller', suggesting a distance from urban grief. The fondest alliances I saw in Bhith Bhagwanpur were those between adults in the third ashrama and children not yet in their first: grandfathers telling stories, grandmothers smuggling sweets. The fourth ashrama is that of the sannyasi, the renouncer.

In a small mud house next to the mangled mango orchard where our tents were pitched lived a Mahatma, a 'Great Soul'. His full name is Swami Sarba Prakashanand Paramahansa and not one syllable of it commemorates the name he was born with. He was, though he does not care to recall it, a lawyer, a freedom fighter, a man on the run from the British police, a politician supporting J. P. Narayan. For fourteen years, after his wife died, he disappeared. He does not discuss where. Seen again, he had shaved his head, shed his possessions, except a water-pot and staff, dressed in an ochre robe and doffed his identity. With difficulty he was persuaded back to the village he had known; and then, only on the strict condition that auld acquaintance be utterly forgot and that he can relate to everyone afresh—outside kinship, outside foreknowledge, as Atman to Atman, Self to Self. As if to establish his transience, he still takes to the road now and then. Before dawn, while we lay alongside, he did his yoga exercises, his meditation, washed yesterday's robe and hung it on a bush to dry. Before the farm children were riding on bullock-back to the fields, he was sitting on his porch. He collected nuts and berries and passed them out as sweets. The village regarded him as a mighty ornament. All his visitors touched his feet. He ate very little. He listened to village disputes if they were brought to him, but never volunteered for village politics. When, on one or two evenings, he lent his hut to the Surrey Group, the village action committee that met to work out in what simple ways a sophisticated Engineering Department in a British University could help a village in need of a simple pump, some simple sluice-gates on a new canal, small gadgets that the village blacksmith could maintain, the Mahatma sat outside in the dark throughout. He had been a pupil, a householder, a forest dweller. He now represented the wisdom of loosening the grip on life (with a small 'l') in order, as he might claim, to open himself to Life. That he was once Shivesh's uncle drops away like yesterday.

Why, I asked, did he find it necessary to separate himself from his former self and leave home? 'To be nearer to God,' he replied, 'with the object to have peace of mind.' 'And the idea,' I pursued, 'is that this peace and this nearness to God cannot be achieved while a man is in society?' 'That,' he proffered, not presuming to make up anyone else's mind, 'is our experience.'

Without button-holing him (if such a thing is possible on an ochre robe) or making him feel haunted, I spent all the time I reasonably could alongside the Mahatma of Bhith Bhagwanpur. After a time, it seemed possible to observe the village as he might observe it. He saw the local elephant, Bhith Bhagwanpur's sole taxi, ferry bride to groom or groom to bride for one or two weddings that he did not attend. He sat alongside, keeping well clear of the hearth, at a ceremony in his front yard at which four brahmin priests recited Vedas and offered a fire-sacrifice to secure a good harvest. He heard the morning clatter and bray of drumming and chanting from the Shiva temple that lies just beyond the village, but he never went there. He saw school children and their teachers cart their painted clay image of the goddess

Saraswati from the classroom to the temple pond and drown it, but he did not join the procession. The nearest he came to seeming to worship the gods was the morning we left, when he stood by his hut as villagers dropped garlands of flowers over our heads. As the old bus lumbered from the blighted mangoes to the cart-track, he waved.

'As you renounce,' he once said, 'you also renounce the gods.'

3

ISRAEL
The Chosen People

If the question were, 'In which city—Benares or Jerusalem —do they worship many gods?', there seem to be strong reasons for choosing Jerusalem. On the Temple Mount at the Dome of the Rock and the Al Aksa Mosque, Muslims wash faces, hands and feet and prostrate themselves in the direction of Mecca. Through a small gate, patrolled by an armed guard and deeper in the ruins of the Second Jewish Temple, Jews in prayer shawls kiss what remains of the Western Wall and say their prayers. As if neither Muslims nor Jews existed, Christians pace out their own Jerusalem in the steps of the Master—the Via Dolorosa, Calvary, the Holy Sepulchre. To a newcomer it was like moving through a haunted house where ghosts from different eras move past and through each other dreaming of the time when the house was entirely theirs and behaving as if that time were now. Suddenly a pilgrim's leg, blown off by one or other kind of extremist, jolts the sleepers awake and for a second or two they appear to look at each other, but very soon the habit of separateness returns.

When I gave these impressions to Rabbi Pinchas Peli, a friend of *The Long Search*, he said that two groups of people had a right to talk about Jerusalem: those who had just arrived and those who had known about it for a very long time. Six generations of Pelis have been Jerusalem Rabbis. Where else, he says, would you find Jews near their Temple, the muezzin calling the Muslim faithful to prayer, and the sound of Christian bells, all in one city and all in worship of One True God? He speaks of Judaism as the father of two daughters—Christianity and Islam. My less generous intuition is that Judaism is the father of two sons who admire, envy, need, wish to supplant, wish even to murder, then wish to mourn the one without whom they would not have existed at all. Such thoughts are deeply maddening and would probably never have surfaced without a nudge from one of the more powerful recent Jewish prophets—Sigmund Freud.

Of all the *Long Search* journeys, the search for the Jews was by far the most taxing. It was not undertaken in one journey but in a series of frenzied forays over three or more years. Two of the most resonant and wounding rumpuses within the *Long Search* team happened in the course of searching for the Jews. Where other films ran their course, found their shape and put themselves to sleep on celluloid, the search for the Jews was an argument that, once started, would not stop. Witnesses were summoned years apart, filmed, added. The jury was never asked to retire. Eventually the film was not so much completed as suddenly twirled into a particular, confected shape and deep-frozen. From it startled Jews stare out in surprise that the talking should have stopped, the movement been arrested. Some filmic wizard must have wormed his way into this argumentative Jewish paradise and paralysed it with a spell. By rights then there must be another whiter wizard, prince, warrior who will fight his way in with a counter-spell, cast it, watch the ice melt and the tongues set about it again. Films are sometimes said to have life, but the Jews have it more abundantly. Was it, I wonder, just an accident that the search for the Jews became the lightning-conductor for so much seemingly unconnected *Long Search* turmoil? There is a nice story about the Baal Shem Tov, the eighteenth-century Jewish master, who lost his way going from one room to another in a strange house and found himself down the cellar. Immediately he began to investigate the *mezuzah*, the small parchment container on the doorpost that carries key Jewish scripture. A bystander raised a mild objection: 'Just because a man loses his way, does there have to be a cause? Couldn't it just be an accident?' The Baal Shem Tov answered: 'As far as I am concerned there are no accidents.'

'What', I used to ask until the question asked itself, 'is a Jew?' 'I don't have any idea,' said a Rabbi in Westchester County, U.S.A. 'What is worse—I have too many ideas.' I suspect that there is one set of answers when the question comes from a Gentile, quite another set when the question comes from a Jew. The answer to a Gentile usually starts with a demolition of the thought that the Jews are a race. Those Jews whom Gentiles say they can recognize as Jews are merely similar Jews and, with a history of closed societies, it is natural that some Jews have become more similar. But one walk down one Jewish street in Jerusalem, where Jews have assembled from remote corners of the world and resemble each other not at all, should convince all but the most impenetrable racist that a phrase like 'the Jewish race' carries no meaning. The Jews, in their own various accounts, are a Nation and a People, a Holy Nation and a Chosen People. Their defining features are not genetic but 'religious', though again, the word 'religious' will not quite do. 'Religion' is a Latin word and carries a smear of cultism. The idolatrous Romans are an ancient enemy.

'Did God, in the Jewish account, speak to the Jews?' There was a breezy upwardness about the question at the start of three years as if one answer would do and a monosyllable at that. Some Jews gave it: 'Yes.' But the Jews who became friends held back. That God spoke they would admit, for a start. But they hesitated on the word 'God', knowing they had no guarantee that what I thought they thought and what any of us thought had any bearing on what God may be. As for 'spoke', the word was acceptable in a manner of speaking. But if 'spoke' implied a speaking mouth and a human shape to carry the mouth, then there was cause to hesitate. On the matter of 'speaking to the Jews', the thought is too elided for comfort. 'God spoke', whatever that may mean, not just once but, in the Biblical account, in a sequence. What He said to Adam He said to all men, posing the greatest question: 'Where art thou?' God of course knew where Adam was, but did, and does, Adam? 'God spoke' again. His servant Abraham 'heard'. His servant Abraham by 'hearing' obeyed. At that moment, he became the proto-Jew, the first 'hearer' to transmit the past. Again God spoke—to Noah—and out of the dialogue emerged the seven great commandments that guarantee the oneness of God and the possibility for Gentiles of being 'righteous' and having their share in the world to come 'whatever that means' (Rabbi Peli's footnote). Again God spoke—to Moses and, through Moses, to mankind, on Sinai —and the Torah, the Law or, better, the Teaching, was delivered. Michelangelo, following a common misrepresentation of a Hebrew word, represents Moses wearing horns. The mistaken word properly means 'with a radiant face'. He also, in line with generations of lesser Christian painters and chisellers, solidifies the Teaching on a Tablet. The Jews, again, hesitate at anything quite so specific. A Teaching was given, perhaps on Tablets, perhaps by inspiration. Who knows? And sometimes at this stage in the discussion I sensed an undertow of 'Who cares?' All my questions drifted Godwards, towards theology, towards the definition of areas that may simply have to be left dark. Bit by bit, battle after battle with the Jews, I was persuaded that my approach was a very Christian approach; that my 'open-mindedness' was my own mirage; that knowing names and places in common, sharing the Flood, the Ten Commandments and the Psalms of David does not guarantee insight into what the Jews are about, what the Jews are for.

In the opening moments of the Jewish *Long Search* film Elie Wiesel, sitting among his books in New York, words the distance between the Christian question and the Jewish answer: 'Think about it. God decided for the first and last time to reveal Himself on Sinai. For the first and only time He was going to speak to His human race. And you would expect God to give you a lecture on theology at least. After all, it is His domain. Or on mysticism: He would explain to you the beginnings and the ends; He would tell you how He created the world, because it is not given in Scripture. Instead what He did was to give all kinds of commands about human relations. "Thou shalt not kill", "Thou shalt not lie", "Honour thy father and thy mother". Why did He do this? It was so simple. But this is the lesson. God can take care of Himself. What He had to give man is the dignity of man.' God, in other words, did not say 'Judaize the world', but 'humanize the world'.

I now think, much too late to do anything about the film but not too late for the other long search which is less visible and longer, that the search for the Jews, as it took place on and off during the time of travelling and talking, became fog-bound on Sinai. Nearly every encounter boiled down to an effort to find an acceptable form of words to describe Torah, the Teaching, and the Covenant. It looked Godwards. Perhaps we could have learned from Jesus, that remarkable Jewish teacher, how we might have gone about the Jews. In His parables on the subject of stewardship—how the owner of a vineyard leaves someone in charge and goes away—in no case does He recommend that the steward should lean over the gate gazing at the master's departing footprints. Rather he is supposed to work in the vineyard;

and his work will not be judged according to the richness of his longing to see his lord again. Longing could even get in the way. If this line of thought had been pursued, the film might have been less talkative, but busier. Or perhaps busy as well as talkative. Space would have had to be found for cheese-cake, Jewish charity, politics, business, comedians, with two recent mini-Messiahs—Marx and Freud—making their different attempts to lead people from different sorts of slavery and into the promised land. There would have been Jews who would have applauded this approach. Equally there would have been others who deplored it. Wherever there are two Jews, said Rabbi Peli, there are three opinions.

The Pelis, Pinchas and his wife Phina, are Orthodox Jews, or perhaps an exacter word would be 'orthoprax'. They do the traditional things. They remember and observe the Sabbath. They eat kosher. They pray as prescribed. Their right opinions, their orthodoxy, involve action. Though Pinchas does not wear the eighteenth-century court rig of the big black hat, long black coat and side curls, he was born in one of those parts of Jerusalem where they are still worn—Mea Sherim—and thinks that one day all Jews may be grateful that some few of their number opted to appear to 'freeze' in a by-gone age in order to free themselves to be Jews in the age in which they actually live. Once or twice I walked in Mea Sherim. In origin it is a garden suburb outside the walls of Jerusalem though the garden, if it was ever there, has now died. Its founder, an English Jew, Moses Montefiore, offered Jews a cash inducement to live there, such were the hazards of not being closed up in the city. The gates (one of the meanings of Mea Sherim is 'a hundred gates') were originally to shut out the unnamed hostility of the surrounding region. At the same time as they shut out, they shut in, marking off the extreme orthodox from their neighbours. Now that the waste places have been swallowed up by the enlarged city, the gates of

Protestant churchgoers in the U.S.A.

Young Jewish boy with *tefillin*

Mea Sherim separate its inhabitants from other Jews. Two enormous slogans were painted in white on interior Mea Sherim walls: 'Jews mourn twenty-seven years of rebellion against G-D', i.e. mourn the twenty-seven-year existence of the State of Israel; and 'Judaism and Zionism are diametrically opposed'. (I wonder why they were in English? Were they rapid sermons to the pilgrimages of American Jews who come to the homeland, stay at the King David Hotel, visit the Holocaust Museum and come to Mea Sherim to find out how the other Jew lives? Did they represent the majority opinion in Mea Sherim?)

During filming our camera pedestal was attacked by a ferocious ringleted little boy who would not be convinced that we were not an Israeli camera team and therefore not, automatically, an enemy. Pinchas Peli, who accompanied us, was much occupied explaining us to hostile inhabitants and came in for his own share of dressing down; as soon as they sighted us, the Mea Sherim men pulled their hats over their eyes and accelerated past us. It was not clear whether the image now graven on the film stock came under the commandment about graven images; or whether they felt that a part of their presence, of their 'soul', deserted them if they left themselves behind on celluloid. Mea Sherim is clearly tourist-proof. It aims to be assimilation-proof. In Eastern Europe, or wherever the original inhabitants came from, there was little danger. The Christians did not wish to be Jews and the Jews did not wish to be Christians. Suddenly, in a state called Israel, Jew calls to Jew, secular Jew to religious Jew, observant to lapsed, new to old and the gates of Mea Sherim seem to be needed, by those who need them, as never before.

At moments during the search for the Jews when something had disturbed and alarmed me—a visit with Rabbi Peli to the Holocaust Museum in Jerusalem, an account by Elie Wiesel in New York of his time as a boy in Auschwitz and Buchenwald—a certain quality of question always followed. It took different disguises but did not vary underneath. To Pinchas Peli, sitting on the cemetery wall outside the Museum, it went: 'What would you say to a Jew who decided that he had had enough of the God who had chosen and not protected him, and wished to merge with the rest of us? Would you blame him?' 'I should not blame him,' came the reply, 'but I would pity him.' Certainly, went the theme, he would seem to have removed himself from some dangers. At the same time he would have given up his greatest source of pride, his role as witness for the good and the holy and against evil.

There was a similar little crisis in New York. Elie Wiesel, sitting in his apartment just off Central Park, had just recalled a classic incident, of which he was part, in one of the concentration camps. Once, he said, three Jews who were scholars, heads of academies, decided to put God on trial for what He had done to His Chosen People. Evening after evening, sitting on the beds, with young Elie Wiesel absorbing the scene like a bleak cub reporter, the men argued the case with great gravity, knowing that their verdict would tell on the hearers and fame of it would spread. After great discussion they brought in their verdict: 'Guilty'. 'And now,' said the Head of the Tribunal, 'let's go and pray.' Thirty-five years later, that memory is waiting for Elie Wiesel to make a short story or a play of it. And his intention, when he works on it, is to introduce one new character, a character who would take God's part, argue that His ways are just, that the punishment prepared for six million of His people is proper. That character, says the writer, will be Satan. Again, out of my infinitely milder disorientation and woe, the same question emerged, this time in the form of an offer of friendship: 'All right. Let's strike a bargain—I will cease to be a Christian and you cease to be a Jew. And I will look after you, think well of

you, enjoy your company and protect you. Will you accept?'
The answer was not rapid, but there was no scrambling or
disorientation about it: 'No. Absolutely not.' The tension
that followed was so severe that I involuntarily relieved it
with what I heard to be someone else's, an alien, laugh. The
answer continued: 'I will not cease to be a Jew because I
would cease to be. Do you think that I could decide that
3,500 years of history should end with me? Do I have the
right to say "enough"? And David and Abraham and
Moses and Isaiah and Jeremiah and all the thousands and
thousands of martyrs and sages and teachers and prophets
all end with me? I would never stop.'

The words 'Let's strike a bargain—I will cease to be a
Christian and you cease to be a Jew' were partly a device to
secure an expected reaction; partly a genuine wish to wipe
out history and start again; but most of all, though at the
time quite unconsciously, it was one of those 'heads I win,
tails you lose' offers which it was not only right that a Jew
should reject but at which he could be angry.

There have been times, on these journeys, when I have
denied being a Christian. For instance, in Indianapolis,
when rabid Baptists asked me if I was saved (which adds up,
in their context, to being a Christian), I answered 'No' with
a good conscience. In Romania too when old East *v.* West
battles were being fought yet again, I ducked the fray. I do
not, as far as I know, belong to the Elect. Nor do I have any
way of knowing whether the Pope was being proper and
pontifical or merely peevish when he allowed his emissaries
to plant a note of the excommunication of all the Eastern
Patriarchs on the altar of St Sophia in Constantinople on
16 June 1054. It may even be possible for Christ to wish a
man not to be a Christian if 'being a Christian', as interpreted, involves overwhelming stupidity and error. Whatever answer I give to the question 'Are you a Christian?', so
long as it is an answer in good conscience, does not make me

less of a person. Much in my own tradition supports me.

For Elie Wiesel and for any Jew, it is harder. To be a Jew, as far as I understand the term, means to accept Jewish history, the historic nationhood of the Jews. And this is a nation covenanted to God. It is good, as Elie Wiesel puts it, for a Jew to believe in God, to fight God, to plead with God, tell Him He is wrong, plot against Him, send Him into exile. But it is not possible to be a Jew and yet be indifferent to God. God makes him a person and a Jew. The Jewish God is worth taking trouble over. Out of the trouble comes the Jewish cutting edge, fine-honed by argument. 'Hath not a Jew eyes? Hath not a Jew ears?' is a sound human plea as Shylock makes it in court in *The Merchant of Venice*. And even that witless gathering is silent and touched for a second or two. They would not have understood if he had said: 'Hath not a Jew a Covenant? Hath not a Jew a task to do? Hath not a Jew history?' Shakespeare probably did not know either, or perhaps he would not have let Shylock, a punctilious man in all things, cry out for 'the Law' and 'Justice', when Shylock knew better than any present that his 'Law' explicitly says: 'Thou shalt not murder.' But then, if Shylock were not a greedy monster the tinniness of his oppressors would be so repellent that the play would be quite without heart. The age-long Christian wish for the Jew not to be the Jew is one of the pieces of Christian history that have been well absorbed and remembered by both sides. It has also led to one or two decent jokes . . . like that of the man who went up to a Jew and struck him. When the Jew asked why, the hitter replied, 'You killed our Lord.' 'But that was ages ago,' said the Jew. 'I know,' said the other, 'but I only found out yesterday.' And the other, a response to some new developments in Christian theology, on which a Jew wryly observes: 'Well, they've decided there is no such person as Jesus. But the Jews still killed him.' It will take more than a papal apology to eradicate the shadow, that still lurks, of the Jew as a threat. But perhaps a shadow brought into the sunlight will be sufficiently well defined and handle-able that it may in time throw back its own question: 'What is it about me, who am only a shadow and a foreshadow of you, which makes you so frightened?'

Three thousand years and more of Jewish energy and debate have gone into keeping the Jews distinct from their neighbours, and particular. Sometimes, as when the Nazis decreed that all Jews must wear a Star of David on their backs, their neighbours have lent a hand. The six hundred and thirteen commandments that, according to Jewish tradition, the Jew must keep, tie him to God for sure. They also separate him graphically from his neighbour, who is thought to have done all that can be expected of him if he observes seven. Am I, I used to ask Rabbi Peli, a second-class citizen in your eyes? How am I to read your condescension in thinking me capable of remembering seven principles while you absorb and observe so many more? Am I, as my pocket calculator would suggest, 87.571428 times stupider and less able than you? The voice rises and the heels start drumming. Am I a child, sitting at table, facing a plate of mild mush while my elders, claiming how burdensome it is to be adult, work their way through five courses and a change or two of wine? What makes my father give my elder brother privileges that he does not give to me? What are these six hundred and thirteen errands that he is thought capable of doing and I not? The more these complaints are given breath, the more they express themselves in the language of sibling jealousy. The phrase 'the Chosen People', scaled down to single family size, sounds alarmingly like 'Father's Favourite'. It is, of course, not adult, responsible, rational, happy, liberating, to corner and rough up father's favourite; but, as any Jew reading his own Scriptures knows, with their tales of Cain and Abel, Esau and Jacob, Joseph and his brethren, it is how some families are.

On mild Sabbath evenings, with these family tensions well banked down, Rabbi Peli used to tell me about the two poles of 'particularity' and 'universalism' in Judaism: how the Jews have an obligation to be distinct; at the same time, how their distinctness points towards a future universal commonwealth in which separate peoples will, each in its own way, serve the One God. He quoted, on the universalist theme, the prophet Micah: 'Each man shall dwell under his own vine, under his own fig tree undisturbed, for the Lord of Hosts Himself has spoken. All people may walk, each in the name of his god, and we will walk in the name of the Lord our God for ever and ever.' (Micah 4:4–5.) If, however, as I sometimes gave the impression, nothing would satisfy me but the six hundred and thirteen commandments of the Jewish Law, I was reminded that the doors were always open and 'we would welcome you with open arms'.

Jewish missionizing lost heart, not surprisingly, in the days following the conversion of the Emperor Constantine to Christianity. A Jew who converted a Christian and a Christian who became a Jew were both done to death. Christian supremacy and vengefulness have worn down with time and it is again possible to undertake some mild Jewish proselytizing. Pinchas and Phina Peli are in regular touch with Japanese groups who are looking for some affiliation with, if not absorption into, the Jews. In Israel I attended a class for would-be converts. It was a class of three and a teacher, so nothing like a landslide, but enough to make the point that being a Jew is not just a matter of having the right grandmother.

Naomi Raaman lived, when I met her, with her husband and child in a new concrete village, guarded by armed men and surrounded with barbed wire, about five miles south of Bethlehem. Her pupils, all girls, were Dutch, Spanish and

American. The Spanish girl had most to say. She had been brought up a Roman Catholic with the idea of the Jews as the killers of Jesus, and described her first sight of a Jew at the age of twelve when she was alarmed to find how ordinary he looked. Interest in the Jews and in Israel grew and three years earlier she had come to live there. Once in Israel, she made the discovery that being a Jew is also a religion and that it is possible to join. The advantage, as she saw it, of Judaism over Christianity as she knew and had practised it, is that, for a Jew, every detail of life, matters of cooking, dressing, speaking, are religious matters. It is a religion and a life. The Sabbath is not the only holy day of the week, although the holiest. The Christianity she knew she found to be disorderly—Sunday observance and Monday derangement. The Judaism she now practised she saw as all-inclusive and orderly.

It clearly gave Naomi Raaman no particular pleasure to hear the version of Roman Catholicism from which her pupil appeared to be on the run. Jews are unused to hearing Judaism spoken of as a sanctuary for renegade Christians, though they have some experience of matters the other way round. To become a Jew, as she was careful to explain, need not be a step forward. If the new Jew loses heart, becomes slack, fumbles the life of a Jew, it will be a step back. The Jew is not offered salvation but a task. Better not take it up at all than take it up and leave it half done. No teacher could have been less eager to make converts, to advertise her classes, to offer discounts. Anyone converting should know what they are undertaking. To know what you are undertaking cannot be easy when to be a Jew means, first of all, to make that people your people, that God your God, that history your history.

The history of a large section of the Jewish people ended at the railheads from which the concentration camps collected their inmates and which, as Elie Wiesel in New York bitterly observed, the Western leaders refused to bomb. The history of an unnumbered section ended in assimilation with the Gentile world where all, Gentile and Jew, lost their God together. The history of a vital number led into socialist and Zionist politics, first in Europe, then in Israel. They remained Jews but their relationship with the Jewish God underwent changes. They have been described as 'orthodox secular Jews'. It was in a Kibbutz called Ein Gev, sitting under the Golan Heights, beside the Sea of Galilee and founded in 1937 by orthodox secular Jews, that I learned of a move, in a hitherto utterly secular Kibbutz, to build a synagogue.

When I asked one of their number, Mukki Tsur, what he meant by 'orthodox secular Jew', he replied, 'It means a Jew who believes in the non-existence of the Jewish God.' Believes in the—? 'Non-existence of the Jewish God.' Do you mean, I asked, that there is a space left not to believe in Him? 'Yeah. Right.'

The Kibbutz Ein Gev had a rapid start. At the time there was a piece of legislation covering this area to the effect that once a new building had a roof it could not legally be removed. Anything less than a building with a roof would have been torn down by British police at the end of the day. The founders of the Kibbutz gathered their forces and their friends and beat the police by completing the first building, roof and all, within the legal time-span. 'According to the Jewish tradition,' said Mukki Tsur 'first you do and then you think.' The first settlers were from Hitler's Germany and from Eastern Europe, communist, socialist, Zionist. The energy that had raised a building in one day could not easily be contained in the rest of the buildings when they were completed and, in the fifties, the community split on issues of politics and support for Ben Gurion. Half the members left. About ten per cent of the remainder found themselves twenty years later proposing to build their own synagogue.

'Isn't the building of a synagogue,' I asked, 'about the last thing you would expect in a secular foundation?' 'I would say,' came the reply, 'it's the first thing you would expect . . . Politics as a way of redemption, I think, is in crisis.' And he thought that religion . . . ? 'I am not thinking that religion will save us from politics. But I think we should enrich our consciousness beyond politics, not in order to escape politics, but in order to live in more dimensions. The synagogue is an extension of the cultural and spiritual life of this community.' And are the secular Kibbutzniks, who have cleared the ground already and are preparing to build again, acting first and thinking afterwards or the other way round? 'Some are coming back to their childhood. Some are looking for the lost childhood they never had. Some are looking for spiritual things. Some are looking for God as a question mark.' 'Is it feasible', I asked, 'to worship a question mark?' 'Yes, because the question discovers what you are looking for.' (We were sitting near the reeds that fringe the Sea of Galilee. It was too misty to see to the opposite side. Recently shells from the Syrians on the Golan Heights had swung over the rooftops and hit the water just as a reminder that Ein Gev is in a tight corner.) 'This movement of looking for religion is a way of self-affirmation more than self-negation. There are people who would like to commit suicide into religion, to jump from the secular world to the religious world without having any transitional period and without having any time for hesitation. But I believe that the religious ground is fertile only when we hesitate.'

Currently the most renowned suicide and deliberate dead-end in Jewish history is that of nine hundred and sixty Zealots in A.D. 73 in the great three-tiered mountain fortress of Masada in Judaea. It was constructed by order of Herod the Great with its own water system, swimming pool, bath houses, reception halls, private apartments. When the nine hundred and sixty arrived there for their last stand it was deserted. Forty miles away, in A.D. 70, the Romans sacked Jerusalem and for the second time the Temple of the Jews was destroyed. Masada held out for three more years. In A.D. 73, their leader addressed the survivors along these lines: 'Where is now the city that was believed to have God for her founder? She has been torn up by the roots . . . Old men with streaming eyes sit by the ashes of the Temple . . . If only we had all died before seeing the sacred city utterly destroyed by enemy hands, the Holy Sanctuary so impiously uprooted . . . God Himself without doubt has taken away all hope of survival.' Rather than be taken by the Romans, the nine hundred and sixty killed themselves. The only record of those events and of that speech is to be found in the work of Josephus, a writer and diplomat of Jewish origins who, if the war had been that of 1939–45 rather than the Jewish rebellion, might have been called a collaborator for he worked for and justified the ways of the Roman conqueror. The story slept for nearly two thousand years. Then, in 1927, the poet Yitzhak Lamdan used the line: 'Masada shall not fall again'. And the climb of the Masada deaths back into Jewish consciousness had begun. Underground fighters went to Masada to take their oath of allegiance in the years leading to the creation of the State of Israel. Professor Yigal Yadin claimed in archaeological digs and influential writing that Josephus's account, though that of a traitor, had been accurate. There was speculation within Israel on the 'Masada complex', a tendency to compare the position of the nine hundred and sixty Zealots with that of the modern Israelis, dedicated, beleaguered, but resolved that, this time, Masada should hold out.

It seems reasonable to suppose that, if the story had been

known and the nine hundred and sixty had been beleaguered Christians rather than beleaguered Jews, some churchman would have made a loving record of the event and they would now be venerated as saints and martyrs. But Jewish teachers of the time either never heard the story or saw fit not to report on it. A number of them, though, tell a story that is far less spectacular. During the Roman siege of Jerusalem a learned man, Rabbi Yohanan ben Zakkai, was smuggled from the city to safety. He approached the Roman commander with the innocent request that he be allowed, with a handful of students, to set up a non-combative school at Yavneh, somewhere in the countryside, for the study of Jewish Law. Thus the Romans, at the same time as they laid waste the Temple and destroyed Jewish religious life in Jerusalem, helped lay the foundations of modern Judaism. The Rabbi established a *yeshiva*, a sitting-place, and he and his students set about learning what God willed for them, scattered, without a temple, outside their own city. They were the survivors.

An account of this double event, death at Masada, survival at Yavneh, was an early idea for the opening sequence of *The Chosen People*, the *Long Search* film account of the Jews. A helicopter was hired to swoop round Herod the Great's deserted terraces with a film cameraman on board taking what would have been an unforgettable opening sequence. A desolate wind. Wheeling kites. The voice of the lost leader speaking the words that Josephus reports of him: 'God Himself without doubt has taken away all hope of survival.' But it was not easy to achieve the proper deadliness in the more tangled situation of modern Israel. As we prepared to film the desolate plateau, busloads of young Israeli boys and girls, with the Torah Scrolls, carried on before under a swaying canopy, started to snake their way up the hill, singing Israeli songs and playing their guitars. Once they reached the top, and with proud parents taking home-movies, they were crowded into the small ruined synagogue, the scrolls were unfurled and the young aspirants were 'called to the Law'. They became *bar-mitzvah* if they were boys, *bat-mitzvah* if they were girls—sons and daughters of the Commandment. On the ruined wall of the synagogue, while the reading of the Law was completed, stood a soldier with a machine-gun at the ready in case of trouble. The story of how best to survive if you are a Jew is tidier when read in accounts dating from two thousand years ago than traced in the present. In the event and in spite of the visual glory—which film-makers can rarely resist—the story of Masada and its dead was excluded from the final version of the Jewish film—as if to say that, though Jews in their millions have died hopeless deaths, the message of Judaism is that the Jew has a holy obligation to survive and go on fighting.

During one battling Jerusalem attempt to pin the Jews down, to have some solid morsel to go home with, I asked Rabbi Peli to give me an A.B.C. of Judaism—nothing too subtle, just a child's guide. Judaism, went his reply, is a three-way system of communication. The first is the Torah, the Teaching, God speaking the Word. This line starts with God and moves downwards. Next—and the order of events has a meaning—comes man's response, the listening, the prayer, the engagement, how young Samuel replied when he heard the still small voice in the night: 'Speak, Lord, for thy servant heareth.' This, the second line of Judaic communication, goes from mankind upwards. The third line is horizontal, the communication of man and man, life in the cities, work in the world, business, justice, how to make a good meal, how to decide with a neighbour the placing of a fence, what freedom is, what are the rights and wrongs of restraint. Communication in any of the three directions seems to mean engagement: not compliance, the smoothing over of difficulties, the laying down of arms, but the hammering out of a meaning and a course of action. When God speaks, He does not necessarily soothe. When the Jew speaks back, he does not necessarily agree to what he thinks he is hearing. Communication between man and man is sweeter when it means peace but it may mean battle and may be none the worse for that. The only sin seems to be incommunication, pulling out the plugs on the Teaching, breezy insouciance about what to say back, indifference between people. The warriors of Masada lost their battle; the scholars of Yavneh won it. Out of those bent backs, peering eyes, jabbing fingers, alert ears, nimble wits, this teasing abstraction called Judaism, which had me pinioned and gasping in many an exhilarating (and infuriating) bout, was somehow born.

Their latter-day offspring still argue, sway, tussle and pray in modern *yeshivas*, religious seminaries. They also, when they have to, fight in Israeli wars. By all accounts, some of the most dedicated fighters were taught combative thinking first of all in the religious academies. The very name, 'Israel', commemorates a fight without quarter in the Book of Genesis. Jacob, the mysterious story goes, spent the whole of one night wrestling with a man he did not know. The bout did not end even when the stranger put Jacob's thigh out of joint. Before he would let go, Jacob asked to be blessed. The adversary asked him his name and, hearing it, said: 'Thy name shall be called no more Jacob, but Israel', which means 'he who wrestles with God and man and wins'. There were desolate times in the fight for a film on the Jews, so that I wondered what could be the Hebrew for 'He who fights with the children of Israel and loses' and whether I should change my name.

In a new building in central Jerusalem is an American *yeshiva*. We were guardedly welcomed, had our credentials searched (only to be expected in such an embattled city) and were allowed to watch, attend prayer, ask questions, communicate. There were more picturesque events in the Jewish journey—a dancing procession of Bokharan Jews carrying a new Torah scroll to the synagogue and facing a reception committee of dancing older scrolls that had come part way to meet it, young foreign students trekking to the fields near Safed in North Galilee as part of a course in Jewish mysticism, the clamour of the Jerusalem flower, fruit and meat markets in the hour or two before Sabbath starts—but none that seemed to keep us on our orthodox course quite like the days spent alongside Jews studying.

The noise of morning prayer at the American Seminary in Jerusalem was deafening—stylistically at the other end of the scale from Quakerism. It would have made more immediate sense if the central Jewish prayer were 'Shout, O Daughter of Jerusalem'. Instead, it is, in Hebrew, *Shema*, 'Listen', 'Hear, O Israel, the Lord our God, the Lord is One.' Bodies swivelled from side to side and backwards and forwards as if the whole room had just trapped its thumb and was living through the inevitable wait between the bad happening and the easing off of the pain. From time to time prayer shawls were thrown over the head and face, and thumb and forefinger were pressed into the eyes. Even the word 'Amen', which European Christians have a way of turning into a unanimous sigh, became among these boys a dissonant clamour of individual affirmations. It was too near Christian worship to have the charm of utter strangeness, and too strange to be utterly comfortable. Above all, it demanded a redefinition of the words 'Hear' and 'Listen'. 'How does God speak to you?' I asked. 'He does not speak to me,' replied the sharp, pale bearded boy who had taken me on. 'I understand Him through my learning and my actions. That is how I listen.' Learning, praying, living in the *yeshiva*, as far as I saw it, was a scene of constant engagement. The gearing of the engagement could vary—top gear at the height of prayer and study, a lower gear for a moment of recovery and recoil—but no coasting, no slipping into neutral, no Zen attempt to disengage, to get the knife-edge of bare attention between the oncoming thoughts.

A part of prayer was the respectful removal from the Ark, the scroll cupboard, of the Torah scroll, hand-written out on parchment, rolled in on its rollers, covered by a decorated cloth. The Torah in this sense—as the scriptural base of Judaism—would be more familiar to non-Jews as the Books of Moses: Genesis, Exodus, Leviticus, Numbers, Deuteronomy. As the hoisted scroll passed among the worshippers, they kissed it. Is this not (I asked at the first available opportunity) idolatry and is a Jew not covenanted to fight idolatry? Response to the question varied. From Rabbi Peli, who is orthodox, came the reply that the Torah is a letter written to every Jew from his Father in heaven. Love of the letter may not supersede love of God or love of one's neighbour: but, this side of idolatry, a kiss is permissible. A more liberal opinion on the same issue, picked up in New York, went that, when you needle into it, idolatry in some form or other is a fact of life. Religion cannot alter this fact, but, by drawing attention to it, can keep the tendency to idolize in check. From the Torah Scrolls, one of the students read the portion of Scripture for the day.

After prayer and in the same room, other books were produced and Talmudic study began. By Talmud, I understand a study in which there is no last word. Nearly two thousand years ago attempts, not so far superseded, were made to assemble, give a shape to, add commentary on the Oral Teaching, the Tradition of fighting for an understanding of what God willed for His Creation. To embody, live, rehearse the Talmudic arguments and submit them to question is to develop stamina and muscle where Jews hitherto have most valued them—in the heart and the brain. Study is done out loud and in pairs. Energetic openness to God in prayer moves over into energetic openness to God in study. There is a mark on the page. What does it mean? How should we act on it? Similarly—a point made explicitly in the *Long Search* film—musicians face a score, another mark on a page. How should they interpret it? How should they act on it? How should they play?

After the study session, the same energy and engagement carried over into answers that came to my questions. Yes, it is possible to fall into cleverness for its own sake; but truly that is not the purpose of study. No, the noise of debate is not distracting. It is an echo of the upheaval that attended the delivery of God's Word to Moses on Sinai. One meaning of 'Torah' is the words on the scroll as copied, read, carried about, covered, the mobile token of the particularity of the Jews. At the same time Torah is everything, the whole of a life, the whole of study, all politics, all endeavour, the rights of this nation, the rights of all nations.

'Can you ever say,' I ventured, 'that you have something in your mind that you cannot quite get into your mouth?' 'When anyone says that,' came the riposte, 'he doesn't know what he is talking about.'

At this point an arguably blasphemous question formed itself to be asked. God, in the Jewish account, spoke. The life of a Jew is working out what God could have meant and applying it in living. If God knew what He meant to say, surely He should have been able to say it. Why should He need the Jews or any other group to complete a sentence that was only half spoken, to make God's mind up for Him? Or does God not know His own intentions till some arguing, battling, resourceful, tireless part of His human creation sets to work to clear His mind for Him?

On second thoughts I take back the word 'blasphemy'. There are Christians and Muslims for whom the thought of the uncompletedness of God could sound blasphemous. Most Jews may think so too. But not, I think, the Jews I grew to love and admire, and who raised the questions that will not lie still. They might well argue that it is a pretty impractical, abstract, theological point to be making; but, if the alternative was no communication, no speech, no engagement, they would choose to discuss it.

4

SRI LANKA
Footprint of the Buddha

My earliest lesson in what I later knew as Buddhism was delivered at the water's edge on the beach at Scarborough in Yorkshire. I must have been about three. I was seeing the sea for the first time. When my father asked why I did not paddle, I said, so I am told, 'I'll go in when it's stopped moving.' With greater insight (not to be expected in one so young and scared) I should have realized that not only would the sea go on moving endlessly but that the air around me would move too, that the sand between my toes was in process of change from rock to pebble to grain, that my skin, flesh and bones were cycling, declining, re-forming, that the jangling cluster of thoughts and feelings lacked any continuous substance. I could not have the assurance of the hymn-writer who wrote 'Change and decay in all *around* I see', as if he were somehow exempt. Human existence, says the Teaching of the Buddha, is unstable, impermanent, unsatisfactory. It is necessary to pierce through to some understanding of this instability, this discomfort, and learn how to handle it rather than constructing temporary shelters like belief in the immortal soul, hope of a reward in heaven, faith in God, all of which will be washed away by some oncoming tide.

Because of one translation of one key word, most English speakers start with the joyless notion that, to a Buddhist, to be alive at all is to 'suffer'. Existence is suffering; wanting and not getting is suffering; wanting and getting is suffering; meeting is suffering; not meeting is suffering; parting is suffering—as if the face of the world were soured into some endless, pained wince. The 'suffering' word in Pali, the language of one vast body of the most ancient Buddhist scripture, is *dukkha*. Its opposite is *sukha*. Somewhere behind both words lies an image of the action of an axle and a wheel. If *sukha* is the joy of a wheel revolving on a smooth axle, no rust, no grit, no judder, then *dukkha* is obstruction, the resistant squeal of faulty bearings, the grating of substance on substance without lubrication. The first of the Buddha's Four Noble Truths is the fact of *dukkha*—a truth to be grasped. The rest of them cover: how *dukkha* arises; the bliss that follows from *dukkha*'s overthrow; the Eightfold Path leading to the bliss of *dukkha*'s overthrow. Rather than risk the gloom of faulty associations, *dukkha* should probably stay as it is and join the language as a new word. The most useful thumbnail definition of *dukkha* that I know came from a Buddhist monk in California (though it may not have started with him): '*Dukkha*,' he said, 'is the attempt to make reality repeatable.' The sentence itself is very repeatable and each time I spin it round it seems to dig deeper and deeper.

Of all the *Long Search* journeys, I think the journey to Sri Lanka and the initial search for Buddhism was the one that began with the greatest expectations. If, as I gathered, the astute Church of Rome had understood nearly a century ago that Buddhism was to be a great challenge to Christianity in coming days, and had set beavering Jesuits to master and become expert in Buddhist scriptures; if the insights of the most modern physics seem to lie alongside the Buddhist world-view without difficulty; if Alfred North Whitehead had traced the decline of both Christianity and Buddhism to their failure to get together; if Buddhism had been vulnerable to none of the anti-God, anti-Heaven, anti-Creation attacks that have made Christianity wince; if anti-religious scoffers stopped scoffing when they reached the Buddha, then I felt, not for the only time during these journeys, that I should be paying the B.B.C. for letting me search, not the other way round.

In May 1975 one of our number, Peter Montagnon, had gone to Sri Lanka clutching an increasingly damp little list of eminent Buddhist monks who might be suitable as guides, participants, censors, obstacle-removers for the search that lay ahead. From time to time after a day's driving and talking, he would record his findings on a small tape-recorder. It was from the transcripts of this tape that I got my first impression of the hazards that we were all about to face: not the clean lines of the *Dharma*, the Teaching, as it appears rinsed and sweatless in the cool accounts of Buddhist scholars, but the tangle of politics, high-mindedness, doubt of our motives, combativeness and sanctity that would face us once we took a real camera to a real place on a real search.

The golden thread that runs through these evening notes is the tale of the first mention, the daily pushing to one side and the eventual discovery of the Venerable Ananda-maitreya, who sometimes held my hand and sometimes slapped down my pretensions on the eventual journey. He was not, for some reason, on the original list of grey eminences, though he had been Vice-Chancellor of the Buddhist University in Colombo, spoke English, knew England. Peter Montagnon first heard his name from the driver in whose car he scoured the island: Henry Rupasinghe, a burly ex-politician whose reasons for turning from politics to chauffeuring we never quite dared to probe. Daily, as Peter stepped back into the car after a meeting with yet another recommended monk, Henry, scraping into first, would mutter something about the right man being overlooked. There are folk-tales in which the searcher, thinking himself far away from the answer he is looking for, finds that it has been alongside him all the time. As a last resort, Henry was listened to, Anandamaitreya was met, and that particular stretch of search was over.

My most adhesive memory of my short-term teacher of Buddhism, the Venerable Anandamaitreya, is not of any words he spoke, nor of his tirelessness, his light tread well on in his eighties, his rigorous life-style, but of his chuckle. It came, for instance, at the end of a small exchange in which I had challenged him to put Buddhism in a nutshell. He accepted, and his reply went: 'Avoid evil; do good; and purify your mind.' (By 'mind', he meant something warmer than 'thinking'.) 'Not easy,' I mused. 'Very easy,' came the back-hand volley, 'if you understand it.' 'The Teaching of the Buddha,' said a teacher in a Buddhist Sunday School where rows of bright children parroted their way through a litany of Buddhist pieties as a first step to understanding them, is 'critical in spirit, dialectical in argument, positivistic in its conclusions, synthetic in its purpose, mystical in belief and, above all, rational in structure.' In other words, and without quizzing each of those loaded words for its real meaning, Buddhism, as that teacher taught it, is generally acceptable by any educated European who has rejected God, turned away from blind faith, repudiated dogma, unseated superstition. Buddhism, as he saw it, has not made those unfortunate commitments that are now sucking in and mincing Christianity.

This is the flavour of the Buddhism I first learned from the Venerable Anandamaitreya: tireless teacher, fierce rationalist, compassionate guide, exemplary religious simpleton (this to be understood as the height of appreciation and esteem). It was much later that I learned of his respect for horoscopes, his knowledge of his past lives, how he consciously draws 'magnetism' from the food he eats and the air he breathes, how he saw a ghost-monk walking on the hot coals at the great shrine of the god Kataragama in the south of the country. This is not to say that he tells one tale to visiting Europeans and another to himself and his fellow Buddhists. Rather, that the clear outlines of Buddhism seen from a distance blur once you land on it and start asking questions.

Long as his name is already, the Venerable Anandamaitreya adds to it, according to local custom, the name of his birthplace, Balangoda—a small town with one main street, quiet but for its dark Hindu temples, and with one main Buddhist temple on a hill. The priest in charge there was in his nineties. The Venerable Balangoda Anandamaitreya is his junior. As we approached, the junior took from his robes a yellow handkerchief, spread it on the floor, knelt on it and prostrated himself before his senior. When I first met Anandamaitreya (it is not out of disrespect but terminological exhaustion that I reduce him to one name from now on) he sat on an adult chair and I sat on a nursery stool. All laymen are seen as the spiritual inferiors of all monks and gain merit by admitting it. All monks owe the same respect to monks ordained before them and receive the same respect from monks ordained after them. The Triple Gem, the Buddhist invocation that the children in that Buddhist Sunday School chanted till it scored itself indelibly on my memory-plates, went:

> Buddham Saranam gacchami;
> > (I take the Buddha as my refuge;)
> Dhammam Saranam gacchami;
> > (I take the Dharma as my refuge;)
> Sangham Saranam gacchami.
> > (I take the Sangha as my refuge.)

In other words, I stand by the One Who Woke Up to the Truth; I stand by the Teaching he preached; I stand by the community of monks who live by the Teaching and carry it out into the world. As they sang it out, Anandamaitreya and his fellow monks sat impassively by, their fans aligned on their knees. Out of the mouths of babes and sucklings, over and over again till I can still hear it, came the three-part focus of the Sri Lanka search.

Anandamaitreya had the idea, I think, that to call Jesus Man and God made Him in some way impenetrably complicated, whereas to call the Buddha 'a man, an extraordinary man, but a man' (which he did) made him more graspable. Both Jesus and the Buddha, I should have thought, are impenetrably complicated the moment either of them has to be explained. And to call the Buddha 'an extraordinary man' when he is said to be one of a select band who have broken the cycle of birth and rebirth and penetrated things as they really are, is to stretch even the word 'extraordinary' till it cracks. Later I was to meet some of the Buddhists of the North—of Tibet and China—where the Buddha seemed to dissolve into Buddha-nature, Buddha-ness, essence of Buddha, till in Japan he disappeared entirely. In Sri Lanka he was presented in a way thought, perhaps, to be appropriate for a beginner—flatly, without rainbows, as a Teacher with a Teaching.

The interior of the Buddhist temple in Balangoda makes one big, coloured, teaching aid. Life-size and larger-than-life-size plaster likenesses of the Buddha and his disciples are arranged in instructive tableaux that start with his miraculous birth as Prince Siddhartha—a child preaching on a lotus-flower—and proceed through his exit from his life as a prince, his time as an ascetic, his vigil under the Enlightenment Tree, His Waking Up to the Truth, his First Sermon, his Mission and his Pari-nirvana, the complete cessation of births and deaths. On an adjacent wall is a gallery of other Buddhas, twenty-four in number, like reflections in a hall of mirrors. These are not former incarnations of the one we know as Gautama the Buddha or Shakyamuni, but former fully-enlightened Buddhas who ruled former eras while the organism that, 2050 years ago, became Gautama was still spiralling up to Buddhahood. At the end of the temple gallery stands the serene statue of the Buddha Who-is-yet-to-be, the Maitreya Buddha (a name too like Messiah-Buddha not to give any Judaeo-Christian a slight jolt). He is presumed to be at this moment re-birthing and re-deathing his way towards us—unless he is here already. All the Buddhas, however, teach one Buddha Truth.

Though in no other way does the Venerable Anandamaitreya resemble Greg Dixon of the Baptist Temple Indianapolis, he resembles him in this: he too sees it as his sole aim to propagate his particular Gospel. The differences, though, as far as I understand them, tell a story. The Baptist is after your soul; the Buddhist, if you are so far deluded as to think that you have a soul or any continuous self, is out to convince you otherwise. The Baptist says God made you; the Buddhist discourages you from idle speculation. The Baptist encourages you to accept Jesus; the Buddhist encourages you to accept the Buddha, and the Buddha encourages you to accept nothing blindly from anyone. The Baptist says the world is good, though spoilt by Satan; the Buddhist says the world is neither good nor bad, merely unsatisfactory, uneasy, woe-laden. The Baptist talks of the washing away of sins; the Buddhist talks of the piercing of ignorance. For the Baptist, heaven is where God is; for the Buddhist, Nirvana is where all the unsatisfactorinesses, woes, clingings, births and deaths are not. The Baptist speaks of Heaven as perfect bliss; the Buddhist speaks of Nirvana as perfect bliss. The Baptist preaches one life, one death and Heaven or Hell to follow; the Buddhist preaches many lives, many deaths and Buddhahood, at length, to follow. There is one gateway to salvation for the Baptists—Jesus Christ; there is one gateway to salvation for Buddhists—the length of your own body, the clarity of your own understanding. Jesus says: 'I am the Way, the Truth and the Life.' The Buddha says: 'I point the Way and I point the Truth.' As for the Life, if the word means in any sense the chain of itches and woes, gains and losses that we experience here, the Buddha would seem to point away from it.

My recollection of Anandamaitreya is of a man teaching. One evening in Polunnaruwa, the old capital of the island, in a tourist hotel, I called on him as a courtesy, knowing that he had not eaten since noon and would not eat again till next day, and that I was due to go in a clamorous bus-load for a curry and mosquito attack in a dank restaurant built out over a lake. He was sitting on his bed reading. I, as usual, sat below him on the floor. He assumed I was there for more of the Dharma and spoke of how to handle an enemy. We both settled in for a sermon. If you recognize that this thing you think of as 'you' is a process and that thing you think of as your 'enemy' is a process, you have great difficulty knowing where you should attack. If you think to attack his body, all you attack is the mere instrument of his mind. If you think to attack his mind, where do you propose to start? The thought that hurt you is as dead as the 'you' that the thought attacked. What revenge then can you take? Very little that makes any sense. You can try to make sure that the offending thought is properly banished from your enemy's mind; and, once clear of him, doesn't come and roost with you. Of the possible 'excluding' techniques, you should try the meditation of Human Kindness: extending Loving Kindness first to yourself (for the feeling of enmity often flourishes on lack of a proper self love); thence to all living creatures, including, of course, your enemy.

During one such sermon in a hotel bedroom in Kandy, a waiter brought a tray of tea, and whereas his usual style had been to flick his napkin over a window-sill until we thought to give him a tip, this time he sat and listened. He could not have stayed long enough to pick up much of the drift and his English extended little further than 'You leave today?'; but it seems he somehow gained merit by the sheer act of pausing in the presence of the Teaching being taught. Extensive conversations with Anandamaitreya were taped at intervals throughout filming. The last took most of two days. When, at around seven on the second evening, I said that I had asked my last question, he allowed himself to look relieved and he let himself be driven the eight or so miles back home. Next day we discovered that he had left us to attend an all-night gathering at which he had preached for a further three and a half hours.

A Buddhist monk, a *bhikkhu*, is allowed to own eight objects: three articles of clothing, a girdle, an alms bowl, a razor, a needle, a water strainer (to strain off, I should imagine in Sri Lanka, dead mosquitoes). The robes, on the Buddha's instructions, were to be the wrappings of the corpses in the charnel yards, sewn together as an enveloping reminder of mortality. Token gestures in that direction remain—in one tradition a panel of patches. But the *bhikkhus* of Sri Lanka wear a bright saffron orange, a dazzling sight in an island that is, in its habitable parts, mostly bright green. The Buddha taught that it is the duty of a *bhikkhu* to teach and preach for the good of the many, for the happiness of the many, out of compassion for the world. He also taught that the *bhikkhu* must let the Teaching work on himself, must cultivate himself, lest he become merely a mouth. These two tendencies—to cultivate oneself and to turn one's attention to others—ideally coexist. In practice, in Sri Lanka certainly, there are forest-dwelling monks and town-dwelling monks—one group cutting themselves off from secular society to accelerate their self-cultivation; the other living surrounded by laity, serving in temples and teaching in schools. Our search too had to fork two ways—one townwards, one towards the forest.

Anandamaitreya did not accompany us to the Forest Hermitage at Waturuwila and gave reasons which sounded like those a bishop might give for not entering another bishop's diocese. We were accompanied by Nandasena Ratnapala, who is Professor of Anthropology at the Buddhist University in Colombo. His particular interest is the Veddas (two d's), the Sinhalese aboriginals who still exist in pockets here and there. His favourite sleeping place (I have his word for it) is up a tree where the Veddas sleep. His declared intention, in relation to me, was to persuade me to spend a holiday with him among the Veddas up a tree, and to lay hands on the diary I used to write up in the evenings. His anthropological enthusiasms included the quirks of searchers. He had himself the lithe, slightly arched body of a tree-climber. He wore on his head what looked like an enlarged egg-cosy and he was usually nearing the end of a small cheroot. Whereas I might have seen Sri Lanka Buddhism entirely through Western eyes, he at least made me wonder how the Noble Eightfold Path, the Four Noble Truths, the quest for Nirvana, might sound to a tree-dweller. When we parted at Colombo airport he gave me a pot Buddha, a *bhikkhu*'s fan and a brightly painted bamboo flower-holder. It is only now, as I set about trying to reclaim Sri Lanka from my memory, that I begin to see how much of the fun of that search had to do with his wryness, his ability to make out-of-the-way connections, and his sudden bouts of mirth.

The Hermitage of Waturuwila stands in a heavily forested part of the island. In wet weather, patient leeches on either side of the drenched approach paths wave their prehensile filaments in the hope of connecting with something through which blood might be flowing (e.g. a human leg). It is said that they can keep up this hopeful ambush for as long as five years without success, and still be alive. On my first visit, the rain was stopping.

The Hermitage is first seen from a cart track in the valley —a white dome among the trees. At close quarters it is extensive under a forest camouflage. There are monks' quarters, a special meditation block with eight single rooms, each with an enclosed corridor for undisturbed walking meditation, a Buddha hall, a variety of rock shrines, and an imposing assembly room roofed only by an impending rock, with stone seats running round the edge. The founder of Waturuwila, the Nyaka Thera (Chief Monk), is alive, though he was taking things steadily after a heart attack. His recognizable likeness can be seen in a series of rough-and-ready wall paintings that decorate one of the monastery porches.

The story, as it was told to me, is that, as a young man in search of greater seclusion, he came across this great rock in a high forest. There he sat to meditate, fed himself as best he could, and looked to the rock to be some sort of fortress against the appetite of wild animals. The wall painting shows him seated mid-rock, evidently unperturbed, while the claws of fierce animals scratch away below him. The story goes on that, though his arrival in that forest was known to no one, a pious lady in a nearby village dreamed that they had a visitor. A small band of explorers set out following dream instructions, and came across a solitary monk on his rock. The arrival of such a man is seen as conferring great merit on the adjacent communities. Soon they were starting to build round him. Other monks joined him. When the community grew too large, those with a taste for greater solitude moved to off-spin hermitages. In some cases they resettled caves that are known to have been occupied by Buddhist monks two thousand years ago. Now Waturuwila is something of a pilgrimage centre, and from time to time the laity gather to pay respects to the monks.

Doing so, they pile up merit. The lay incursion that we had arranged to film was the ceremony at the end of the Rain Retreat—the Kathina Ceremony.

For the three months of the Rain Retreat it is customary for Buddhist monks to stay put wherever they happen to be. According to the tradition, the Buddha himself instituted this retreat, after hearing complaints that his disciples were moving about in rainy weather and endangering the plant and animal life. Respect for life includes not laying oneself open to accidental murder. It is the responsibility of the laity, during this time, to make it easy for monks to stay in retreat undisturbed. At the end of the retreat, there are said to be ceremonies within the community at which any difficulties encountered between the brethren who have been so long at such close quarters are ironed out, and from the laity the *bhikkhus* receive cloth from which to make new sets of robes. The Kathina Ceremony is the handing over of the cloth.

On the afternoon before the full moon night of the Kathina Ceremony, we joined the massing pilgrims on the cart track up through the forest to the Hermitage. A sermon from one of the monks was being relayed over loud-speakers hung in the trees. We removed our shoes well before the outer courtyard of the Hermitage, and ooch-ed and ow-ed our way over flinty pebbles on our way in. Down at the bottom of the winding steps that led to the Hermitage's first level, there was the odd soft-drink seller, vegetable and fruit merchant. No tradesmen ventured higher up. The devout washed their feet in a fountain before entering the inner areas. Bunting in the Buddha colours hung from the trees. In the Buddha hall the ordination of a monk was taking place. We were introduced, as something of a wonder (both they and us), to twin boys of about nine years old who, it is claimed, had in a previous life been Tibetan monks killed in a bus crash in Andhra Pradesh in India. Their father claims that their story began to emerge when he found them at about three years of age in tears and trying to tell him something about dying in a bus. Over the following weeks they sobbed out their story. Now it is widely accepted that their claim is respectable. On the following day we filmed the Chief Monk, flanked by two other venerable *bhikkhus*, sitting in poised meditation, their fans on their knees, while in front of them the two boys sat in the lotus posture, and with their eyes closed chanted in Sanskrit and in Pali. Facing this group was a large congregation of the laity, their hands together in sign of respect, sitting on the ground and listening.

Whenever I approached a Buddhist layman with a question about why he or she gave alms, refrained from meat eating or drinking intoxicants, went on pilgrimages, spent time in meditation or pious reading, the most regular answer was that all such actions bestow 'merit'. It is meritorious to scoop a spoonful of vegetables and rice into the *bhikkhus*' begging-bowl, to listen to the preaching of the Dharma, to hear the recitation of a discourse of the Buddha, to waft a fly gently from the face rather than swatting it in vengeful fury. In search of the Buddhists of Sri Lanka, I started to think of 'merit' as a powerful, floating spiritual coinage, to be accumulated, even hoarded, sometimes transferred to another account, but surely tied to a Buddha-standard that precludes revaluation. At death it is thought that these unseen assets lend their weight in a process leading to a new and, to be hoped, better birth.

How then did I stand—English, reared a Christian, with a fistful of doubts and questions, padding round a forest hermitage in the middle of Sri Lanka and bobbing my respects at any person or thing that appeared venerable? What are my hopes of a better birth next time? This was not a question I had had in mind to ask. It was forced on me during a merry and fearless conversation with a group of devout women. When I met them they had enjoyed the satisfaction (and gained the merit) of cooking a meal for the *bhikkhus*, a privilege they had booked a year in advance. Nanda Ratnapala interpreted. How much of the boldness of the Buddhist put-down that follows came from the spokeswoman herself, and how much was salt added by the translator, I have no way of knowing. I guess, though, she meant exactly what she appeared to say. We were talking about how all of us will pay in our next lives for the transgressions, the meat eating, the lying, the alcoholic intake, of this. Does that mean then, I asked her, that I have done something wrong in a past life and am now being punished by being born a Christian in England? Her reply was immediate and unguarded: Certainly; certainly. I must be working out my transgressions. Is there, I wondered, any hope for me? Once again the answer did not back away: Certainly—if I work for an improvement from now on, my future lives will show it. Indeed I must have collected somewhere the merit that had propelled me out of England and towards Sri Lanka and Buddhism.

I liked that woman. She did not make convenient adjustments because she was talking to a foreigner. She radiated real concern about my past mistakes, my present potential, my chances in the future. Certainly her view was exclusively Buddhist, even nationalist Buddhist, but it took me back to the warm and exclusive Christianity of some of my stauncher Christian relatives. And it sounded real. She sought me out the next day on her way to her pilgrim bus; we exchanged addresses and she invited me to come and stay with her whenever I cared to. She would give me a bed and food. The village priest could teach me Pali and show me how to read the scriptures. That is, if I was serious about the quest for Nirvana.

To some ways of Buddhist thinking Nirvana appears to be a constant presence and a constant possibility. It clamours to crowd in on us. It is we who are too clouded and ignorant to let it happen. The commoner view in Sri Lanka—for the idea of either Heaven or Nirvana lying about us needs the touch of a poet or a saint or a child to bring it to life—seems to be that Nirvana, though outside time, is not now but later, and that there exist three ways of attaining it. The first way is to happen to be one in that precious chain of Fully-Enlightened Buddhas, the most recent of whom was Guatama. The second is to be an Individual Buddha, who reaches Nirvana for himself but carries no one with him. The third is to be a disciple of a Fully-Enlightened Buddha, to receive from him the Teaching and, through him, Enlightenment. It was so with the disciples of Gautama. Their proximity to a source of wisdom carried them through. But in the last two thousand years, the traces of the last Fully-Enlightened Buddha have receded and fewer and fewer people have found the inner light with which to follow him. All they have it in them to do is to circle round and round, re-born and re-dying, something like (I mean no offence) circling aircraft which are denied their clearance to land at their ultimate, longed for nirvanic destination. In the meantime they are required to try to follow the Five Precepts appropriate to a Buddhist layman—not to destroy life, not to steal, not to misuse sex, not to lie, not to take intoxicants—while their merit accumulates.

By about 4.30 the following morning the Kathina Ceremony began. The organizers had some difficulty luring the laity from the higher levels of the Hermitage, where the film electrician was rigging his lights in the assembly room with its rock roof, down to an assembly point at the foot of the hill. The loud-speaker appeals became crisper. The sign that the procession had begun was first a whispering, surging sound from the bottom of the hill—hundreds of voices murmuring *Sadu, Sadu, Sa*, meaning something like 'May you be happy', 'Well done' and 'Amen'; then the sight of men under a canopy humping a bale of cloth for the *bhikkhus'* robes. As the canopy passed, bystanders fell in behind until the whole body of the pilgrims made one line stretching up from the end of the cart track below and into the Hermitage. The sky was clear. The moon was full. On the stone seats that skirted the irregular walls of the assembly cave sat the full company of Waturuwila *bhikkhus*. The cloth was placed at their feet and the processing pilgrims followed with their gifts. Those who had already given or had nothing to give lined the pilgrim route and touched the offerings as they passed, so as to share in the merit. The women who had been concerned for my welfare in my next life beckoned me into line and I spent a contented hour touching passing brooms, bars of soap, folded brown paper, blankets, more cloth, towels, bottles of medicine. The *bhikkhus* sat impassively. Perhaps they were meditating on the great words in the Lord Buddha's 'Greater Discourse on the Void'. He speaks to his disciple, Ananda: 'And how, Ananda, comes the teacher's undoing? Here, Ananda, some teacher retired to a secluded abode— to the forest, the root of a tree, a rock, a hill cleft, a mountain cave; a charnel ground, a woodland solitude, an open space, a heap of straw. While dwelling thus in retreat, priests and laymen from town and country visit him. When that happens, he goes astray, hungers, succumbs to craving, and reverts to abundance. This teacher, Ananda, is said to be undone by the teacher's undoing.'

I spent many disturbed nights in Sri Lanka—some because, outside the big towns, our lodgings were often rooms with unglazed windows and I never grew quite to relax with the midnight scuttlings of rapid lizards; others, I think, because what I was experiencing during the day needled into me at night. I kept pencil and paper at the bedside and made half-awake notes of anything that persisted out of sleep. One dream was so powerful that it shocked me wide awake and the following account is pretty well as I wrote it at the time.

It is night. I am working alone at home in London, at a table lit by an oil lamp. I suddenly sense that the front door of the flat is not closed. I take the lamp and walk down a corridor to see. As I reach the end of it, I notice that a bedroom door is open. By the light of the oil lamp I see my father standing in the doorway in a piteously feeble state, dressed in dirty white rags and scarcely able to stand. He died in 1971. He appears to be holding on to something for support. As I move with the light I see that he is clutching the arm of another figure, a younger and stronger and calmer version of himself. I want to help, cannot move, wake up.

Next morning the dream seemed more real than the car I was driving in, the film location it was driving to or Nanda Ratnapala sitting beside me. Trying not to make it seem as weighty as it felt, I retold the story. Nanda offered what he called a 'Sinhalese and Buddhist' interpretation of the dream, adding that, of course, I should not take too much notice. My father, he said, was in his current state a very weak being struggling for re-birth as a man. The stronger, supporting image is himself as he could be re-born if more merit could be added to the merit he was struggling with already. Since I was seeing him struggle, it was up to me to supply the merit. The next step, if I were Sinhalese and Buddhist, would probably be to find a beggar, buy him food or give him money and have it understood that any merit that followed should be transferred to my father. With both of us cultivating an air of detachment and curiosity—a thin veneer in my case—we went in search of a beggar.

We passed a very bent old woman who would have done but I hadn't the nerve to tell the driver to stop. Then a blind beggar, but the lights changed. At last, in the local temple, Nanda showed me a possibility—a man who had been discharged from a hospital workless and was employing himself tending the lights round the temple stupa, the relic dome. I had to stand by and be pointed at while Nanda explained to him for whom and from whom the merit should move. I gave him money. He shook my hand and gave a careful account of when he would sit in the temple, how long he would stay, what he would recite. The film crew, in the meantime, was busy at its task of filming Buddhism. When I next saw Anandamaitreya, I told him what we had done. Quite right, he said, without a blink.

Gods too are on the spiral of birth and re-birth. And, before a god can reach Buddhahood, so says tradition, he must be re-born as a man. Likewise, before a woman can reach Buddhahood, she must be re-born as a man. Which would seem to assign the gods and the women firmly to second place. Naturally, as underdogs, they have much to say to each other; and in great secrecy, in haunts that lie off the Noble Eightfold Path and away from the Four Noble Truths, they say it. Here they are joined by those men whose will to climb to Buddhahood is weak or is suffering a set-back, and even by those who are normally committed climbers. For Buddhist monks have been known to resort to the gods. Surely the most extraordinary episode in the whole Sri Lanka journey was the night visit to the shrine of the god Dadimunda. Henry Rupasinghe drove us there through heavy forest. Without forewarning, he stopped the car, switched off the engine and wound down the window so that we could hear the pandemonium of night animals and birds. There was a small bamboo hut alongside, where the light from an oil lamp just reached through the wall cracks and touched the edges of the undergrowth outside. After a time we drove on. Within a mile of the shrine we heard the drumming.

The god Dadimunda is a convergence of many forces: he is the nature god who inhabited the rock from which the shrine itself was hewn; he is the chieftain who, in the days of the Sinhala kings, did the hewing and became a god when he died (as there have been moves to perpetuate the assassinated S.W.R.P. Bandaranaike as the god Banda); he is the re-emergence, in a Buddhist context, of the Hindu god Vishnu; he is that god who, in Buddhist mythology, did not flee when Mara, the Evil One, attacked the Buddha, but crouched under his chair shortly to emerge with a big stick; he is god of all Sri Lanka's devils. He still carries his stick.

The temples, the image houses, of the Buddhists have been, when I have seen them, airy, open, unmysterious; for much of the time, quiet. The shrine of the god Dadimunda is dark, numinous, with the god concealed behind a sequence of veils. As we approached, the overspill crowd was pressing at the steps. Inside, the shrine priest was preparing to test the claims of eight or nine people who were claiming that a god or a spirit had possessed them. The ritual began with a recital of the virtues of the Buddha, followed by a eulogy of the god. The candidates assembled before the priest, pressing sprays of arica blossom between the palms of their hands. There was one young man and one boy of about ten. The rest were women and one a young girl. The drummers established a loud rhythm and kept at it. Though the young man's arica spray quivered, he showed no sign of possession. The little boy showed even less. The women, by contrast, soon began to hoop themselves round in time to the beat and whipped at the bystanders with their hair. At the height of the frenzy, the priest seized them by the hair and spoke to them, or through them, and to the occupying spirit. One claimed to be under the influence of the goddess Pattini, another under the god Kataragama. The young girl and her mother claimed possession by different goddesses, the mother by Kali. The small boy had been brought there by his parents after showing signs of strange abstraction and dizziness, but he simply stared the priest out and stood still. The young man, whose father had been priest at a sub-shrine, was next in line for the priesthood, but his claim would be invalid unless a god took hold of him and used him. The women appeared to satisfy the priest and themselves, and could return to their village with heightened prestige and, perhaps, work as mediums. At the very least, they had succeeded in giving themselves new elbow-room in a tight, male-dominated society.

When the temple had cleared of worshippers, two of us were allowed the special privilege of a sight of the god. We knelt before the curtained shrine. First one veil was drawn, then a second, then a third, then a fourth. The small god-image stood darkly in his recess, holding his stick. He is said to be guarded by cobras. There were indeed two cobras flanking the god and facing our way. I say they were wrought in some gilded metal; my companion says they were live.

There was a certain amount of pious Buddhist hostility to the inclusion of the god Dadimunda in a search for the Buddha. Had we not understood that the Noble Eightfold Path bypasses gods and demons, and pushes on to Nirvana, renouncing these colourful distractions? I think that, as far as we could, we had. But the god Dadimunda has his place in a journey to Sri Lanka, I should have thought; not because god-worship is tied up with Buddhism but because Buddhism is thought to be tied up with tolerance, and in Sri Lanka the gods and the Buddha appear to have lived alongside each other without a Holy War or an Inquisition or the death of either for two thousand years. Perhaps I should have whispered in their ears that, in the high days of roaring monotheism in the West, the shrine priest, his acolytes and the whole ecstatic, bacchic dance corps, Buddhist, quasi-Buddhist or neither, could well have been frizzled as witches.

5

Rome,
Leeds and the Desert

Just once or twice *The Long Search* lost its usual footing and
found its true direction. The occasions were rare, unforce
able, unpredictable and usually incommunicable. One suc
happened in Rome during a conversation in the Monastery
of Sant' Anselmo with Rembert Weakland, an American
monk who was then Abbot-Primate of the Benedictines and
is now Archbishop of Milwaukee.

We had ranged over Faith, Doubt, Papal Infallibility
Ecclesiastical Wealth, Abortion, Birth Control, Liturgica
Reform, Monasticism, the Place of Women, the Second
Vatican Council, Missions, the Teaching of Children
Conservatism and Change, Relations with the Protestants
with the Orthodox, with the Religions of the East, with th
Religions of Marx and Mao, some of the topics round whic
much current debate in the Roman Catholic Church seem
to assemble. The camera was whirring away contentedl
and we went in assurance of getting meaty observations t
mix in the filmic stew we called the Search for the Roma
Catholics. As happens, the film ran out and Abbot Weak
land and I were told to 'relax' while a new magazine o
celluloid was slotted on the camera.

It was then, in a dawdling silence through which th
inerasable sound of the Rome traffic drifted up the hill an
through the garden, that I turned to Abbot Weakland an
said: 'Do you know—I do not understand one word of th

Lord's Prayer.' He did not, I am glad to say, presume to help, to explain, to fight for my soul or to put words into my mouth. Neither spoke till the camera was ready again to devour us and the interrupted talk flowed once more. But we both knew that for a second or two we had touched the level at which any real search takes place—beneath the forms of words, the creeds, the debate, the propaganda, the self-justification, the sparring.

The story of the search for the Roman Catholics ('Catholics' from now on for short) is one of a movement from seeming security to real insecurity, from splendour towards the cracks in the splendour, from the comfort of firm answers to the bracing discomfort of large questions. Of these, the largest, and the ones I tried throughout to stay with, were questions about Jesus.

'It's a great difficulty,' I put to Abbot Weakland, 'to have to accept that, at the birth of Jesus, at a particular time and in a particular place, something became available which had not been available before. Even after two thousand years of Christian conditioning, it is hard to accept. Must we accept it?' Behind the question is a niggling unease at what seems like the rupture of history and the favouritism of God. Must we, to be Christian, accept that the wisest man B.C. lacked something of crucial worth which the stupidest Christian A.D. has as a free gift? Must we accept that the wisest person outside the shock-waves of the Gospel cannot achieve some crucial thing that the most careless Christian can take up or leave as he or she pleases? The Abbot's reply went: 'I would say yes. I wouldn't want to water down that aspect. If one takes the Christ-Event as God entering human history, then God makes something available to man which he did not have previously.' Before that claim, though I have heard it all my life, I have to rock on my heels a bit and ponder.

It would seem so much easier if Jesus Christ could be just

one of the many and recurrent incarnations of a Great Wisdom. He would then join the Buddha and Lao Tse and, for all I know, some Hindu master alive today, as one of the many Masks of God. Indeed I have seen pictures of Jesus in exactly this position, placed reverently on the family altar in a Hindu household, alongside the Lords Rama and Krishna, and overseen by Kali, the Great Mother. But I have rarely met a Christian whose ecumenism stretches so far. To see Jesus as a Western alternative to Rama and Krishna would seem to be, not Christianity but a form of Christo-Hinduism. Indeed there is current in India an alternative account of the life of Jesus. He is said to have been a great yogi whose obscure years before his public ministry were spent in the East. At the crucifixion, in one of those yogic feats by which it is known that an adept can put himself into a state of deep slumber and suspension, Jesus kept Himself barely breathing. At His entombment He resummoned His vital powers, and His followers smuggled Him away. He returned to India where He lived to a ripe old age and lies buried in the Himalayas. Though His supposed burial place is not one of the mighty holy places of the Hindus, it exists. The value of that Hindu account to someone sprung from a line of Protestants and out in pursuit of the Catholics, is that it is likely to throw all Christians together in agreement on what Jesus is *not*. He is *not*, in their view, a Hinduesque holy man. He is *not* one of many Incarnations. He is unique. He is the fulfilment of Jewish historical prophecy, rather than an embodiment of persistent cycling Hindu wisdom. He existed in time. He exists for ever. He stands at a crossroads. He hangs from a cross.

At the same time it seems unlikely that there exists some unbreachable wall between those who follow the Religions of Revelation and those who follow the Religions of Self-Knowledge, with Jews, Christians and Muslims on one side hugging their uniqueness, and Buddhists and Hindus on the

other, blurring their edges in an endless process of acceptance and tolerance. Human beings are not so tidy. Nor, I
respectfully suggest, is Jesus. And some of His words have
about them an oriental circularity. They speak of rebirth
and going back: 'Unless you become as little children, ye
shall in no wise enter the Kingdom of Heaven.' They
recommend to generations of pushers the virtues of not
pushing: 'Consider the lilies of the field.' They make dying
a part of living: 'Whosoever will save his life shall lose it . . .',
failure a part of success: 'The first shall be last.' The unsettling truth seems to be that whenever Christians have
claimed to have reached a settlement, found security, dug
themselves in, taken a line, their subtlest enemy has been
not the polytheist, the communist, the heretic, the Buddhist,
the Muslim, the Jew, but Jesus Himself, the vine that unseats
the wall, the root that makes the plaster crack. I was
determined that, as far as the choice was mine, the search
for the Catholics should not swing about the super-rigging of
the Latin Church, among the historical postures, the
liturgical disputes, the political manoeuvring, but should
try, as far as these words make sense, to keep an ear open
for Jesus.

It is a short linguistic hop from Jesus the root to Jesus the
radical, and the search for Catholicism forced me to make
it. The trim balance of Protestant as protest and Catholic as
conservative did not hold. I was handed, like an escaping
prisoner of war in films about occupied France, from radical
Catholic to radical Catholic, till it became hard to see by
what sleight of hand and success of enemy propaganda the
Catholic Church has ever been passed off as irrevocably
reactionary. Once or twice I picked up another Catholic
flavour; as when I had to hold the coats while one friend,
once Catholic now lapsed, told another friend, once Con-
gregationalist now Catholic and a fighter for the retention
of the Latin Mass, that Catholicism was 'utterly evil'. But

generally the Church I think I saw was one in vigorous debate with itself and in mid-convulsion. Any picture I took of it is no more valid than (someone somewhere has used this image before) a still frame taken from a moving picture of a leaping cat. It is the leap. It is not the leap. It is the cat. It is not the cat.

A quiet rumbling of things to come began early in conversations with the Catholic adviser for the filming—Bishop B. Christopher Butler, who is a Benedictine monk. His description of how he became a Catholic in early manhood shows nothing like alacrity. He calls himself, in those years, a 'dissenting Catholic', out of sympathy with many areas of customary Catholicism, all the more convinced that Catholicism was his way. He described walking up the steps of St Peter's in Rome at the start of the Second Vatican Council, a prelate among prelates, with no great hope that, under the weight of their copes, so many bishops would be likely to waft the debate off the floor. He describes the pleasure, disbelief, almost alarm with which he saw the debate rise—conservatives and reformers, all at their most eloquent. Would he describe the Second Vatican Council of 1962–1965 as the greatest upheaval in the Church since the defection of Martin Luther? No, he said, he would call it 'as revolutionary as the break of Christianity with Judaism'. And that was two thousand years and several empires ago.

Since such words as 'revolutionary' and 'radical' seem set to thread their way through this account, it is worth clearing the soil away from their roots. A radical need not be a libertarian. Nor need he expedite change. Nor need he be a threat to tradition. A radical, in the sense of the word in this context, refers himself back to an original intention and adjusts his ways accordingly. He may decide that the radical needs of the moment are to try to stand still. In which case he is going to have to grab hold of his radical intention and run, for everything about him and in him moves, breaks up, solidifies, re-forms, whether he likes it or not. But a true radical may not drift. Revolutions too need not all be seen as rolling out towards the new and alarming. They can roll back to the old and forgotten or down to the rooted and original. The most radical revolutions have it in them to roll all ways at once.

When earlier I said I felt I had been handed from Catholic radical to Catholic radical, I should perhaps have added also—from monk to monk. The search never settled in one place long, saw little of Catholic family life, leaned towards theological chat, was relentlessly high-minded, shunned excess and appreciated spareness. It was also firmly monastic. That is not to suggest that the way of the monk is divorced from life, but it is divorced from life as most people know it. Jesus started by calling disciples from their nets, taking them to desert places, making them give up jobs and homes and family. Only later did His way settle in cities. Perhaps to pass from monk to monk as an approach to Jesus will do at least as a start.

There is no monasticism in Islam (the Qur'an speaks out specifically against it) and there are, apart from converts to Christianity, no Jewish monks. Yet the monastic impulse in Christianity seems to have shown itself first in nothing more than the withdrawal of certain people from cities and into deserts, and in both Judaism and Islam deserts are places of power. The Prophet Muhammad received the Qur'an not while plying his trade, but while withdrawing to pray. And the Children of Israel were not a people till Moses took them into the wilderness and God bonded them. John the Baptist lived in the desert. Jesus withdrew to it to return to His roots. Satan did not lurk under the porticoes of Capernaum to catch and seduce the Master while He was busy healing the sick and preaching. He confronted Him in the desert. There is a fine line between withdrawing to a blank space meaning alienation and sickness, and withdrawing to a blank space meaning sanity; just as there is a fine line between joining the crowd from a terror of loneliness, and joining the crowd as a movement of health. But the desert-presence seems constant in Christianity. It need not be a place of dry bones and hot stones. It can be, more humbly, the enclosure of ten minutes in a busy day in which to be blank. But without fertilization from the desert, religious orthodoxy seems to show a tendency to shrivel, to start to imitate itself, to lose its swing.

For a thousand years there have been hermitages on the startling peaks of Montserrat, the saw-tooth mountain that cuts through the plain about twenty-five miles inland from Barcelona, chief city of Catalonia in north-eastern Spain. Now there is a great church, a monastery, guest houses, shops, a hotel or two, car parks, a funicular railway. From three sources in Montserrat, I heard the tale of a monk who wished to reclaim some lost time and be, once again, a hermit. At first the Abbot of Montserrat, whose word is law to his own community, refused permission. The supplicant was of a sickly disposition and to fend for himself on a mountain top would need toughness. But the pestering paid off. The monk was allowed his eyrie. His health improved. He farmed and built and prayed. He was, I suppose, living out his vocation. But he did not stay. Whereas he had had three visitors a year while he was down with the rest of the community, he now had three thousand. The absoluteness of his stand exerted a magnetic attraction to people less capable of his particular form of self-abandonment. He is there no longer. He went with a group of like-minded hermits to live on an island off the coast of Japan. But the rigour of his example still haunts the place he left. Why else, with so many other things to talk about, should these three people—a boy from Barcelona campaigning to bring about a Catalan Socialist Party, a Barcelona psychologist with a particular interest in new Latin-American theology, and a vigorous old Montserrat monk—tell me his story? The vigorous old monk, by the way, was eloquent on the subject of 'the Golden Age of Monasticism'—a supposed time when monks were respected, laity was devout and the living was easy. There has never been any such time, he said.

Montserrat means many things to many people. To the day-tripper up from the hot beaches of the Costa Brava it may mean three hours in a high, cool place, ten minutes in the middle of the day in the Basilica to hear one of the world's great choirs sing a hymn to the Virgin and a Catalan carol, a ride in a cable-car and an ice-cream. To a pilgrim on foot it is certainly the end of a steep road. To a Catalan separatist, it presumably means separate Catalonia. To a mountaineer it means a mountain. To Catalan newly-weds it means a seal placed on a union at the only place in Catalonia with the traditional right to bestow it—the Shrine of Our Lady of Montserrat. To many who had given up hope and had their hope restored, it means a miracle.

There is, in one corner of the forecourt of the Basilica of Montserrat, a room that houses the ex-votos. These are offerings made in gratitude to our Lady of Montserrat for her help. They are sometimes lively paintings—done in a homely, vigorous, unselfconscious style—of calamities averted: an impending death-bed scene turned by the presence of the Virgin of Montserrat who appears in a radiant cloud in a corner of the room; a scene of masons falling from scaffolding without harm; a scene of derailment on a railway track without loss of life. They are sometimes tell-tale objects—car-keys hanging alongside a photograph of a wrecked car, a leg-brace no longer needed, a wedding veil offered by the bride and groom. They are sometimes plaster and plastic effigies of wounded limbs and sore places. It is, of course, an unerring cradle-Protestant nose that would find out the ex-voto room at Montserrat and ask Father Miguel, the Guest Master, to explain. He explained

first of all that, when he came to Montserrat, the offering
made a small mountain at the feet of the statue of our Lad
in the main church. They had now been cleared away to
corner. That should be taken as a hint to the faithful. To th
dubious like myself, he could only speak for himself. H
would hesitate before pronouncing on what might be super
stition in others and what might be faith. 'You cannot judge
you see. You cannot judge.' He suggested, kindly, that i
would do me good to deny myself the use of abstractions lik
'prayer', 'faith', 'love', 'superstition' and see, rather, 'peopl
who—pray, believe, love, expect miracles, do not wal
under ladders, carry a lucky charm'. It will then be dis
covered that they do much else besides. 'Right,' I though
to myself, 'I will incarnate my abstractions.' But the wi
wilted. If I must listen to every person as sense and nonsens
and not hurry to decide which is which, I should reduc
myself to silence. . . . Well?

I know of at least one secret tunnel which connect
Montserrat with Rome, for it let through the memory of th
conversation in which I said to the Abbot-Primate of th
Benedictines: 'I do not understand one word of the Lord
Prayer.' The same issue arose in Montserrat. What, ye
again, does it mean—to pray? 'Everything,' said Fathe
Miguel, 'is prayer when everything is a real response to th
consciousness you have of the Reality of God.' I could hav
said I did not understand a word of that either, but th
word 'response' let in some light. God, it seems, speaks firs
and to pray is to respond to a statement by God; not th
other way round where a man has to prod a dozing Tita
awake by shouting in his ear. The prayerful response is th
appropriate response in the light of God's statement. It ma
be contemplation and adoration: Abraham's prayer wa
adoration. It may be complaint: Job's prayer was th
prayer of complaint. In the face of injustice and cruelty,
may be a fist crashing down on a table and a shout of 'No

Montserrat, in spite of its bland, spacious air, has been much wounded. There are small red crosses embedded in the grass in the monks' garden, commemorating some of their number who must have said 'no' when the side that said 'yes' had the guns. They were shot during the Spanish Civil War. 'Montserrat,' said Father Miguel, 'is a pluralistic house. By that, I mean that not everybody thinks alike.' Or, as he graphically put it (moving from the language of war to the parallel language of church history, and bracketing the Counter-Reformation Council that condemned the heresies of Calvin and Luther with some future gathering that may carry the Church through to a new age)—'Some are Council of Trent and some are Vatican Three.' But I wonder if there are Montserrat monks who fought on opposite sides in the Spanish Civil War.

Bullet-marks from those days streak across the ends of houses in the village of Farlete about half a day's drive from Montserrat. Franco, the goat-herd, who lives in the open most of the year round, saw I was a stranger and told me, in appropriately decelerated Spanish, that in Russia there are no shops and no bars and 'they do not live the good life we live here in Spain'. Farlete is no more than a low-lying crossroads with a church. The nearest city is Zaragoza where there is another great shrine of the Virgin—the Madonna del Pilar. In 1956 a man on a bicycle, prospecting for property, came to Farlete and looked over a dilapidated Marian shrine on its outskirts. He was one of a small Catholic order of monks called the Little Brothers of Jesus and he was looking for a place to use as a Novice House. The first generations of novices had trained in southern Algeria, but politics rather than the desert became too hot and they were required to move. At first they had considered Scotland, but early approaches met Presbyterian opposition. Then a sympathetic Archbishop of Zaragoza suggested Farlete. This approach met opposition from the local parish priest. Would it not be confusing for the villagers to have alongside them monks who did not dress as monks, worked on the roads, in the farmyards, collecting garbage, delivering water? The Archbishop overrode the priest and the Brothers prepared to move in. Since then the Archbishop has passed on and his successor is not so sympathetic. He it was who took the statue of the Madonna del Pilar to the bedside of the dying Head of State, General Franco. He, too, clearly had doubts about monks in camouflage. It was to a surly village that the first novices came. Rumour spread that they were Protestants. Eventually a villager, seeing them lugging great stones out of the wilderness that runs from the house to the hills, lent them a donkey and cart. This was the breakthrough. By the time I stayed in Farlete, village and Fraternity had locked into partnership.

The Little Brothers lay emphasis on two aspects of the Life of Jesus. The first is His obscurity: until He was thirty, He worked, they assume, in Nazareth, presumably as a carpenter. The second is that He withdrew to the desert places when He wanted to pray, i.e. to listen to His Father. The Brothers (and the Sisters too, for there are four times more women than men following this particular vocation) work in the world, do rough jobs, identify themselves not just with the poor in spirit but with the poor in pocket. They also relate themselves to their own deserts. For Brothers and Sisters elsewhere, it may be a garden-shack in a nearby town, the loan of a retreat house, a room somewhere. For all of them, it is a space inside them. For those in tight corners it may only be a space inside them. They tend this desert and this Nazareth life-style as their chosen way of relating to Jesus.

Perhaps because this way runs alongside lay life and blends into it, some Catholic laity are following it too. There are secular communities which married people, single people, priests can join. Sooner or later they are bound to be accused of communism; but sooner or later a line may have to be drawn, painfully no doubt for those who panic easily, between communism that seems inseparable from the Christian idea of community, and communism, the rag-bag label for all forms of rule that are not either feudal or capitalist.

The Little Brothers of Jesus came into existence obscurely in 1932, the Little Sisters in 1939. Their inspiration, Father Charles de Foucauld, was assassinated in his community of one in Southern Algeria in 1916. The gap between 1916 and 1932, how a dead seed lay so long in the ground and suddenly sprouted, is a longer search than the one I am currently writing about. De Foucauld, even in the hagiographic accounts of him so far available, is a cryptic figure. His family were French, military and wealthy. He joined the army, did well, then suddenly less well, as if someone were sawing away at his foundations. He broke with his mistress, plangently named Mimi, and followed his regiment to Algeria in 1881 to help in the quelling of a Muslim revolt. Once in the desert, he stayed, shed his uniform, disguised himself as a Jewish Rabbi and undertook scientific research, later published and much admired as *The Reconnaissance of Morocco*. The rest of his life reads like that of a man trapped in disguises, wondering who will release him, who will pare him down to the bone, reduce him to elements, restore him to himself. He returned to the Church from which he had drifted, became a Trappist monk, took work as a gardener in a convent in Nazareth and planned his return to the desert. The Fraternity he had hoped to found he never founded. But, on manuscript evidence from his fifteen years in the desert right up to the day of his death, he never gave up hope. There is a great line of Blaise Pascal which runs: 'I have often said that the sole cause of a man's unhappiness is that he does not know how to stay quietly in his room.' That seems to be a problem which, from some source (from

Jesus, he would surely say), Father de Foucauld solved.

As it is not safe to assume currently that a Spanish navvy, at least in the vicinity of Farlete, could not possibly be a monk, so it is not safe to assume that a woman throwing rose petals down on a traditional Corpus Christi procession of the mayor, corporation and army commanders could not possibly have a mind of her own. This was the lesson of Daroca, a small town not far from the Little Brothers and not far from Zaragoza.

Daroca's claim to Catholic fame is that during the Moorish Wars a miracle occurred. Some corporals (the cloths on which the consecrated bread rests in the Mass) were carried by an army chaplain to beleaguered troops. When he unfolded them, the wafer had somehow imprinted itself in a bloodstain. The cloths are now housed in the parish church of Daroca, and each Corpus Christi are carried in procession through the town with bands, the army, the mayor, what the parish priest called 'the authorities'. I remember the phrase because he left the procession to urge us to film them. It is not unusual to hear Catholics describe some of the more florid structures that have grown up around Catholicism in the last five hundred years as a reaction to the Protestant Reformation and, more recently, to the loss of the Papal Estates. The miraculous corporals of Daroca could be described as a reaction to the overwhelming sweep through Europe of Islam. To anyone who has been awed by the radical simplicity of the Little Brothers, Corpus Christi in Daroca looks like Catholicism stuck in a very old groove, and that is how I marked it down at a glance. Daroca procession=magic=authoritarianism=the military=clerical pretensions=the subjugation of the laity.

Throwing rose petals from a balcony next to that from which we watched was a group of women; among them— Señora Gil, wife of Ildefonso-Manuel Gil, a native of Daroca and teacher of Spanish Literature in Brooklyn,

U.S.A. Was she happy, I asked, with the Church as she found it? Not exactly, came the reply, she would like changes. Such as? Well, for instance, birth control. She thought the Church should change the ruling on contraception. It was only, she added hastily, her opinion. Would she, if the Church did not change its teaching, cease to be a Catholic? Certainly not. 'I was born a Catholic. I am a Catholic. I wish to go on being a Catholic.' Through her, we met Victoria, her young daughter, daunting in the way that the perfectly bi-lingual cannot help but be. She continued the demolition of the clichés of the day. What did she think, I asked, about the mayor and the army and all the authorities parading in what was a religious procession? 'I thought Jesus was interested in poor people.' She was not thrown. 'Jesus is interested in everybody,' came the reply. 'Even the mayor?' I ventured. She put me down with the gravity that seems to come easily when you are intelligent, well-taught and eleven years old. 'Jesus is interested in everybody who is good and, whoever isn't, He will help them to be that way.' Fire-crackers were exploding down in the street. The procession had been to its terminus and the bands were leading it back to the church. Below, the bearers were leaning in under the monstrous ornate casket that houses the miraculous cloths. What, I asked, if I say to you that I do not believe that story about the battle and the priest and the bloodstains? What if some unscrupulous retreating Catholic commander thought his troops needed a miracle and gave them one? 'Believe it if you like. But if you don't really want to believe, you don't have to.' 'So it's not right at the heart of things? It's not what matters most?' 'No. The Christian religion isn't based on that one story. You can still be Christian and not believe in it.' 'What is the one thing you have to believe in to be a Christian?' 'Christ and God and the Holy Spirit.' 'Christ doing what?' 'Christ saving the world.' 'How did He do that?' 'Well, He came as

a human being to the earth and He let everybody understand more about God, so that they could be believers.'

I am not sure which is the greater miracle—the venerable
cloths or the indeflectability of Victoria Gil. 'If someone,' I
asked, 'wasn't a Christian but was doing his best wherever
he happened to be, would you want to make him into a
Christian or are you quite happy for him to go on being
honest in his own way?' It was a bit like making an enquiry
for oneself under cover of enquiring for a friend. The reply
was reassuring. 'If he's honest and good and thinks that he's
right, I think that's O.K. He can do whatever he wants.'

For the time being, the issue that marks Catholics off
from other Christians, from Orthodox East and Protestant
North and West, is that of the Pope. Did Jesus want the
Popes to guide the Church? Or did He leave the guidance
to all the bishops? Or did He leave it to individual
Christians, strong in the Spirit, guided by the Scriptures? I
say 'for the time being' because it has been known for the
passage of time to alter landscapes without human intervention, very much as the view from a floating log reduces
today's mountain to tomorrow's molehill. Four or five times
on these journeys I saw Pope Paul VI—not to speak to but
to gaze at: once when he installed twenty new polyglot
Cardinals—Argentinian, Ugandan, Philippino, Indian,
British, American—and rose from his chair to embrace the
last one who looked like an afterthought, the Archbishop of
Hanoi suddenly propelled westwards on a surprise visa from
Vietnam; once, when he concelebrated Mass in St Peter's
with his new Cardinals, and about two hundred out-riding
priests took Holy Communion out to the people; the rest
when he blessed the crowd from his palace window. At a
distance and to a stranger, fresh from Farlete, he had the air
of a man who might rather have been a Little Brother; or,
more precisely, a member of a new sub-order that was the
subject of a merry debate one evening among those monastic

avvies. It is to be called *Les plus petits frères des petits frères*, nd it is for people like me with soft hands. As he entered t Peter's, His Holiness leaned out of his litter as if to lessen he gap between himself and the hands that waved up to im. He stopped at the bottom of the altar steps to hold the and of a sick woman. He mounted the steps as if every step hrank him. Every word he said was audible (with the help f a microphone), every gesture visible, as far as is possible n a basilica the size of an airfield. But if his wish was to be lose, totally available, totally understood, the servant, the ast, then the building, the distances, the chair that ferried im and, more than all, the mysterious words he spoke at he altar, set him apart. What did he mean, quoting Jesus, This is my body which is given for you?' The really earching question in papal Rome is not: What does a 'rotestant make of a Catholic? or, What does a Catholic nake of these buildings? But, What does anyone make of his Jesus?

The last days in Rome were toned up by the arrival of a Catholic family from Leeds: the Dryhursts, Jim, Judith, hree daughters and a son. Para-papally, they inspected the 'orum, the Villa Adriana, Tivoli; threw coins and, where ossible, each other into fountains, ate ice-creams on the rinciple that the least shall eat most and the most shall eat east, the Coppa Olimpica being awarded to a doughty even-year-old girl. They supplied, too late to do anything bout the monastic, celibate cast of the journey as a whole, he element of family. If, say, they or a family like them had een the whole focus of the search, it would have been a earch for Catholic community rather than through Catholic communities. Its questions would have started nore domestically—daily bread, clothing, rent—spread vider—grandparents, employers, teachers, exams, urban lilemmas, ubiquitous pagans, government legislation, Catholic parenthood campaigns, Mass on a kitchen table where two or three are gathered. It might, if the site were Leeds, have spread to the Little Brothers, for there is, in a Leeds back street, a Fraternity where, when I visited it three brothers lived out their bit of Nazareth by doing rough jobs and found their desert where they could. (When I asked Brother Guy, working in his dye factory, not proselytizing, not preaching, what he thought he meant to the men working alongside, he replied: 'A question mark, I suppose.') It would have moved very little. The orb, the universe, implied in the word 'Catholic' would be a bubble with a small circumference. But this circumscribed search might, in its homelier way, have sent down deeper roots.

It might have touched the issue of femininity and asked why all the religious traditions we are touching on are dominated by men. It might have raised the matter of the sly Judaeo-Christian trick that makes Eve and the Serpent together responsible for all our woes. It could have wondered why, among Christians, Protestants in particular should have been so alarmed at the respect paid to the Blessed Virgin, when it is clear that, without her collaboration, the Redeemer would not have reached the world in the way that Christians have always claimed He did. It might even have found a new axis for faith, one that joins Chinese wisdom and Western Revelation in one discoid diagram of Yin and Yang: the Masculine Redeemer, the Feminine Enabler. It would certainly have been radical.

6

JAPAN

The Land of the Disappearing Buddha

The first Zen Buddhist Abbot I met on the long search was, just to confuse things, an American. He is teacher-in-residence at the Zen Centre in San Francisco, with its satellite settlements half an hour's drive up the coast at Green Gulch Farm, and four or five hours' south and a trek inland at the mountain retreat of Tassajara. He is not responsible for anything that appears in the Zen Buddhist section of *The Land of the Disappearing Buddha*, nor does he appear in the film; but he practised Zen for many years in Kyoto, supplied me with letters of introduction to people he admired in that town, and taught me stage one of Zen meditation. Three years later I am still at stage one; though the cumulative effect of sitting daily—however faultily—with knees and seat in a tripod, eyes unfocused, back straight, hands and tongue still, breath noted, is incalculable. It does not make me anything as label-able as a Buddhist, but it makes me a sitter. Sitting does not make me calm and easy but it makes me calmer and easier. If I were a machine flung about the world taking and evaluating samples of its religious traditions, this slight confession would be irrelevant. Since I was anything but a machine and found the travel, the exposure, the shocks, the responsibility, the impossibility of the whole endeavour hard to live with, a slight confession has its place.

Richard Baker has a hyphenated 'roshi' after his name. 'Roshi' means literally 'old man' and is a usual title for a Zen master. Only a master can enable another master. Baker-roshi's master was Shunryu Suzuki-roshi, founder of the San Francisco Zen community. One Saturday morning in San Francisco I attended one of Baker-roshi's talks for the Zen community and interested outsiders. His theme was Gutei's finger, one of the great Zen stories.

Gutei, so the story goes, used to answer questions on the nature of Zen by raising one of his fingers. A young pupil took to imitating him and, when strangers asked the boy what the master taught, the forward pupil would raise a ready finger. Hearing about it, Gutei summoned him and cut his finger off. As the boy was running away in pain, Gutei called after him. The boy turned, Gutei gave his customary teaching: one of his own fingers raised. The boy could no longer imitate. He had to find his own way. In that moment he was enlightened and became a great master. In Suzuki-roshi's day, said Baker-roshi, certain things were possible because of the nature of the master—a certain flavour, a certain ease, a certain expansiveness. Now these days are over and it may seem that colour has departed. One day it may return. In the meantime, the community must practise Zen, without making comparisons, without forethought and afterthought, without reward. At that moment the quality of my listening certainly changed. So, I believe, did the quality of the listening around me.

The path that led from England to the Zen Community in San Francisco was a devious one. It led through the Benedictine Abbey of Ampleforth in North Yorkshire, where Dom Aelred Graham, author of *Zen Catholicism* and doyen of those Roman Catholic monks who have joined encounter groups and prospected for Zen in California, gave me a fistful of names. Along with the names he gave me such slight hopes that any of them would see me that I resolved not to try. On a rainy Sunday in San Francisco I met a psychologist at a damp performance of the Beethoven *Missa Solemnis* in a Congregational Church. He offered to guide me through Union Street, where he said I should very likely find the headquarters of one or two movements that might figure in a search for the new religions of West Coast America. In the headquarters of Esalen, the pioneer of encountering, I uncrumpled Dom Aelred's forlorn list during a conversation with the lady minding the bookstall. She turned out to be Dulce Murphy, wife of Michael, one of the names on the list and friend of Richard Baker-roshi, another name. She left my number with the Zen office and I departed with no great expectations. A day or two later a phone call from Richard Baker reached me just as I had returned to my room for a supply of paper handkerchiefs, feeling it was about to be one of those days when I was likely to sneeze. If I could be at the Zen Centre in Page Street in thirty minutes, I could pick up a lift to Green Gulch Farm and meet him for lunch. Lunch lasted on and off for the rest of my stay in San Francisco. Japan was suddenly a country not in the Far East across the great landmass of Europe and Asia, but in the Far West out from the Golden Gate Bridge and across the Pacific. The search for Japanese Buddhism had begun.

Green Gulch is a farmland creek running down to a beach and the sea. Most of the structures are wooden, face the Pacific and look Japanese. After perhaps an hour's conversation—just the Abbot and me—we sat down to lunch with his wife and three or four Zen students. Soon a tall young man with the nicely-aligned back, neck and head of an inveterate Zen sitter joined us and Baker-roshi introduced me: 'This is Ron Eyre—a closet Buddhist working on a series of films for the B.B.C. called *The Level Ascent*.' The language of suddenness, spontaneity, swooping down on the moment with the deft abandon of a skilled butterfly-catcher is familiar to those who cultivate Zen. The split second in which I could have put in a correction, tried to nail down 'the truth', passed unused. We swopped hellos. Walking by the sea later that afternoon I found myself confiding to a Zen Abbot of three hours' acquaintance that perhaps the most important single thing to have happened to me in years was a change in the position in which I sleep. I used to sleep, I said, curled up, my shoulder at right angles to the bed. Now, for some reason, I sleep flat on my chest with my hips swivelled. 'There, you see,' he nodded. 'That's why you cannot make a film about Zen Buddhism. It is all so unnoticeable, slight and ordinary that no one would credit you.' I went to Japan.

It was deeply inconvenient, once my foot was firmly placed on the Zen path, to find that not all Japanese Buddhism was Zen. Of the thirteen traditional schools of Japanese Buddhism, Zen, in the matter of numbers of followers, comes about fifth. Well ahead are the Pure Land Schools with their twenty million adherent families. The battling Nichiren School nurses a vigorous chick called Sokka Gakkei that draws devotees in their millions to a great futuristic temple under the slopes of Mount Fuji, and tells them that the day of Gautama the Buddha has passed and that thirteenth-century Nichiren is the Buddha of the new age. Zen, of them all, is the warrior's way. Of the three Zen masters I met in Japan two had served conspicuously in the Japanese armed forces in the Second World War. One, Omori-roshi, a master swordsman, was preparing to take his life in the best warrior tradition when the American bomb fell on Hiroshima. Then, in his own account, the rules of war changed. He now teaches in a small Zen institute attached to his house in a suburb of Tokyo. He must be over seventy. His silhouette, showing up against the light screen in his practice hall as he teaches sword-fighting to a plump Okinawan a quarter of his age, is that of a boy of twenty.

Who, I asked Master Omori, is the Buddha? He pointed to me, to himself, to his fighting stick. 'I am the Buddha; you are the Buddha; this stick is the Buddha.' There in one sentence he posed the Japanese Buddha problem and left me scrabbling for new bearings. The Buddhism I had met before, in Sri Lanka, had seemed tidy. Or rather, when I tried, with my tongue wedged in the corner of my mouth, to do a kindergarten sketch of Buddhism, no one had jogged my elbow. No one tried to derail me by calling me 'Buddha'.

If, with hindsight, I were to try to find a white stick with which to tap my way towards the Buddhisms of Japan, I should choose, until someone knocked it from my hand, a folding device consisting of two hinged Japanese words. They are *jiriki* and *tariki*; *jiriki* meaning 'self-help', *tariki* meaning 'help of another'. And the question I should be asking as I tapped away would be: what is the nature of the power that makes me truly what I am? Is it a power within myself that needs to be employed, stretched, harnessed? Or is it a power beyond and outside me which I am powerless to control or obstruct, though my self-conceit may whisper otherwise? Do I take action and have life or do I take no action and have it more abundantly? If anyone thinks that playing with *jiriki* and *tariki* is pretty theoretical, I can only say that a white stick is pretty theoretical until it stops you running your nose into a lamp-post and helps you to turn a corner. Things, in relation to Japanese Buddhism, seem to me to be as desperate as that.

How eleven of the thirteen schools of Japanese Buddhism would range themselves on the scale between *jiriki* and *tariki* I cannot say, as the journey did not go their way. Of the two remaining there seem to be strong reasons for regarding Zen Buddhism as the extreme of *jiriki* or self-help, and Pure Land Buddhism as the extreme of *tariki* or dependence on another. At least that would be a first placing.

The name 'Zen' is a clue to its nature. It has been described as a Japanese mishearing of a Chinese mishearing of a Sanskrit word meaning 'meditation'. Though there is enormous Zen literature and a proliferation of Zen disciplines — sword-fighting, tea-making, flower-arranging, archery—no Zen master suggested study or athletics as the way in to understanding. All spoke of za-zen, sitting meditation. At first sight and certainly at a first attempt, Zen sitting seems strenuous. The knees are stretched sideways and lowered to the ground, the seat is raised on a cushion, the back is arched and stretched so that the spine settles on a tripod of knees and seat. The chin is pulled in, the head and neck are held at full stretch as if a puppet cord were attached to the top-knot and pulling the body straight. Nose, chin and belly are in alignment. As if that were not enough, the tongue is stilled on the roof of the mouth and the eyes are defocused in sight-lock just ahead of the nose. Some teachers suggest laying the merest thought of the figures one to ten and back again over the outbreaths. Others recommend that the outbreath be accompanied by a coextensive repetition of the figure 'one'. To call this Zen Buddhism is as inadequate a ploy as to call the recitation of the Apostles' Creed Christianity. Yet it seems fair to say that, where many a Christian will answer the question 'What is your religion?' with the recitation of a creed, many a Zen Buddhist will answer the same question with a recommendation to sit as instructed. Since no credal position is taken in sitting, it is quite possible to be a Christian and to sit. Some do. No Buddhists, however, recite Christian creeds.

Zen is fatally easy to talk about. And talk about Zen, in my experience, often starts with a story of an occasion on which Gautama the Buddha did not speak. Near the end of his life, so the story goes, Gautama was asked to preach a sermon. He stood before his audience and, instead of offering a discourse, he held up a flower. Those present awaited a footnote, a word of explanation. One disciple, Maha-Kashyapa, smiled. The Buddha, noting the smile, said: 'There is a supreme Dharma, a wonderful Truth. Words cannot reach it and words cannot teach it. That truth I have just handed to Kashyapa.' Round that silence there had accumulated an enormous body of literature, an extensive series of Zen practices and a Zen tradition. It is possible to buy in Japan a *daruma*, a small, legless, self-righting doll in the shape of a scowling old man with a blanket round him. One model, about an inch high and designed to dangle from the mirror of your Datsun, has eyes on stalks that pop out when the body tilts. This Buddhist patriarch, who carries in Japan some of the legendary glory that the West reserves for Father Christmas, St Christopher and Robin Hood, is Bodhidharma, an Indian monk of the sixth century A.D. who is said to have taken a doctrine of Buddhist meditation to China, where it became Ch'an Buddhism, and to Japan where it became Zen. Bodhidharma (or Daruma, as adapted to Japanese) is credited with distilling Zen into four famous phrases: 'A special transmission outside the scriptures', 'Not standing on written words or letters', 'Direct pointing to the human heart', 'Seeing into its nature and becoming Buddha'. With a slight shift these pungent phrases can carry poison, and I should guess that such a shift has sometimes happened as Zen has moved westwards to take a place in the common Western vocabulary. In their shifted state the phrases would be: 'The fellowship of those who cannot read', 'An early end to the quest for any form of exactitude', 'The supremacy of appetite and whim', 'Self-inflation'. Any form of religious practice, as far as I have observed, has to carry the vices of its virtues and Zen is no exception. It does not degrade masterly Zen to set alongside it whimsical and brutal Zen. Nor does it degrade a Zen master to allow him his occasional whim.

Any meeting I have had with a Zen adept has been memorable not for anything like steady discourse, but for the occasional jolt. The whole approach to and friendly absorption in the Zen Community in San Francisco, starting from Baker-roshi's sudden phone call, was one of the little cracks on the head. The style carried over into Japan. Ryoko-in is an exquisite sub-temple in the great complex of temples in Kyoto called Daitokuji. There I met Nanrei Kobori-roshi. Quite why it should suddenly be necessary to describe the detail of the approach road to the little room in which we talked, is puzzling; but the meeting, the words, the cup of tea were part of a process that did not begin with a bow and a handshake and did not end with the inelegant wobble with which I stood to replace my shoes and make an exit.

The approach from the gate of Ryoko-in to the sliding paper panel of the entrance hall is along a paved path. The stones are irregular and between them grows moss. At about a foot from the ground on either side of the path is a series of bamboo poles slung between supports. The path from time to time expands an extra stone's width from one side or the other. The bamboo rail follows. Beyond the rail is a moss garden—low, rich moss shading into the light brown earth. No leaves on the moss and no litter. The door of Ryoko-in is not visible from the gate but becomes visible as the path turns. On a support beam near the entrance to the building is hanging a bell and a small hammer. Warned how to make my presence decently felt, I removed the hammer and tapped the bell lightly twice. From within a boy's voice chuntered and stopped. A shuffle of footsteps. The screen ahead of me slid to reveal a young monk of about twenty, kneeling, wearing black and, as he bowed to touch his head on the mat, the sight of his scalp came and went beneath a quarter of an inch of black, scrubbing-brush hair. Invited to enter I strove for a gentle, consonant way of removing my shoes, knowing that whatever way I chose would take more time and be messier than absolutely necessary. At least on this occasion I placed them neatly side by side; not, as on a similar occasion in Sri Lanka, tossing them defiantly aside because on that particular day I felt rough and lacked the self-restraint to know and check myself.

The boy led me silently along wooden bridges that skirted, on one side, a gallery of uncluttered, perfect rooms; and on the other, spare, deliberate gardens. In one of the gardens is a famous stone lantern. Alongside it is a tree that has lived to a ripe old age with judicious doses of *sake*. Each step I took along the floorboards sounded thunderous. The boy ahead of me seemed more to collaborate with the ground he walked on and made no sound at all. Later Abbot Kobori was to tell me that a man transmits his state of mind along the fibres of a wooden floor and announces himself long before he comes into view.

The room we sat in was furnished with tatami floor coverings and two cushions. In a modest alcove there was one flower in a bowl, and a scroll painting of an empty circle traced in a thin sure line. Only after a time did what I took to be bare walls start to show themselves. Each of the panels was a scene of cloud and water. A mountain slope stood in mist, showed its outline, disappeared. Down below, floating on nothing, was a slender fishing boat. Why, I asked the host, is this room so little furnished? 'We furnish it,' he answered, 'you and I. In some rooms, like the kitchen, there must be pots and pans. But where guests are received it is better not to impose furniture but let it grow, just for that meeting, out of the time of day, the wishes of the guests, whether there is talk or silence.' In the house of someone professing a 'religion', I remarked, it is usual to find a few religious emblems—a cross, some candlesticks, a Koranic inscription. Yet in that room there was a flower, a circle on a scroll, and us. Where is the Buddha? Or has he disappeared? 'Well . . . er . . .,' came the reply, 'there is Buddha for those who do not know what he is really. There is no Buddha for those who know what he is really.' There are words. There is space between words. There are words that make space. There is the side of a mountain. There is mist covering the side of the mountain. There is mountain mist. In the road beyond the garden wall a seller of what Abbot Kobori nicely called 'evening dishes' rings his bicycle bell and shouts. I am emboldened to try a little philosophy. The Buddhists, I embark, sometimes speak of no-soul, no-self, the deluded notion that we have a continuous permanent being. Would it be correct and Buddhistic to compare our deceptive sense of continuous self with the illusion of a small raft that happens for a time on a stream when leaves fall, swirl and gather in a continuous platform, where they stay until someone stirs them with a stick and once again they disjoin and float away on the main stream. Raft and no raft. Platform and no platform. Soul and no-soul. 'How silly,' said Abbot Kobori.

I continued on firmer ground. Zen meditation, to look at, seems very strenuous, I ventured. The knees have to be properly grounded, the back stretched, the head and body in alignment. It seems very formal. 'Yes. In the beginning it is conscious, formal. Everything is so in the beginning. It cannot be natural from the beginning.' At which, with his back looking effortlessly straight and mine beginning to ache a bit, we both laughed.

What, I asked, is the most important thing that a man should do with his life? 'To know himself,' came the ready reply, 'not only through ideas but through his total being. I believe it.' And by what device would he recommend that a person should start to know himself? 'I say za-zen, sitting meditation. If a plant needs to break the surface of the earth and emerge, it cannot do so with its flower displayed. It has to draw all its force into one point and push. So it breaks the

An Orthodox Jew

Following page Buddhist monks
receiving alms
in Sri Lanka

Roman
Catholicism:
The Pope
and Spanish
children

surface. Once the surface is broken the bud can burst, the leaves can trail, but for the moment of piercing there is need to draw together, to know one-pointedness of mind. One-pointedness of mind can be achieved in za-zen.' I wondered ruefully why my floating leaves were silly and his piercing leaves were sensible, but brushed the thought aside as Zen manuals on sitting and not thinking recommend. It felt safer to stay with the technical details of sitting. Isn't it, I mused, troublesome to have to count on the outbreath, whether a count of one to ten and back again or a repeated count of 'one'? 'Counting,' he observed, 'is like chewing-gum. It has taste at the start and no taste later. If counting loses its taste, I would judge that the one counting may come to reach some spiritual heights.' Beyond the screen and across the walkway was the garden gathering shadows. What, I asked, makes a good garden? 'A man makes a good garden.' Who does this man think I am, I grizzled inwardly, some sort of idiot? In my pocket was a piece of paper with a note of the matters I intended to raise. I took it out and scanned it. 'Scripture,' he had proffered, 'is nothing but a footnote to mind-essence.'

The one remaining unasked question, at least of those planned, was about the koan, the Zen problem. These, as far as I had read, are a meditation device in use in one of the two main Zen schools, for throwing the mind off its tracks, breaking its deadly conditioning. They are problems needing an answer. No answer can come from usual thinking. The three most exercised koans are: 'In a dog, is there Buddha nature or not?'; 'What was your original face before your mother and father were born?'; and 'What is the sound of one hand clapping?' Having at least read so far but opting to suggest that I may not have, I asked, with what innocence I could, for an explanation of the use of a koan. The dialogue that followed was set about with trip wires and I managed to find and fall at them all, I think. 'It must be concrete,' he said. 'Do you have a koan?' I had to fumble to find the next handle: 'Do I . . .? Do you mean, you want an example?' He nodded. 'Well . . .,' I made a move, . . .' I suppose the most famous is: "What is the sound of one hand clapping"?' 'So,' he shrugged, 'show me the other one?' 'Another koan, you mean?' 'No, the other hand.' At stalemate, he took me and put me on my feet. 'This koan is Hakuin's koan. He made it. It isn't mine. One hand clapping is a very good question for those born in the Tokaguwa period with a background in Buddhism as well as Confucianism. It may do for the Japanese mentality. Now a Westerner may have an interest but I do not believe that one hand clapping is a universal question. The question must be the simplest possible question. The question is my own awareness of myself. A Zen monk has to speak seriously, not in an abstract way but facing real persons you know, dealing with real suffering spirits. A koan is a thing which one has. It does not have to be given. Everyone has it but often it is obscured . . .'

By this time dusk outside and mist on the painted mountains had joined to blur many of the distinctions that had been clearly there when the conversation started. We stood in preparation for parting and the young monk, who, I imagine, had been sitting sentinel behind one of the screens, slid in to take away the tea things. Kobori-roshi gave him some instruction and my attention wandered over the darkling wall, the flower and the exquisite ancestral circle in the alcove. On an impulse, and forgetting for the moment whether I was me or someone else, here or elsewhere, I flung my arms up and enjoyed a long pleasurable stretch. At lightning speed and without noise—for my last recollection was of him standing near the doorway and talking to the boy—he shot across the room and gave me a resounding thwack on the shoulder with the flat of his hand. It made the same sound as rises off the backs of Zen sitters in the meditation hall when the patrolman with the stick brings down encouragement on the shoulders of any who, for a moment, give up the struggle to wake up. I turned round wondering what new ritual this could be. He looked encouraging and saw me out. What the blow 'means', why he did it, what it refers to, whether or not I am allowed to hit back, he did not explain. But whereas for the scriptural, textual part of our meeting I have to look up my notes, the thwack lingers on, without effort.

Kobori-roshi had nudged me towards an impasse but my nose was not pressed right up against a wall and it was possible to look around and appreciate Kyoto: some of the three thousand Buddhist temples and fifteen hundred Shinto shrines; the Zen rock gardens in which ripples of pebble-chips swirl and eddy round grounded rocks; the monthly fair at the Kitano Shinto shrine. Here a Shinto priestess did a sword dance to drum accompaniment for the relief of some ancestral stress; in his own little temple, a Buddhist priest gave out fortunes which, if you did not like, you could hang on a nearby reject tree; a religious beggar peddled the discourses of the Buddha from his fur pouch and wailed a line or two as an appetizer. Near the railway station, of which Kyoto has only one, there is a high concrete tower with a rotating disc and observation deck at the top. This is modern Kyoto and the publicity pamphlet that comes your way with the entrance ticket tells you that the tower is specially designed to harmonize with the traditional Kyoto landscape. Here too real-estate double-think can make you doubt your sanity. There are those in Kyoto, one said to be a recent candidate for mayor, who have been overheard voicing their regrets that Kyoto survived so well the bombing of the Second World War. More empty spaces cleared of old temples would have given prospecting builders more elbow room. After Tokyo, the air of Kyoto, at least at the time I breathed it, was freshish. Not so that of industrial Kobe, where pungent factory fumes paint your throat with a poisonous tincture even as you drive in with the car windows sealed. It was in Kobe, after the near impasse with Kobori-roshi in Kyoto, that I met my Zen Waterloo.

Yamada Mumon-roshi is superintendent of two monasteries—one in Kobe and one in Kyoto. For one who does not over-much believe in fairies I am surprised how the language of gnomes, water-sprites and leprechauns offers itself first at any attempt to describe what he looks like, how he has mastered and uses the art of being there and not there. But there is nothing fey about him. He settles on his cushion as unaffectedly as an old twig and he keeps a grip on his abbot's thwacking staff with the air of one who means business. He does not speak English but he likes biscuits. For most of his life, so the story goes, he wandered Japan as a travelling preacher. Only later was he persuaded to take a grip on settled communities. When we parted he gave me a little book of broadcast talks. He is one of the few religious figures in Japan who could rattle a prime minister. When I asked him if he ever hit anyone with his stick, he said he would enjoy waking up one or two politicians, but they hardly ever come to temples.

His monastery in Kobe has none of the aristocratic lineage of Kobori-roshi's Ryoko-in and Yamada Mumon himself has the unsettling placelessness that I would expect in an incompletely reclaimed tramp. At the doorway of his temple is no elegant screening but a bold wooden table carrying a cheerful broad bowl of flowers that reminded me of the entrance to a Methodist chapel at harvest festival time. The office in which we first met had the solid frame, decent plaster and uninspired institutional paintwork of a poor but nicely maintained country railway station. He was sitting on a cushion. Next to him was a small two-bar electric fire. He was hearing the troubles of a businessman. Any troubles I had were warded off for the time being with the offer of a cup of tea and a particularly succulent jam biscuit that Mumon-roshi said was his favourite and of which he left one or two generous flakes resting on his beard for later. He gave permission to wander where we liked, talk to whom we liked, knowing that if any secrecy was required in spiritual matters it would be as secret to us if we gazed at it and did not understand as if some veil were drawn to keep us out. At the first meeting he was light and mobile with much to laugh about, though as it was in Japanese the detail was withheld. Later, at a formal interview with a translator alongside, he dropped over his face the mask appropriate to one being scrutinized and left me to make the first move.

'Master,' I began, cautioned by the interpreter to make myself clear for he was unused to translating dialogue of a religious nature, 'is there a connection between za-zen, sitting meditation, and having compassion for other creatures, and, if there is, what is the connection?' Before he answered he let out from his middle what sounded like a husky groan. 'Sitting in za-zen,' he said, 'I become nothing and everything becomes nothing; that is to say, I and everything melt into one. Once this "heart" is realized, when seeing a flower, the flower is I; when seeing the moon, the moon is I; things all become I. I think there is no greater love than this.' Only back in England, when Yamada Mumon's words were checked over by someone who knew the Christian gospels, did it become clear that the Zen Master was cross-referring to a verse in St John's Gospel. 'Would you', I pursued, 'describe an enlightened man as someone who sees that everything is himself?' Another pause held in the pit of the stomach and squeezed out. 'It is not such a simple thing. There are four states. *No I and no other*—absolute *mu*—that is one. At another time, *disregarding the other and putting the interest altogether on self*. Sometimes it is *to disregard self and put the interest wholly on the other*. At another time, *I am and you are.*' So saying he picked apart the answer that was lying concealed in my question and left me with four more questions.

The word *mu* became something of a code word in Zen conversations. It implies negation. But it pays to tread warily when a Buddhist starts talking negatives—emptiness, nothing, the void, snuffing out, Nirvana. By such tokens he handles their opposites too: fullness, everything, potential, coming to life, bliss. *Mu* is emptiness; at the same time *mu* is the purest action, undistracted being. Anyone brought up on the great opposites—good and evil, black and white, happy and sad—may be tempted at this moment to throw in the sponge, which is perhaps what your Buddhist tutor would like you to do. So long as throwing in the sponge is not an act of negation!

'Could the Master explain how someone in Europe far away from Japan could begin to learn about Zen?' 'It is said,' he replied cagily, 'that in Europe and America Zen is popular. I do not know how far they understand it.' On another occasion he was mischievous in a different way. He said that Zen in Japan is dead and will have to be re-imported from America. All this time Master Yamada Mumon sat, it seemed, like one on a riverbank fishing on a hot afternoon, very alert and nearly asleep. He did not smile. 'We like it very much when you laugh,' I ventured. 'What do we have to do to make you laugh?' As soon as he heard the translation, he rocked forward with mirth. 'That made me laugh,' he said. And immediately his face went empty. Or full. I resumed the cross-talk. 'Can Zen ever be popular,' I said, 'or must it always be something for the élite?' His reply to this question took me by the scruff of the neck and propelled me back to my own neglected tradition. 'Jesus said that unless the heart becomes that of a little child, no one can enter Heaven. Now surely, you say, an adult cannot become a child; and this is a difficult saying. Za-zen is becoming a child.' There seemed nowhere else to go. 'If you had one thing to say, Master,' I began, knowing I had got to the end, 'would it be that?' His answer settled down in a series of shortening sounds: 'The baby has no knowledge and no experience. It is a zero. Yes.' We sat without scrabbling to fill the air with more chat. On the wall, framed, was a fine brush-and-ink drawing of Bodhidharma, Daruma, the Zen patriarch, his face all but obscured by his blanket, the jutting eyebrows just visible. The Daruma drawing that I remember best of all is a back view, no face, no arms, no legs, just blanket. Not even blanket, just a wavy line. And even that trailed away into nothing.

Daily the young monks, who rise early, sit, garden, mend their clogs, do their laundry, beg and sit again, come to the Abbot, tell him their koan and give the day's answer. They sit in a long, still line along the gallery a short distance from the Master. A senior monk sits at the head of the queue in front of a large bell. A ring on a small handbell announces that the Master is ready. A note on the large bell signals the approach of the first candidate. The walk is emptied of bustle, foresight and hindsight. At the drawing back of a screen or the turning of a corner, the advancing monk kneels and touches his head on the ground, raising his upturned palms to a level higher than his head as if to suggest that if possible he would put himself beneath the floorboards.

The first koan, as whispered by the kneeling pupil to the Master, was inaudible. For an answer the pupil raised his head, took it a foot or so from the Master's unblinking face and roared like a dog: '*Mu!*' The koan, as became clear later, had been the Zen chestnut: 'In a dog, is there Buddha nature?' The answer did not suit the Master. He expelled a long husky sigh, and said words that sounded to an alien outsider without the language very like: 'Why the hell do you turn up here day after day giving the same damn-fool answer to the same stupid question?' The tail-end of the initial groan or sigh faded away after the words were ended, and the Master reached down and rang his bell of dismissal. In reverse, the young monk bowed and prostrated his way from his Master's presence. What the Master said was: 'You must put your strength into the abdomen, be collected together where there is no "I" and no "world" and grasp firmly the state of absolute *Mu*. *Mu* with the lips alone is no good.'

Later the Master gave tea and another of his flaky jam biscuits. He now wore woolly check carpet-slippers as if it were the end of the day. 'How many Zen koans are there?,' I asked, still imagining that the right accompaniment to a cup of tea was a spasm of prattle. 'One thousand seven hundred,' said the Master. 'And how long does it take for a monk to come up with an answer that satisfies you?' 'About three years,' he replied. 'Sometimes longer. If it takes much longer, perhaps he should give up.' 'And,' on I battled, 'is a man expected to answer all one thousand seven hundred in one lifetime?' 'Yes,' came the unannotated reply. After tea Yamada Mumon said goodbye and trod lightly away in his slippers. A fair gust of wind, I thought, and he would blow away. A slight panic seized me: 'I think he has forgotten me already.' I had an impulse to sprint after him, pull on his arm and say: 'Do you remember me? I am the person who ate your biscuits and asked all those questions. You can't have forgotten already. Who has superseded me? What is occupying you now?' But I stood my ground and let him disappear. I do not think anything was occupying him.

Long ago (on some other journey, it seems) there was talk of a white stick and two opposed words, *jiriki* and *tariki*, self-help and help of another, Zen being out on the far side of *jiriki*. But it is no longer at all clear what self-help can possibly mean. If za-zen makes the world and I one, the moon and I one, the flower and I one, what is the end-point of self? The death of the 'little self', as pictured by thirteenth-century Zen master Dogen is 'to lift up one's body and mind and forget them by throwing them into the life of the Buddha'. But who is the thrower and who receives the throw? This is suspiciously like the language of *tariki*, the reliance for help on another. It is a language familiar in conversations with Pure Land Buddhists. It is the language that my chief, though unofficial, Pure Land adviser in Kyoto claimed I did not know how to handle. Here, blind as I was, I had to throw away the white stick of *jiriki* and *tariki* and fumble ahead as well as possible.

The Pure Land is spoken of as a Western Paradise, a world of bliss, the opposite of all that makes life on earth acheful, unstable, transient and threatening. It is not Nirvana, for it still has some measure of colour and dimension. But from the Pure Land, Nirvana is just one unimaginable step. It is the hope of the majority of Japanese Buddhists to find rebirth in the Pure Land after death and, from the Pure Land, to reach Nirvana. Word of the Pure Land, in their view, was brought in among men by that same Buddha Gautama whose discourses in Pali are the sacred texts of the Buddhists of Sri Lanka and who held up his wordless flower and transmitted Zen. Through the discourses of this Gautama, mankind has word of Amida, Buddha of limitless Light and limitless Life, and of his great Vow. The story of Amida Buddha's vow is enshrined in a venerated Pure Land Buddhist Text and tells of a monk called Dharmakara who made forty-eight special Vows. Of these, the eighteenth vow goes: 'Upon my attainment of Buddhahood, if the beings in the ten quarters, who have Sincere Mind, Serene Faith, and Wish to be born in my country, with even ten utterances, would not be born therein, may I not attain the Highest Enlightenment . . .' Carrying the burden of this Vow like a Saviour who carries on his shoulders the hopes of the world, Dharmakara then began his journey to Buddhahood, *did* attain Highest Enlightenment, and became Amida Buddha. By his Vow and the completion of his journey, all suffering creatures have the promise of rebirth in the Pure Land. They can lean on Amida Buddha and float across with him. They need faith, not a paddle. Help of another will carry them through where self-help fails.

My first blurred awakening to a trace of the grandeur and immeasurable promise of the Pure Land came in a conversation at Ryoko-in with Zen master Kobori-roshi. He was trying to help me to give a meaning to the word *Mahayana*, the Greater Vehicle, the overall label of the Buddhisms that went north out of India, spread through China and reached Japan. The vehicle in Mahayana, he explained, is greater in the sense that it will carry a more generous span of people, not just a handful of spiritual pioneers. Talk of a 'Greater Vehicle' came oddly from a Zen master, for much that I had seen of Zen—the spare elegance of a Tea Ceremony, the ceremonial severity of Zen archery, the life-and-death borderline poise of Zen sword-fighting, the precision of Zen sitting—made it seem like work for specialists. If he had spoken of Zen as a light, one-or-two-person skiff, that cuts through the water and makes the greatest headway with the smallest ripple, he would have been describing what I think I had been seeing. But nothing I saw in Zen seemed to bring to mind the ponderous roominess of a great flat-bottomed barge.

Who then, whose life, whose example, whose attitudes, I asked him, would he point to as the best example of Mahayana, the Greater Vehicle? Without hesitation, Kobori-roshi named Shinran Shonin whom he called 'one of the bravest of Buddhists'. Shinran, twelfth-century monk and rebel, is the mightiest proponent of Shin Buddhism, the Buddhism of Faith, the Buddhism of the Pure Land. He spent twenty years among the renowned Buddhist temples on Mount Hiei, outside Kyoto, learning a Buddhism that he found to be too scholarly, too lordly, too remote from the people. He came down the mountain and learned, from a new teacher, the Buddhism of Faith, Buddhism for all, reliance on the Promise of Amida Buddha. The Buddhist establishment hounded him and his teacher, drove them out into exile where Shinran, taking a momentous step for Buddhism, married, raised a family, became, in his own words, 'neither monk nor layman', neither privileged nor hopeless. He preached the Nembutsu, the invocation '*Namu Amida Butsu*' ('I rely on Amida Buddha') and thousands found hope. It is hard to read a brief life of Shinran Shonin and keep the thought of Martin Luther entirely at bay.

The Way of the Nembutsu, the Way of Faith, is called the Easy Way. The phrase is Shinran's. I pursued it to a shoe-shop in a suburb of Tokyo where the owner, a devout grandmother, spoke of the Pure Land as the love of a parent for a child, of the Buddha's Compassion as a stream of warm light. In the alcove of the living-room over the shop was a scroll painting of the Bodhisattva Kannon, that ubiquitous, leaning, slender lady who pours salvation down from her undrainable vial and so resembles some depictions of the Virgin Mary that, when early Christian missionaries discovered her in China, they thought that the Church had somehow arrived there before them. Then I wheezed my way along an industrial waterfront, where the fumes of the factories blister the larynx, to meet a successful factory owner who holds monthly Pure Land services for himself and his work force. The one I attended had hymns, worshippers in rows and a preacher in a Geneva gown, a Buddhist tribute perhaps to the success last century of Protestant Christian missions. Lastly, one of the two Pure Land Patriarchs in Kyoto gave me an audience. His lineage is traceable back to Shinran and sideways to the current Emperor. He spoke, as did all the Pure Land Buddhists who strove so hard to help, of Amida's Great Vow, of the Buddha's Compassion, of human powerlessness and frailty. But it was not until I met an expatriate Australian poet, who lives in and loves Kyoto, knows the blind alleys up which Judaeo-Christians can drive themselves and is himself a Pure Land Buddhist, that some blurred idea of the enormity of Shinran's challenge and the impenetrability of the Nebutsu started to flicker through. His name is Harold Stewart. On Pure Land matters, he became my implacable and attentive adviser. The Easy Way would have been easier and, as he would claim, misunderstood, if he had not dogged my straying heels and snapped at them.

It is not difficult for anyone brought up a Christian to understand that entry to Paradise or to the Pure Land may be denied to the clever, the wealthy and the powerful and may be given to the humble and meek. Chapter and verse of the gospels tell the same story: how a sick woman touches the garment of Jesus and her faith saves her; how the father of an epileptic son cries out, 'I believe; help thou my unbelief,' and his faith saves him; how the thief on the cross asks to be remembered when Jesus comes into His kingdom, and obtains a promise. But in all these cases the person saved makes some little gesture of faith, some smallest move, some cry. Yet Shinran taught that any gesture is too puny to count. Even the Nembutsu itself, the saying of the saving phrase, is the working of the Buddha in the breast of the one who says it. It is not to be thought of as a small coin to offer in exchange for an inestimable bargain. 'One who strives to accumulate merits through his own efforts', wrote Shinran, 'is not in accord with Amida's Grand Will, since he lacks absolute faith in its power.' 'Even the virtuous can attain rebirth in the Pure Land, how much more so the wicked!' 'The Nembutsu may lead me to rebirth in the Pure Land or may land me in hell—I simply don't know.' 'Were I the kind of person who becomes a Buddha through other, strenuous religious practices and yet landed in hell through Nembutsu, I might regret having been deceived by my teacher. But because I am absolutely incapable of any other religious practice, hell is definitely my place.'

Not to be able to lift a finger, to deny the 'I' any power to help itself, to pile up no merit, to be capable of nothing but a word of thanks to Amida Buddha for what he has already done, then to take no credit for this word of thanks because even that can never generate with you, is too vast a burden for the 'I' to take: the 'I' that worries, competes, needs boosting, is hard to keep afloat. What can I do to inherit eternal life? Nothing! Hard, uncrackable, draining doctrine.

Harold Stewart lives alone in a small hotel in Kyoto. One day he collapsed with a violent heart attack. In the hours in which he waited for someone to find him, he claims that he experienced not so much fear as some insight into his own powerlessness and the alien, though compassionate, nature of the promise that, if he were to happen to live, would sustain him. At that moment it ceased to be difficult to give up self-help. Self-help gave him up. Recovered, he is tirelessly busy, writing, fighting for Kyoto against Kyoto, leading the blind, making the same effort as if his salvation depended on it. Which he is assured it does not.

7

EGYPT

There is no god but God

A moment to cherish on the search for Islam happened late one evening as I was sitting with two Muslims on the floor of a mosque in Cairo. They were a husband and wife, Dr Abul Fadl and Dr Zahira Abdin. He is Professor of Chemical Pathology, she is Professor of Paediatrics at Cairo University. The mosque is the private property of Dr Abul Fadl. He uses it for his own religious exercises, but mostly as a place where groups can meet for the study of the Holy Qur'an and of the Life and Sayings of the Prophet Muhammad, and for the repetition of the Name of God.

Early in the evening about thirty men and one or two boys had sat on the carpets in a great circle, each with a simple wooden book-rest on which were placed the books for study. In the group were a retired general, a bank manager, a headmaster, a shopkeeper, a few civil servants and a High Court judge. Dr Abul Fadl, his face radiant, discoursed on the life of the Prophet. The group then took instruction in the proper style for the recitation of the Holy Qur'an. Tea and cakes were passed round as if they too might be a foretaste of Paradise. Dr Abdin and about half a dozen other wives, their heads covered, sat behind a curtain near the entrance and listened. Strangers were admitted for only the first stretch of the meeting, and were then asked to leave. Sitting outside, we had, in one ear, the squeal of brakes in the narrow street as drivers exercised their own form of that creative driving that is such a feature of Cairo; in the other, from the mosque, the sound of rhythmic chanting as the group drew one or other of the Ninety-Nine Beautiful Names of God in and out on their breaths. Sometimes, said Dr Fadl, he and his companions move as they pray. If they had been dervishes, they might have whirled. Dr Abul Fadl seemed more animated after the three-and-a-half-hour exercise than before. We talked on for a further hour or two, sometimes on film. There is an Arabic proverb: 'Slowness comes from God; haste from the Devil.' The pace of the evening was slow.

Throughout, Dr Abdin had held her peace obscurely behind the curtain. Afterwards, as Dr Abul Fadl and I talked, she threw in various off-stage remarks. To adjust or amplify at yet greater length what her husband was saying, she now and then drew the curtain aside and peered round. At last, drawn by an overwhelming curiosity and wish to contribute, she drew herself out from her seclusion, slid across the carpet and sat alongside us, asking first if we minded. We talked more of the life of the Prophet, Heaven and Hell, the speaking out of the Holy Qur'an, the difficulty for outsiders of accepting that God's last word is in Arabic, the Islamic ideal of community, marriage and divorce, the Sufis or Muslim Mystics. Suddenly Dr Abdin turned to her husband and, nodding in my direction, said: 'This man is more serious in his search for Allah than many who call themselves Muslim.' It was a small shift, occurring after weeks of meeting and talking. But, for a moment, the heavy curtain that hangs between Muslim and non-Muslim was tweaked aside and I was allowed to slide along the floor towards them. It outweighed, in my estimation, all the hospitality, the open-handedness, the tireless teaching, the warm attentiveness, that had come my way as an Unbeliever. For once I ducked free of my label.

To most non-Muslims who have a view on the matter at

all, Islam is the religion that owes its shape to the Prophet Muhammad. To all Muslims I spoke to in Cairo, Islam is the religion of Adam, Abraham, Noah, David, Mary, Jesus and all the Prophets. It is, therefore, the oldest religion. Whatever Adam experienced, with mind undistracted and senses orderly, as he talked to God in the Garden in the cool of the day, is Islam. Whatever Abraham underwent as his knife approached his son's throat to offer a sacrifice needed by God, is Islam. The gesture with which Noah abandoned dry land and, on the promise of God, took to sea in the Ark, is Islam. The total skill which David applied to the writing of the Psalms, is Islam. The trust with which the Virgin Mary let herself become the vessel for the delivery of the Muslim Prophet, Jesus, is Islam. The words of the Prophet Jesus, in agony in another garden, 'Nevertheless Thy will, not mine, be done', is Islam. Islam carries the sense of peaceful submission to God, abandonment to His Providence, unfragmented bare acceptance of His Unity and incomparable Will. A child, too young to separate 'me' from 'you' and 'that' from 'this', knows Islam. 'Every child', said the Prophet Muhammad, 'is born with a Muslim heart.' As the child grows, the heart is cracked and pieces attach themselves to this person and that, this object and that, in a gradual drift to idolatry. Islam is the constant drawing back from the fragments to the Source, from the idols to Allah, from the many to the One.

The Islamic view of the succession of the Prophets of the One True God seems to be a succession of new brooms which swept clean for a time but wore out. God spoke to the Prophet Moses, who delivered the Law to the Jews; but they misapplied it and turned a universal message into a nationalistic mandate. God spoke to the Prophet Jesus, who brought the Gospel, but four inconsistent accounts remain and Christians cannot agree. God spoke last to the Prophet Muhammad through the Angel Gabriel. This time the word was heard and delivered. In the Holy Qur'an there exists on earth, in the Muslim view, a final statement of the Will of God, an earthly copy of a heavenly original. Dr Fadl and Dr Abdin are wise to the uprush of infidel questions that are bound to follow any such bold claim. The Qur'an is in Arabic. Does this not suggest that God has a favourite language? Dr Fadl allows himself a moment of satisfaction that Allah chose an Arab to be the bearer of His last message when 'the rabbis expected it to be an Israeli'. But he does not regard Arabs as specially privileged in Islam. They may be able to read the Arabic but, without submission of the heart to Allah, it will carry no meaning. Islam has an impressive record of racial equality and the practice of the brotherhood of man. The worldwide spread of Islam covers many good Muslims who speak no Arabic. Even to the good Arab Muslim, the Holy Qur'an is still said to be 'virgin'. It can be studied. It can exercise its power. It can offer enlightenment, judgement, support and can issue grave warnings. But it cannot be penetrated. Hence, whenever in English conversation with me a Muslim quoted the Holy Book, he would speak the Arabic first—the impregnable wordage. He would then offer, not a translation but an 'interpretation' or a 'comment' on the untranslatable. The uniqueness of the Prophet Muhammad in Muslim eyes has to do with the successful delivery of the Word of God into this world. The Prophet is Perfect. Christians of some persuasions know the traditional veneration offered to the Blessed Virgin for a very similar reason. She is Immaculate.

Egypt seemed to select itself as the likeliest place for the Muslim search. Stricter Muslim countries would not let us carry away images on celluloid. The one occasion on which the *Long Search* crew landed in Jeddah, in Saudi Arabia, and left the plane to film the disembarking pilgrims, they were led away by the airport police and asked to explain themselves. Egypt has some historical involvement with the

British, and English is spoken. Cairo also boasts the most ancient and prestigious university in the Muslim world—Al Azhar, where Islamic Law is still expounded by professors who sit in chairs, thus setting a style and inventing a terminology which is said to have spread westwards to Paris, Bologna, Oxford, Cambridge, and thence to their many derivatives which still, unwittingly, may carry a trace of an Islamic original.

The first thought for a film story had been to settle in Al Azhar, as a place of acknowledged Muslim orthodoxy, to talk to the Grand Sheikh, the university's president, choose one or two students, to see how they live and what they study in Cairo, go with them to Nigeria, Iran, Indonesia, wherever their homes happened to be, and see how they relate to the Muslim community there. The plan had at least the virtue that it propelled us towards Egypt and we did meet and talk to the Grand Sheikh, though the pull of the two doctors and the shifting ground of doing a search rather than talking about doing a search gradually moved us sideways.

The Sheikh al Islam, one of the Grand Sheikh's other customary titles, lives in an apartment block in Cairo and has a roomy office across the road from the great Al Azhar mosque. To meet him is to join the shifting circle of his retinue. Both at his home and in his university office, the room in which we met was set out with a circle of chairs. New arrivals pay their respects, slip to their seats and wait. Tea is brought. The Grand Sheikh guides the conversation as he pleases and at his leisure. The signal that the conversation was moving our way was the sudden experience of coming under the interested gaze of a roomful of eyes. I had burning questions to ask but such things cool down with delay, and by the time they were translated with nervous devotion by one of the secretaries, pondered, answered, and the answer ferried back again, initial voltage had leaked away. His statements were wary, highly diplomatic, and, to judge from translation, rounded with care. They also suggested that, though airing my doubts and pressing my questions may be good Protestant practice, it is not the general Muslim way.

About his titles—Grand Sheikh, Sheikh al Islam—they attach to his role and his moral authority as Sheikh al Azhar. He is a lawyer; not a pope. He tops no hierarchy. How free, I asked, is a Muslim to interpret the Qur'an for himself and reach a dissenting conclusion that might shock the orthodox ? Freedom of interpretation might, he thought, be possible under certain conditions. First, master Arabic; then, absorb yourself in the Qur'an; then, study the Sayings of the Prophet, the conditions of his life, the structure of his community; then, sit at the feet of the great lawyers who are the successors of one or other of the mighty four who established the four accepted schools of Islamic Law; throughout, live the regular life of a Muslim. Then, ask the question again.

The regular life of a Muslim is to belong to the Muslim community, go the way the people go, do as other people do: pray five times a day, facing Mecca; give alms; fast when others fast; go to Mecca for the Pilgrimage if at all possible once in a lifetime; above all, stand by the Profession of Faith—'There is no god but God and Muhammad is his Messenger.' These are the Five Pillars of Islam and no displays of open-mindedness and tact on my part could hide the fact that I do none of those things; that I am an infidel; even worse, that I appear to think that there are certain forms of separateness and mobility that are not merely possible but desirable. For instance, I think it is possible to try to undertake a sequence of disjointed journeys through what I can see of other people's traditions and call it *The Long Search*. This must be, from the viewpoint of orthodox Islam, a deeply un-Muslim thing to do. From the viewpoint of unorthodox Islam, it may be one of the possible approach roads to Allah. But the tension between the individual and the community, the wish to go it alone and the wish of the community to go it together, seems to be a constant in Muslim life.

The loners of Islam go under the general name of 'Sufis'. At their most lone, they are those individuals, gifted or misguided, whose rejection of idolatry goes so far that they may reject as idolatrous the regular forms of Muslim worship. They have sometimes paid the price of community wrath. The more accessible sufis are groups of devotees who gather round a teacher to study the scriptures, practise the repetition of the Name of God, experience on their pulses His nearness when regular worship may seem to put Him at a distance. The orthodox Muslim community, after a great scholar arose to allay their more extravagant fears, appear to have accepted the solitary quest, but only as an extension of community worship. And they are alert for signs of morbid inwardness in those who undertake it. The Arabic word for the Law, the mainstream pressure to interpret Islam as the application of the Will of God to community living, is virtually the same as the word for a highway. The word for the sufi way is the word for a path. To use the path, you follow and return to the highway. The Sheikh al Islam is a scholar of Sufism. He is also said to be a great sufi. 'What,' I asked, 'is a Sufi?' 'A Sufi,' came back the quiet answer, 'is a good Muslim.'

It is part of the perfection of the Prophet Muhammad that he married (more than once), raised a family, founded a community. The 'migration' to Medina in A.D. 622, where his city-state was founded, is the starting date of the Islamic calendar. The Prophet Jesus is not altogether satisfactory in this respect. He never married. But His Second Coming may be to take a bride and rise to His full prophetic height. The Buddha, who left home, wife, child and inheritance to seek enlightenment, would be nowhere in the Muslim scale of things.

Dr Abul Fadl and Dr Abdin have four children. Dr Abdin combines running a household with directing a university department and managing a charitable hospital which she founded. It is on a bend which one of the main roads out of Cairo takes to avoid hitting the Pyramids of Gizeh and the Sphinx. It began in a hut. It is now a sizeable modern hospital which specializes in rheumatic heart disease in children. When I arrived there to meet her, I overlapped with a heart specialist from Minneapolis who had come to see how she managed, and went away impressed. To the unprofessional eye, she manages with energy to spare. She gives the impression of a natural combativeness that has mellowed, though it sometimes breaks through. She will agree that the application of divorce laws is sometimes unsatisfactory in Islamic communities and blames the failure to observe the 'spirit of Islam', which guarantees fairness between husband and wife. She quotes the Holy Qur'an (Arabic, always, first) to the effect that women have equal rights with men; and the Sayings of the Prophet to the same end: 'God has created nothing He loves better than the freeing of slaves and nothing He hates more than divorce.' The Qur'an, she agrees, allows marriage to more than one wife up to the number of four, but only as long as a man can guarantee all of them equal affection and equal support, and that, except for those of Prophetic stature, amounts to a prohibition. Had I, she asked, met a Muslim with more than one wife? 'Not to notice,' was all I could justly say. Marriage, she insisted, is a legal contract. It can carry whatever terms the parties decide. It was a Christian who pointed out, in unwitting support of Dr Abdin, that for over a thousand years till the Married Women's Property Act of 1882, Muslim women fared better in this respect than did their Christian sisters. 'I really would say,' she concluded, 'that Islam is more of a blessing for women than for men.'

It is an Islamic education to walk round the hospital wards with her, catch some of the shy warmth that comes at her from sick children, see how her doctors and nurses relish her visits; and then to know, at the same time, that it would only need one show of disrespect for the Prophet, one slight to the Holy Qur'an, and she would be all wrath.

Every year, Dr Abul Fadl and Dr Abdin go on the Pilgrimage, the *Hajj*, at Mecca. Now they fly. They once went by boat and on foot. We gave them a lift to the airport. The end of the packing and the issuing of instructions about the contents of the refrigerator were interrupted to feed us liqueur chocolates and Coca-Cola, and to make sure that the drivers below in the road had something to eat. As they darted from room to room, a group of the rest of us, Egyptian and English, sat smiling through the language-barrier on ornate Empire-style chairs, tightly covered with transparent plastic sheeting to keep out the relentless Cairo blowing sand. After so many years, aren't the two of them used to the *Hajj*? Dr Abdin paused, for the benefit of my education. 'Every time it comes new . . . It has a special feeling . . . of happiness to meet someone you love.' Then with a touch of bubbling exasperation: 'It is difficult to explain really.'

Some pilgrims leave home dressed in the two white wraps in which they will eventually circumambulate the Ka'aba, the stone shrine built by the Prophet Abraham, cleansed and rededicated by the Prophet Muhammad. Dr Fadl wore a long white woollen robe over his suit and a crocheted white hat. Dr Abdin, looking more than ever like a Carmelite abbess, wore a white wool robe and a white cotton wimple. They walked down the stone stairs of the apartment block arm in arm, their eyes down, their lips just moving, saying their prayers. The Muslim who goes on the

Hajj must be prepared not to come back.

At Cairo airport the two doctors tussled their way through the barrier. On one side, travellers jostled with porters and children wailed for their lost mothers; on the other, without sound-proofing, the clamour was somehow arrested, the pace dropped. This was the all-in-white pilgrim section. Distraction on the far side of the wooden rail; intention on this side. Women sat masked in white on bundles of luggage. One or two men smoked. Hardly anyone talked. On board the plane, community chanting began: '*Labaika 'llah Humma labaik*.' 'Here I am, O Lord, answering your call. Here I am.' Before he had left for Mecca, Dr Fadl told me a story of forty years ago. As a boy of eighteen he had been at home alone one night when an armed robber attacked the house. He fought the intruder off as best he could, but it was a puny best against an armed man. When help at last arrived, he fainted from loss of blood. The following year he was in Mecca for the *Hajj*. In Medina he visited the Prophet's tomb. As he was standing there, a stranger—not an Egyptian—came alongside and whispered in his ear: 'He deserves your respect and your love. He defended you last year.' By the time he had aroused himself to make all the necessary connections, the whisperer had melted into the crowd. Telling that tale, Dr Abul Fadl was close to tears.

The technology that flew the two doctors to Jeddah and then picked them up and drove them to Mecca is Western technology—not Christian but Western. So is the technology that drills for oil in the heartlands of Islam. The pervasion of the East by the West is subtler than the Crusades and likely to be more effective: and it raises the question of how Islam can possibly handle the shock. The new idolatries may well prove more threatening than graven images. The understandable reaction is to recoil. There was an air of recoil about Dr Abul Fadl's fundamentalist approach to the

Muslim Scriptures. The Paradise he speaks of is literally luxurious. The Hell he speaks of literally burns and renews the skin. When he tells the story of the Prophet's mysterious night-ride to Jerusalem, his ascent to Heaven, his vision of the After-Life, he will not accept it as a dream (which even the Prophet's wife was inclined to do). It has to be corporal fact. But, if this line is pursued, it would seem to lead to a hardening of attitude that could become an idolatry of its own, the worship of things as we think them to be, the worship of alarm disguised as stability. At the same time, to embrace the latest thing, so soon to be overtaken by the next latest thing, is idolatry too.

One evening we swung across Cairo in a taxi with Ibrahim, the Grand Sheikh's secretary, to visit a set of his neighbours. They had rented a furnished apartment in a quiet road, though they had unfurnished it and the furniture lay piled along a wall behind a curtain, leaving a sitting-room bare except for mats, a few shelves, some cushions and a low table. Their anti-acquisitive urge is part of a move to return to the radical simplicities of community life as the Prophet himself is said to have lived it in Medina. These quiet revolutionaries, four boys—two English, one Irish, one American—their wives and children are all converts. Inevitably their rejection of modern times can only be partial. They use the electric light, but not the sideboard. The women keep to the women's quarters, at least when guests are present, but their husbands know about Zen. They wear the traditional Egyptian galabia when most of the Egyptians in Cairo wear Western suits.

Food, lamb and rice, arrived in one generous dish and we sat on cushions on the floor and dipped with our spoons. Three of the community men were present (no wife was seen, though an Islamic tot drifted in after the food from the kitchen). Each handled the situation—of Westerners entertaining Westerners in a style that was native to no one—in a different way. One had an approach that might be labelled, if it were in a Christian context, 'pentecostal': strong in the spirit, given to rapture and inflamed dogma, speech punctuated by brief, fervid, holy explosions in Arabic. The second took quiet pains to justify by argument what they were doing. On the matter of life-style, no one was disposed to argue. It seemed harmonious, simple, what they intended, and was being paid for by the hard labour of, for instance, teaching English in a Cairo day-school. Their being in Cairo was for no other reason than to study at Al Azhar. Once they had studied, they would disperse. The third said very little, accepted unstrenuously that we did one thing, they another, made no effort to bracket us all in the same equation, justified nothing, and was persuasive. It is not altogether sensible to pretend that twentieth-century Cairo is seventh-century Medina. Neither is it altogether sensible to pretend that twentieth-century Cairo—any more than twentieth-century New York or twentieth-century London—is the ideal way to house a living community.

Hassan Bey Fathy lives high in an old Cairo house with an overview of the city and a towering vista of minarets and domes. He is a town-planner, an architect, a philosopher. 'My wish,' he said, 'is to apply the rules of Islam, the tradition of Islam, to circumstances as they are today, entirely modern. In that way I am adding to the Islamic understanding of Islamic principles.' His starting point is to accept certain enormous contradictions. Outside, at one moment, there was a particularly blood-curdling scream of brakes followed by a cacophony of horns that sounded like a wolf-pack. He rose with a sigh and shut a window. 'The exhaust of jet planes and cars,' he said, 'should be coloured crime-colour.' The sound was trapped out. 'Make no mistake. All these fumes are changing the envelope that surrounds the earth.' Then he shrugged and sat down again.

'Tomorrow I fly to Saudi Arabia, by jet-plane of course, to discuss improvements in the running of the *Hajj*.' Two images haunt him. One is that the human race has thrown itself out of a window and has not yet landed. All he can think to suggest is that we should put our fingers in our ears and wait for the crash. The other—more hopeful—is that the human spirit has a capacity to expand under the right sort of pressure. The wisdom that made our prime ancestors stop starving their wives and eating their children—thus starting the tribe—may come to the rescue again; and the tribe of the earth may be born.

He gave me a book of his called *Mosque Architecture*, a small contradictory masterpiece. It is not enough, he says, to put up slavish imitations of old buildings. Nor is it enough to pretend that old buildings have nothing to say. In the greatest Cairo mosques the Sufi sage initiated the master craftsman in the secret laws and symbols of sacred art. The stones imply wisdom. But no modern architect whispers wisdom into the ear of a building contractor. Plans pass between them. Engineering technique pastes over the cracks in intention and, instead of a microcosm, which a mosque should be, we are offered a 'macro-farce' (his one-swipe dismissal of the new mosque in the University of Baghdad). He recommends neither imitation nor arbitrary novelty, but a third possibility: somehow to absorb old wisdom without copying old forms and to use it to reach new solutions. Hassan Bey Fathy and I share a great admiration for one of Cairo's oldest mosques, Ibn Tulun: he from a lifetime of study; I from the sudden shock of entering for the first time a great Islamic masterpiece and one of the world's great spaces. It is now 1100 years old.

Unlike some famous churches where it pays to linger because there is so much to see, the lure of Ibn Tulun is that there is so little. Low crenellated walls mark off a square of ground. As you stand on the ground, you see that they also mark off a great arched square of sky. In the centre of the courtyard is what I took to be an offensive modernism, not destroying the building but ill-at-ease with it. This was a domed fountain, built in A.D. 1292, where the faithful could wash. A gallery of arches moves round the walls and supports the only areas that are covered. Light spills into these galleries from high, glassless, intricate, regular, stone, fret-work windows. There are no side-chapels for saints, no inscriptions other than qur'anic and they settle into the stonework as if the master-builder needed them to strike some secret architectural balance. In the centre of the wall along which runs a double range of pillars, there is a low niche lined with the Profession of Faith in glittering mosaic: 'There is no god but God and Muhammad is His Messenger.' This, a curve round a space, is a vacant finger pointing to Mecca. You could say that Ibn Tulun does all that can humanly be done to wipe the mind clear of idols and centre it on Unity and Peace. The question is: Is that enough for Islam?

Again and again, the search for Islam dead-ended itself on the matter of idolatry. What is an idol? Can we remove it? Scots John Calvin described the human brain as a 'manufactory of idols'. What spiritual bulldozer can raze that sturdy little mechanism to the ground and leave unanimity and peace? Are we talking about a human possibility or a mirage and a cheat?

Little Muslim boys in a village about a hundred miles south of Cairo were learning the whole of the Qur'an by heart. If it were any other book, it would clearly be considered educational malpractice to load so much so uncritically into one small space. Yet Dr Abul Fadl defended the practice and drew the line at criticism. The Sheikh al Islam described the Holy Qur'an as 'the only safe book in the world'. But is it safe from our idolatrous attentions? Is there not a real possibility—a question for

Christians, Muslims and Jews, the traditional idol-smashers of the world—of idolizing the One True God and His One True Word? Is this not the ultimate trap?

'Change,' said Hassan Bey Fathy, in his dusty crow's-nest among the minarets of Cairo, 'is the most obvious, the *only* sign of life. Rigidity is death . . . Any piece of knowledge, any movement of science, even the Qur'an itself, if it brings me to a dogmatic attitude, is wrong. I am reacting to my environment now, as I am, in the twentieth century. I am not an Arab in the time of the Prophet.' No other Muslim Call to Prayer rang round my idolatrous brain-box as imperatively as those few words. 'There is indeed no god but God and Muhammad is his Messenger.'

He walked with us visitors down his stone stairs and saw us off from his doorstep. As we lost ourselves in the evening traffic, he shut his front door, remounted his stairs and, no doubt, as he said he often did, sat by himself.

8

The Romanian Solution

If the instruction that came down from the office of the Patriarch of Romania or from the State Ministry of Cults was that we were to be given a picture of seamless, flourishing and loyal Romanian Orthodoxy, it was followed punctiliously. Reading between the lines became a habit as regular as reading in bed. Generally, during the Romanian journey, we met churchmen on church premises or laymen on church premises. No Christian schoolteachers, factory managers, newspaper men, economists came out to meet us. It is rumoured that Romanian Orthodox priests carry out their sacramental work discreetly and privately for those, mostly in towns, who choose not to attend church for fear of losing their jobs or embarrassing their families. There is no religious education in schools. How much the syllabus requires anti-Christian education I never discovered, though one product of it joined us for a day or two as a relief translator and I was grateful, after all the official talk about 'constructive harmony', for his frank atheistic scorn.

If a Christian education is to be had in Romania, it is likely to begin at home. A child is taught, first, how to make the Sign of the Cross, how to group the fingers, what the grouping means, how to move the group from the head to the heart and across from right to left. A slack Sign of the Cross is a sign of slack faith. Immediately after baptism, a child is 'chrismated' (or confirmed), receives communion and is, from then on, a full church member. A young child, brought up to kiss his immediate family at home, is encouraged to kiss his extended family in church: the icons of the Saviour, His Mother, His Saints, His Angels, His Gospels. Worshippers entering Bucharest Cathedral think nothing of edging their way past a bishop in mid-Liturgy to salute a favourite icon and pay respects to the Gospel on its lectern. It is part of being at home, rather as each new arrival for a family gathering might wave, salute, kiss this or that relative without disturbing the patriarchal business he or she has come to attend. On a wet building site in an industrial town in Transylvania, a squad of tough volunteers were clearing the ground to build a new church. They had a priest—he was standing alongside—but no church; and without a church, the high-rise blocks and industrial estates had no heart. 'Who,' I asked, 'will pay for this church?' 'We will,' came the unanimous reply and it needed no translator. 'Imagine,' I put to them, 'a terrible accident. All the bishops and all the priests are taken away. Would Christianity die?' Again they spoke in chorus—'No'—with a force that surprised even them. A spokesman jabbed at me with a leathery finger: 'While ever there is *one* icon in *one* house,' another jab, 'the faith will live.'

To approach Eastern Orthodox Christianity on the level of history leads to endless complexity: What are the rights and wrongs of the Great Schism between East and West? Is the Pope the Supreme Pontiff (as the Roman Catholics say) or the Supreme Protestant (as the Orthodox might argue)? To approach it on the level of politics leads to complexity too, at least in the Socialist Republic of Romania. How should anyone properly interpret the actions of a communist government that supports the building of new churches, subsidizes parish priests, pays wages to monks and nuns, consults bishops? If a priest has doubts about government policy, is he likely to tell someone like me, when he has no idea how I shall use the information? If a priest has doubts about his Christianity, is he likely to tell me either and for the very same reasons? I believe I met churchmen who had suffered for their faith. I believe I also met churchmen who, with no outside pressure, were communist Christians. No doubt I met some who had opted for safety, and it scarcely becomes the armchair martyrs of elsewhere to think ill of them. I may have met saints. I do not know. But to approach Orthodox Christianity through the body of believers is a possibility. Four-fifths of the population of Romania are Orthodox Christians. They fill the churches. While ever Jesus comes at Christmas, those stout hearts will see to it that He has at least a manger.

It was Easter when we visited Romania and the countryside was in mid-convulsion. At its simplest and grandest, spring came. Wild flowers transfigured the hills. Domestically, houses were scrubbed and painted, windows were washed, Easter cake was baked, Easter eggs decorated. Mrs Havriliuc, skilled community egg-painter, had a few uncompleted on Maundy Thursday evening and proposed to finish them on Good Friday. 'But I thought no one worked on Good Friday,' I queried. 'They don't,' she agreed. Ecclesiastically it was a week of mounting drama. There were queues at Confession, held publicly, with the priest not giving absolution but overhearing what the penitent whispered and confirming the promise of God's forgiveness. There were queues at Communion: very old to very young, carrying candles, approaching the altar screen where the priest calls them by name and serves them a mixture of consecrated bread and wine in a spoon. There were queues to tunnel under and emerge from a large table, laid out to represent the entombment of Christ. There were processions for Easter, to greet a bishop, for funerals, for Sunday worship. No rural community seemed to recognize itself unless, from time to time, it came out of its settlement and went for a great collective walk.

For Holy Week we were in Moldavia, the north-easterly province of Romania. Each night we returned to our concrete hotel in Suceava, the first large town on the main road from the U.S.S.R. to the Romanian capital, Bucharest. It had the air of a truculent spa, telling visiting Russians that Romania is buoyant, breezy and non-Slavic. Our days were spent round and about the great Moldavian monasteries, set among wooded hills where generous abbots and abbesses served us great Lenten meals for which they apologized and ate nothing themselves. Here I met Sister Cecilia, who found my puzzled *Long Search* style irritatingly indecisive; Abbot Cucoşel, who told me about 'angelism' or the fall to the heights, the tendency of the enthusiastic to try to climb to God too fast (What do you do, I asked, when one of your monks is in danger of angelism? 'I stand by the ladder and hang on to his leg,' he replied); Abbess Eutochia, who kept a small dog called Tarzan and sang the services in chapel with a light, pure note; Father Cleopa, who spoke best of any about the Jesus Prayer; Brother Michael, who came to the monastery ten years ago in a school bus-party with his history teacher and decided to return; George Schipor, fresh from the army and bursting out of his demob suit, who had opted to be a monk and, when I asked him what he would be giving up, said simply, 'Nothing.' This vivid gallery shifted the search from what it could easily have been—pious tourism round church property—to Orthodoxy in practice. It also kept it down near the people where I think it belongs. For 'the people' in Romania largely includes the monks, the nuns, the parish priests. They farm their land, tend their orchards, mend their carts, dig their ditches alongside their neighbours. If the clergy had made strong past alliances with the rulers—any of the rulers—the Turks, the Austro-Hungarians, the Monarchy—the communist regime might have found it easier to unseat them when it came to power with atheistic intentions. But an alliance between clergy and people is harder to crack.

Father Cleopa, now retired, received us in the Monastery

Previous page Islamic village on the edge of the desert

Japanese house and garden

Romanian Orthodox villagers at prayer

of Sihastria. Half of his life had been spent tending sheep, half as an Abbot. He still has the tanned pelt of a hill shepherd. He still wears big shepherd's boots. In his sheep-tending days he was recognized mainly by his smell as he made one of his rare visits down to the community. When his predecessor as Abbot nominated him to succeed, there was general disaffection among the other monks. But the Abbot knew, as they did not, that in his solitude, Cleopa had become a master in the early desert fathers, those adventurers who wrote from their scorched marrows their log-books of the spiritual life. 'A monk,' said Father Cleopa, sitting on his wooden balcony, his eye steady as a camera moved in and out on him and a microphone swung into position over his head, 'should keep silent until he is required to speak.' I wonder, in retrospect, who he thought we were, keeping our spirits up with a vacant babble of conversation, carting with us all that machinery. We were not Romanian, which created one gulf; nor professedly Christian, which created another. We had not come to stay, to pray, to argue or to keep silent. I should guess he imagined that we were guests of the Patriarch of Romania being taken on a tour of the religious monuments of Moldavia and that, in some office in Bucharest, he appeared as the equivalent of a listed building. He resigned himself to our scrutiny and, when spoken to, he spoke. His voice came from another time.

'Those who do not have the Jesus Prayer,' he said, 'have no prayer.' I asked him to say that again in case something had been lost in translation. It stood. The Jesus Prayer spelt out and in the form in which it is most readily available to a stranger adds up usually to nine words: 'Lord Jesus Christ, have mercy on me, a sinner,' reduced sometimes to three, 'Lord Jesus Christ'; to one, 'Jesus'; then to silence. As silence, it is not a piece of argument, a statement of dogma, a formulation of theology. Father Cleopa hinted at a precise process, with breathing, posture, bare attention, with which the Jesus-word sinks into the heart where it ceases to have any imaginable Jesus-shape. 'The first law, whenever we begin to pray,' said Father Cleopa, 'is not to "fancy" anything or imagine anything, because God Himself does not come under the sway of the imagination. Fantasy is a stumbling block to our union with God. Fantasies, no matter how good and proper they be, always lead the mind away from God. They pull the mind out of the heart and leave us worshipping simple images.' In this light it is possible to say and understand that 'the Jesus Prayer prevents idolatry of God'.

The monks at Putna, a mile or two from the Russian border, are guardians of the Shrine of Stephen the Great, national hero, exemplary Romanian leader. The mantle of Stephen, in a reading of history that does not appear to displease either the government or the people of Romania, now falls upon President Ceausescu. In his lifetime Stephen, a fifteenth-century warrior king, whom even Pope Sixtus VI on the Latin side of the Great Schism called 'the Athlete of Christ', fought forty-six battles against the Turks, won forty-two and built forty-two commemorative chapels. He is invoked in Romania as the English might invoke Henry V —to show how a small band with the right spirit can tear through vast armies. The parallel between Stephen and the Turks on one side, and Ceausescu and the Russians on the other is not lost on the Romanian people. Romania, as an independent state, has just celebrated one hundred years of life. During that time the Great Powers and the Great Wars have redrawn its boundaries, and its population has arbitrarily varied by as much as ten million people. Since 1947, when the communists came to power under Russian protection, the borders have been stable. Since 1964, President Ceausescu has seemed to be pursuing a policy of 'nostrification', of making Romania Romanian and less a satellite of Russia. In this he has the support of the

Romanian Orthodox Church not just of today but of yesterday, for the story of the fight for an independent Romania can be seen partly as the fight of the Romanian Orthodox Church to give itself and its people a name and a homeland. In former times, the shrine of Stephen at Putna was a rallying point for Romanian nationalists, rather as the Abbey of Montserrat in Spain has somehow focused the struggle for Catalan nationhood. Now Putna is a symbol of Romania's continuous struggle against all bullying neighbours—Muslim to Soviet—and it is restored, defended, inhabited by monks.

There are said to be as many as two thousand Romanian Orthodox monks and nuns, scattered through more than a hundred houses and devoted to the traditional life of work and prayer. Where their houses are national shrines or national treasures, like the great painted churches of Moldavia, they act and are paid as museum curators also. On Good Friday at Putna, busloads of schoolchildren came with their teachers to see the shrine of Stephen the Great, ask the monks questions, look at Jesus, His Mother and His Saints in candle-lit glory peering out from the painted walls. Orthodox churches are full of such mute sermons. There is the Screen, the Iconostasis, which seems to stand in for that other screen which divides us from Heaven. There are doors in the Screen which offer the promise of a two-way traffic: of the people upwards and Heaven downwards. In the Liturgy, the central act of Orthodox worship, the people send their priest on a ritual ascent. They give him their bread and their wine. He brings them the Gospel and Earth made Heaven, the Bread and the Wine coming back from the Source transfigured. Some of the Moldavian painted churches open up inside and out like great picture books. Greek philosophers, Plato, Aristotle, Socrates, like kings and magi, process to the cradle of Jesus. The Tree of Jesse sprouts from the earth, encompasses King David, rises to

Jesus. A great ladder fills one whole outside wall of the convent church at Sucevita. It traverses corner to corner, earth to heaven. Each rung bears a climber. Each climber bears a whole support system of serried angels, their wings aligned, their impulse upward. Here is no solitary pilgrim, blood-brother of Bunyan's Christian, but a commonwealth of climbers. Beneath the ladder are those who fall: lonely, disorderly, arms and legs flailing, trapped by hungry devils whose bellies have teeth. Christians, says the wall, are saved in the Christian community; any who fall, fall alone.

Sister Cecilia sat in the choir stalls at Moldovita convent and, if it had been seemly for a nun to snort, I am sure would have snorted. I had wanted to approach Christianity as if it were new to me. How could she help me to take a first step? Clearly she thought I was clowning. It was quite obvious that I had been brought up a Western Christian— heir to the Crusaders who burnt the treasures of Christian Constantinople on Good Friday, 1204; step-son of the Popes of Rome who so misunderstood themselves as to assume the powers of Western Emperors; cousin to Martin Luther, John Calvin, Ulrich Zwingli, Henry VIII, all those splinter-ing schismatics who make Western Christianity look like crumbling land about to fall into the sea. What new trick was this I was trying? She little understood how far England at least has drifted, how unsafe it is to assume that, on the subject of Jesus, we already know our own minds. She offered a creed. I sighed, weary of creeds. She mistook my sigh for displeasure. She became displeased.

'It's up to you what you want to believe. If you want to believe in God, you have him in front of you—made man.' I fought on: 'But what is my relation as a human being to this God-made-man? How do I get in touch with Him?' 'By believing in Him.' 'How do I do it? What do I have to do?' 'You believe.' She may have met non-Christians with a love of painted churches; and troubled Christians finding the going rough; but rarely, I think, a pagan with an ache.

Later, the sigh forgotten, she spoke memorably of the Jesus Prayer as an endless Liturgy winding round the heart. She spoke of *theosis*, 'deification', that process by which, in the Orthodox tradition, a Christian moves God-wards, gains God-hood, becomes God by adoption. The painted ladder at Suceyita never arrives—at least not in paint and not on that wall or in this life. 'Can you ever say, Sister, that you have arrived, you're safe, you're saved?' She started to shake her head before the question was out, thus incidentally revealing that she spoke better English than she had claimed. 'Never. Man can never say such a thing. Our church fathers never said they had reached the end of the road. They still have a long way to go.'

The painted church at Humor where we waited for Easter was packed with villagers. The overflow waited outside. As the end of the day drew in, the table called the 'epitaphion', which had represented the tomb of Christ all week, was taken away; one by one the candles were extinguished and there would have been total darkness. Sadly, total darkness does not take on celluloid. The villagers tolerated one intrusive B.B.C. lamp, a particularly vivid reminder of the enormity of the darkness, the inaccessibility, and the solitariness that is part of a real Long Search but which no film Long Search can handle.

After long moments of what would have been total darkness and silence, one frail light moved from the altar, through the centre door in the screen, the door of the Incarnation, and out to the people. For the lighting of the first few candles, one gust of wind would have seemed able to wipe out Easter. Confidence grew as the light spread, haphazardly down the church. Parents took light from their children, neighbours from their neighbours, strangers from strangers. Beyond the heads of the congregation glimmered the heads of painted saints, rank upon rank of them;

as the story goes, with large eyes, having seen God, large ears, having heard God, and small mouths because what they have seen and heard they cannot speak about. A hymn burst out. Bells rang for the first time since the start of Lent. Banners were hoisted; fire-crackers exploded; and the whole congregation, candles lit, processed round the outside of the church. The Easter Liturgy followed while we snatched an hour or two's sleep on made-up beds in the parish priest's house. When we returned to the church at about dawn, the Liturgy was still winding its way inside the church, and outside two or three hundred women with kitchen baskets filled with bread, bacon, sweet Easter cake and candles were waiting to have them blessed. Our Easter breakfast, for which the parish priest and his wife, in good Romanian style, apologized, started with plum brandy and white wine and went on to chicken in aspic, salami, baked ham, tomatoes, cheese-cake, Easter cake, strong black coffee and eggs. The apologies were for the failure to supply a cooked breakfast.

Romania is a country of great mineral wealth, including oil-fields, and it is industrializing fast. As we drove away from outer Moldavia and through new industrial towns, villagers in new apartment blocks were spending a quiet evening leaning over their balconies as, in the villages, they had leaned over their gates. How many generations will it take, I used to ask, for urban factory workers to forget the villages they came from, and, with the villages, the Orthodox Church? The answers, from churchmen at least, were all confident; and, in proof, they took me to urban building sites where squads of volunteers were digging out the foundations for new churches. I cited the forlorn example of Western Europe: big cities, wealth, shattered community, empty churches. Remus Rus, the translator from the Romanian Patriarchate who accompanied our whole journey, assured me that Romania would learn from our mistakes. Mr Nenciu, the State Minister of Cults (i.e. in charge of religious affairs) in Bucharest, described as 'realistic' the acknowledgement by the State that the Church exists and that the vast majority of the Romanian people appear to need it. Hence, so long as it supports the nation, the Church has State support. Should the people, for whatever reason, discover that they no longer need the Church, it will presumably wither away.

Very few of the people I met in Romania spoke English. This is not meant to sound reproachful. I do not speak Romanian. Yet it did add to the feeling of distance and strangulation: anything I said had to be ferried through a third party and anything they said took the same route back. Who, I used to think, is Remus Rus, this man at my side? Is he a Government employee working for the Church, a Church employee working for the Government, or neither? Does he know and like, know and dislike or not know England? Who does he think I am? He saw me, I should guess, through two filters: first, as a puritan who took pleasure, as a Romanian Orthodox never could, in deliberately bare, white walls; second, since I had recently returned from Japan, as an entranced Western Buddha-fancier who neglects the spirituality of his own tradition to go in pursuit of someone else's. It was a situation parallel, in some respects, to that of the search for the Muslims where two sides, trying to come into dialogue, projected on each other their own puzzlement and a certain crude stereotype.

The small village of Draganului in Transylvania, the most westerly province of Romania, has two churches: one old and incapable of holding the congregation; one new, nearly completed, with the dimensions of a cathedral. It was being built by local effort and with Government approval, and the President of the Church Building Committee was a long-term Communist Party member. I met him in the house of the parish priest where a small dinner was arranged for the Building Committee, a local bishop, the priest's family and *The Long Search*. It was an exercise in constructive harmony and slow disintegration under the weight of hospitality and the kick of local wine. I think I heard enough of the truth to be impressed, but by no means enough to carry away a sense of the right complexity. Behind the indomitable conviviality, I wanted just one person to tell me that at least once or twice in the last thirty years times had been hard for Christians. Then I would have listened with patience. But they dribbled my questions skilfully up and down the table and, when in doubt, kicked for touch. I went for a certain submission. This man alongside me is Chairman of the Church Building Committee? 'President,' Remus ferried back the answer. And a Communist Party member? More ferrying. 'Everybody knows that.' 'But,' I said, dragging the two propositions together like resisting poles of a magnet, 'I thought Communists were atheists.' A roar of Romanian laughter went ahead of the return translation. 'He said,' said Remus, 'they should be atheists. So those who believe get baptized and those who don't believe don't . . .'

The President of the Building Committee worked as a store-keeper in a co-operative. His mother taught him the Lord's Prayer. He taught his children to be forthright, to do their best, not to bring shame on their father and mother, and now he has built them a church. 'Could he imagine,' I suggested, 'that his children might not be interested in the church he had built?' (For, to the extent that their State schooling succeeded, they would leave their father well behind.) For the first time there seemed to be no ready answer. When it came, it lacked the customary bounce. 'What I say is this: I teach them and it is up to them to choose.' We parted with warm handshakes and resonant slaps on the back. There were one or two structural faults in the night's conversation, but out on the hill a new church, somehow, for some reason, was standing firm.

Compared with the East of Europe, the West, at least recently, would seem to have suffered little for the Faith, except for the suffering that one group of Christians has inflicted on another. And, whatever the rights and wrongs of papal supremacy, no one will deny that one strong command headquarters in Rome has given missionary work a Roman thrust and vigour. What Orthodoxy seems to represent is an alternative possibility: that of 'martyrdom' or witness, rather than mission. 'Orthodoxy', in the words of a Romanian priest, 'does not want to conquer. It allows itself to be conquered and, in being conquered, survives.'

There is an Orthodox Theological Institute for the training of priests in the Transylvanian town of Sibiu. It is one of two such in Romania. It enjoys university status. The professors have State salaries. The students mostly survive on grants from local bishops. Entrance qualifications are that the candidates should be healthy, reasonably schooled and able to sing. A parish priest may not mutter the Liturgy. A hidden qualification is that the candidate should have no wish to make headway in State concerns, except in the sense that all Romanian concerns, including Theological Institutes, are State concerns. Sibiu has nine hundred students, a magnificent choir, and instruction in English. For once the language barrier lifted and I spoke to two ordinands. One was called Ovid; the other, Virgil.

Which is more important, I asked, to be in church and say the Liturgy, or to go round the village, discover who needs help and bring it? 'I think,' said Virgil, 'that both things are equally important.' And, from that position, he would not budge. The Church too has a social mission.

On the question of reform there was no budging either. Did any of them wish to see Orthodoxy change? A parallel question, and about as perceptive, could be addressed to a plant in a very tight pot. Wouldn't it like to spill over, proliferate, split, send out shoots? 'No,' replied Ovid. 'We just have to keep our line, our traditional line.' Sensing that to Western ears such a reply might lack adventure, Virgil intervened. 'We need to revive the Christian spirit, not to reform it.' So the Church renews itself without reform imposed from outside? 'Without reformation,' he confirmed. Then, pleased with his English as well as with his rooted Orthodoxy, 'The Christian Church has this capacity of renewing itself and it will never die.'

Across the Carpathians in Northern Transylvania lies the remote province of Maramures. Here the will of staunchly Orthodox people exerted itself powerfully in the election of a bishop. He was Justinian. For thirty-three years he had been a monk and for seventeen years *starets* or abbot of the only monastery in Maramures—Rohia, a hill community at the end of a long ascending lane. When the old Bishop of Maramures died, the people petitioned the Patriarch in Bucharest to give them the successor they wanted. The Patriarch took note. Justinian was preferred. What agonies he underwent—patriarchal nomination pushing him one way, taste for obscurity and silence pulling him the other— are irrecoverable night-time matters, but they have left traces. His elevation meant a move across the mountains, south out of Maramures to the city of Cluj, where he is assistant bishop. There he inhabits his modestly elegant episcopal apartments with the air of a man who has been dropped in by time-machine and is waiting to be picked up again. His proper habitat would seem to be something sparer, bleaker and further back in time. One evening he let Remus Rus translate portions of his journal, his own spiritual log-book. 'There is a desert in the self. But this desert should not be understood as an empty space but as fullness. Man achieves fullness when he detaches himself and remains alone with God no matter where he is . . . It is necessary for a man to look back on his life from a very distant future and a removed place . . . Our times are a punishment for the worthlessness of us priests as Christians . . . The Christians made a great mistake when they transformed Jesus into a cultic object, into a religion . . .' He once spoke of the coming eclipse of the Christian Church, its reduction to its elements, its purgation, its resurrection in a new shape. It was a prospect he appeared to walk towards with equanimity, trust and something like merriment.

On volume and variety of cooking, Bishop Justinian has trained his housekeeper in a very un-Romanian modesty. At any meal we shared I never saw him take more than a small cup of soup and half a slice of bread. He is known to distribute his income readily to anyone who needs it—to the young especially. No door in his house is locked. It is Orthodox practice that a parish priest should marry, raise a family, be rooted in his community; and that a bishop should be celibate, a monk and able to travel light. All true bishops are seen as successors of the Apostles and of the company that met in seven great Ecumenical Councils after A.D. 300 and before A.D. 800 to hammer out Christian doctrine and define all that needed definition. The Orthodox reject as unwarranted and over-anxious subsequent Roman Catholic dogmatizing. They also reject the imperial spurt which raised the Pope of Rome above his peers. The icon of the Church as, in their view, Christ founded it and meant it to be is simply a bishop moving among and shepherding his people.

Word that Bishop Justinian was returning to Maramures on one of his duty visitations went ahead of us. We took it in turns to eat token amounts of the enormous running-buffet that continued from parish-house to parish-house along the route through the mountains. By the river Mara, boundary of Maramures, the Bishop asked us to dismount from the Romanian tourist bus that we had offered him as episcopal chariot and, as Remus Rus and I sat on the banks trailing

our fingers, he scooped up the chill water and threw it at u
in a Dacian baptism, a rite as uncanonical and inescapabl
as those which mark a first crossing of the Equator. 'We ar
seventy per cent water,' he said. 'Respect for water is self
respect.' He describes himself as a Dacian and claims to
recognize cousins and uncles in photographs of Daciar
warriors as they appear in the bas-reliefs on Trajan'
Column in Rome. 'Old national folk beliefs may be heresies
but they contain the truth as experienced by the people.'

The village of Ieud boasts happy marriages: in a hundrec
years no one has asked for a divorce. It is a spacious cart
track hemmed in by houses. At one end is an old church; a
the other, the foundations of a new one which the Bishop
was due to bless. No sooner was he sighted stepping down
from our tourist bus than the village came to meet him
priest first. Since we were in the days after Easter, the
Bishop's greeting to the people was *Hristos a înviat*! (Christ i
risen) and their unanimous reply, *Adavarat a înviat*! (He i
risen indeed), which gained strength as the crowd thickened
The parish priest apologized for the absence of menfolk, bu
many were at work. All the same, the straggling band tha
accompanied the Bishop down the main street to the ol
church swelled to about a thousand while he was in th
church saying his prayers and vesting himself in cope an
crown, and the journey from the old church to the nev
foundations took on the air of a reverential scrum. Banner
went ahead, dispersing a flock of geese. A throaty hym
burst out. The Bishop, with his holy water carried in
plastic bucket, made his way over the gang-planks whil
adventurous boys, with their solemn black hats clutche
respectfully in their fists, balanced themselves high in th
scaffolding.

The blessing over, the Bishop preached. I thought at fir
that the man behind me was getting asthma. Then handke
chiefs appeared from apron pockets. Soon, alien now as s

often in Romania, I seemed to be the only bystander not in tears. His theme was their national identity and their regional identity: one People and one Faith. 'Be who you are . . . be who you have always been.' It is only thirty years ago that an occupying Soviet army attempted to set up a puppet administration in this area under Ruthenian leadership, backed by a stiffening of Ukrainians and calling itself the Government of the Autonomous Soviet Republic of Maramures. Local patriots ejected the newcomers from the town hall. The experiment was not repeated.

The Cultural Attaché in the Romanian Embassy in London, before the journey started, had been righter than he knew when he expressed his pleasure that we were to go to Romania to film the 'folklore', for on such an occasion as the consecration of this village church the 'folklore', in the sense of striking local costumes, and the beleaguered splendour of a crowned bishop standing on a builder's plank addressing the people, was all we could easily see. The national plight, the deep sense of a people's identity in need of guardians, relief that, unlike their neighbours a few miles away, they had not been absorbed into Russia, were matters quite outside our grasp.

Later, at a lunch in the parish priest's house and in the presence of the First Secretary at the British Embassy in Bucharest (constantly addressed as 'Ambassador'), the Bishop rose again to speak. 'There are three great nations in Europe,' he said, 'the French, the Germans and the British. We regard the French with sympathy, the Germans with reserve and the British with admiration.' We looked shyly at our plates. The Bishop recalled gratefully that the printing of a hundred thousand copies of the Bible in 1968, the first since 1944, had been made possible on a gift of paper by the United Bible Societies in London. He then went on to handle matters we may be in danger of misunderstanding. First, he said, harassment of one kind or another is not new to Orthodoxy. The Turks and the Catholic Hungarians have all leaned heavily. Nor should the Church expect favours. But over the past thirty years 'these mad people [so it was translated] called Communists have dared to do something for our country. You have to understand that we started from zero.' Thirty years ago seventy per cent of Maramures was illiterate; today, all are taught to read. Thirty years ago there was no relief for poverty; now the standard of living is almost unrecognizably higher. 'Do not,' he said, 'confuse loyalty with subordination.' The Orthodox Church is loyal to the Romanian State and it is also loyal to its divinely instituted identity. Afterwards the foreigners discussed the speech and the day. Why had the Bishop made his speech? Had we somehow signalled doubt of his integrity? Who else was listening at that table beyond those we could identify? Was it, by implication, xenophobic?—putting us in our place and out of their country as firmly as the inhabitants of Maramures expelled the Russians from the town hall. Was it the nationalist East instructing the imperialist West? Was it Orthodoxy trying to explain to the Catholics and the Protestants a Christianity they appear never to understand?

Whereas we would have left the village of Ieud overwhelmed by its devout vigour, its pride in two churches, its love for its bishop, we left puzzled.

9

SULAWESI
The Way of the Ancestors

There is a growing number of people in the affluent, industrial, urban West who salivate at the mention of the words 'primitive' or 'primal'. During preparations for the shooting of one of the *Long Search* films in California the password, the Open Sesame, the sign of our seriousness and good faith was the answer to the question: 'What are you going to do about primitive religion?' Never, 'What are you going to do about the Methodists, or the Marxists, nor even the Buddhists'; but, 'What are you going to do about that section of the world's population, decreasing by the hour, which still keeps some of the sanity and wholesomeness that we have lost?' In the making of a version of the *Long Search* films for German television—omitting the searcher and substituting an orchestration of disembodied voices to carry the story—it is revealing that the transmission order of the films was altered and the film on 'primal religion' was transmitted first. In the presentation by an American University of *Long Search* material for use by students, again 'primality' nudged its way to the head of the queue. The opening chapter is called *The Way of the Ancestors—a study of Primal Religions*, is followed by a chapter on the Zulus, and only then does the transmission order of the original films take over.

The allure of 'primality' and 'primitivism' seems to be threefold. First, 'the primal' is understandably taken to mean 'first'; 'primal religion' is thought likely to be the religion of our prime ancestors; the lineality of history would make it sensible to put 'the primal' before the rest. Secondly, 'the primal', with its idea of integrity, oneness, has an appeal for those who wish to reject the complexity of the city, the enfeeblement of the individual in the big corporations, the decline of neighbourliness. Third, after the rapid plundering of too many of the earth's resources, it may soon be necessary to find out how to survive more simply, more 'primally'. To give priority to 'the primal' may be simple self-interest.

It never entered our discussions or our heads that the pursuit of 'the primal', as we secretly envisaged it, was a mirage; that nothing is utterly primitive once it has drawn the attention of outsiders; that we would be standing in front of 'the primal' quizzing it for signs of ecological good sense and nearness to its roots and that 'the primal' would be standing in front of us envying our watches and our ballpoint pens. If we had known ourselves better, the right location for the search for 'the primal' and 'the primitive' is not Sulawesi, Indonesia, but California. There, in forest settlements just off five-lane highways, it is possible to sit by logfires and discuss the 'future primitive', the return to sanity of generations of earth-exploiters, machine-maniacs, builders of cruel industrial cities. The Torajas of Sulawesi, Indonesia, were not to know that we were seeking in them an exemplar of what we should be doing about ourselves. They could not know, therefore, the extent of our frustration and disappointment.

The Torajas are a mountain people who traditionally impress their neighbours with their fighting skills, the quality of their magicians, the singularity of their houses, like great decorated, landlocked boats, the length, complexity and variety of their death ceremonies, their elevated rock galleries from which peer stark wooden effigies of the illustrious dead, the vigour of their fighting cocks. They have their own accounts of the Creation, a great Flood, the withdrawal of the Creator God in a sulk, leaving decisions to the village assembly, the arrival in those high regions of the Toraja Lords who descended from the sky. Christian missionaries (those, that is, who survived long enough to make up their minds about the hardy people they were trying to convert) have been predicting the imminent death of Toraja traditional religion since the turn of the century. So far, and for a complexity of reasons, they have been proved wrong. Christians had a harder time than Toraja traditionalists when the Japanese occupied the territory in the Second World War. More recently, in 1969, the Indonesian Government recognized the old Toraja Ritual Way as a 'religion' alongside the Christian, the Muslim and the Hindu, and the traditionalists have representation in the local legislature. Now Torajaland has been marked off as a tourist area with great potential. Hotels are to be built, and an airport. Tourist guides, not familiar with the ways of the Toraja, are given government training courses. The traditionalists, who have long smarted under the Christian jibe that they are 'animists' and the Muslim jibe that they are 'kafirs' (i.e. infidels), are noting that the tourists are not arriving to gaze at Christians singing slow Calvinist hymns in their little whitewashed Dutch churches or at Muslims at prayer, but at Torajanese traditional huts, rice ceremonies, death ceremonies, the ritual slaughter of pig and buffalo.

The local name for the newly-valued traditional Toraja religion is *Aluk To Dolo*, 'the Way of the Ancestors', as opposed to the Way of the Christians or the Way of the Muslims. If there were no need to draw comparisons, the Toraja tradition would scarcely be a 'religion' at all. It would simply be the way the Torajas have always done things. Toraja society seems to have been traditionally feudal. A class of Kings and Lords ruled. Beneath them were the Freemen. At the bottom and unmentionable were the slaves. Some slaves, called golden slaves, were highly esteemed by their noble masters though they could never break rank so far as to lose their slave status. They were taken to their burials trussed up like pigs and there was a strict limit on how many animals even the slaves who could afford it might sacrifice; for animals killed at a funeral accompany the dead soul to the after-life and it would be unseemly for a slave to appear on the other side with too much livestock. Modern Torajanese are said to know who the free families, the slave families, the royal families are, though slavery was abolished officially by the Dutch at the end of the last century and the name 'slave' would never be uttered in public.

To be an impoverished nobleman in Europe is not such a rarity. Among the Torajas it would be a social catastrophe —not just for the nobility, but for the rest of society too. Rank is gained at birth, but is confirmed at the funeral. Someone of whom it is said, 'Twenty buffalo and a hundred pigs will be sacrificed when that person dies', is nobility acting like nobility, moving from this life to the next with an enormous retinue of four-legged wealth, providing a feast for those who are left behind, holding out to the poor a rare chance of some meat. If there is any traditional Toraja equivalent of the Welfare State it is in the ability of the nobly-born to be buried well and feed a multitude.

To call in the right number of buffalo and the right number of pigs for slaughter at one time takes organization and nerve. Throughout the life of a person, now dead, the family will have offered buffalo and pigs to other families arranging a funeral. Once a buffalo or a pig is accepted, a debt is set up and will have to be paid later. The process of assembling the pay-off for a funeral can take years. In the meantime the dead person is regarded as 'sick', is wrapped in cloths and 'sleeps' like the rest of the family on an east/

west axis. Food is offered to the sick one at meal-times and, once its essence has been removed by its proximity to the mute roll of cloth, it is thrown out to the chickens. If, as is bound to happen at some stage in the decomposition of a corpse, the smell becomes too foul, the family may sleep in another room, but the corpse is not removed. The rank of the person who 'feeds' the corpse should be the equal of that of the corpse. Among the officials traditionally assembled to tend to the needs of the corpse is one who should cut off the retreat paths of escaping maggots and return them to the bundle. It is not yet time for burial even in the belly of a burrowing maggot. There must be Toraja children for whom the earliest and longest-lasting smell of home is the smell of a decomposing grandparent. Once decomposition is complete, the bones are unwrapped and reassembled nearby. This is the opportunity for quick lessons in human anatomy for the more inquisitive young.

The significance of the east/west sleeping position is that southwards lies the Land of the Souls, Puya. Once the head is pointed that way the funeral ritual is set in motion, the soul is dislodged from the body, ritual errors will be paid for dearly, the slow journey of the dead from the land of the living has begun. North and east for the Torajas are lively directions. Houses face north. From the east rises the sun that ripens the rice. The west is the dwelling-place of those ancestors who have gone south to the land of the souls, undergone the ritual processing that turns the newly dead into regular ancestors, and releases them to the skies.

Generous sources of information about Toraja rituals seem not to exist. H. van der Veen, the doyen of Toraja studies, made a Toraja-Dutch dictionary, translated the Bible into Torajanese, made translations of Toraja ritual hymns. A handful of scholars have followed. There is in existence a film of a great Toraja funeral, that of the last King of Sangalla, in which his sole remaining wife is seen weeping at his coffin and being buffeted about in a traditional Torajanese carrying-box on the way to her husband's funeral field. *The Long Search* Toraja film contains a tourist-infested sequence taken at the funeral of the very same woman and I spent, beforehand, a dazed afternoon sitting on a rushmat alongside her well-wrapped corpse. The source of most of our information and guidance was Eric Crystal, who is attached to the Centre for South and South East Asia Studies in the University of California at Berkeley. He speaks Torajanese. His information does not necessarily tally with that of the men who shot the earlier Toraja film; nor with that of a doctoral thesis on 'The Religion of the Baree-Speaking Toradja of Central Celebes', which was presented at the University of Leiden in 1956 and which I read with no feeling that we had both been looking at the same place. These observations are not meant to set one authority off against another, but to bring to anyone who imagines that most things are known, agreed on, documented, the news that this is not so.

The last Queen of Sangalla, a childless woman, lay in an upper room in a traditional thatch and bamboo house. Her corpse had been swung into a north/south direction, indicating that the funeral process could begin. A woman relative of equal rank, wearing gold earrings but otherwise in unadorned black, was sitting beside the corpse on a mat. We sat off the mat. Eric Crystal chatted to her and she encouraged us to stay for the feeding of the 'soul' which is presumed to be in the vicinity, detached from the corpse but lurking. Soul food is cold: corn, cassava and wine from the tuak tree. The wine, which was promised instantly, was a long time arriving and we asked to be excused. Tuak wine is the juice of the tree, tapped into a bamboo funnel and carried frothing, strapped to the back of a carrier as an offering at a feast or to slake the thirst of a noble corpse. Next to the Queen's traditional house is her alternative residence—a modern bungalow with electric light.

Not far away was the funeral field. Spacious bamboo booths were under construction enclosing a broad grass field. Towards the centre of the field were the megaliths to which the buffalo for slaughter would be tethered. These hefty monuments would have been dragged to the site—by slave labour presumably—for former funerals. It was with some reluctance that Eric Crystal agreed to attend for the filming of the last Queen's journey. The ceremony, in his view, had been compromised. It had been widely advertised in the tourist offices of the world; the Director-General of Tourism in the Central Government in Jakarta was expected to attend and make a speech. The B.B.C. crew were allocated booth 48. Near neighbours on the right were a German tourist group gathered under the protection of an organization called Mactours. Across the compound another booth housed a mixed group of French and Americans who had been sleeping on the site so as to miss none of the action. It was a five-day event leading to a mile-long jog with the coffin to the burial place, its lodging in a hole in the rock and the placing of a commemorative statue (a *tau-tau*, they call it) in a high spectators' gallery among a crowd of others.

The last Queen's funeral, which seemed to me to be in all ways excessive, must have been tame compared with similar events in the past. Traditionally, at the end of the five days, the whole funeral village would have been set alight. On this occasion (the price of bamboo having risen) one token house was burnt. This, a fine two-storey edifice, was the resting place of the coffin during the period of the public celebration. Toraja ritual specialists, whose Torajanese name is *tominaa* ('the one who breathes forth', i.e. the one who speaks the special high language of the gods), controlled the main events. They huddled together on the top storey of the corpse's lodging house and set up a dancing chant that, with luck, might lead to trance. An intrepid little

American lady wearing a crocheted hat and toting a mean Pentax mounted the ladder for a better view of the hyperventilating men, but was smartly ejected and sent back to ground level. Lines of women in paper gilt crowns set up unison rhythmic chants, moved their feet and bodies little, stroked the air in concerted movements of the hands. Reluctant buffalo, as if to die soon was not enough, were spurred to fight each other, but, unless a clash was forced on them, backed away. Kick fights broke out—a rough game for young men in which the idea seems to be to immobilize an opponent with a quick jab from a bare foot. Buffalo were led to the megaliths and tethered. Their throats were tickled to make them stretch with pleasure and, once the skin was tight, it was lanced with a long knife. Little boys ran forward with bamboo funnels to collect the blood, sometimes finding it best to shove the funnel down the expiring animal's pumping throat. Not far behind the little boys were the cine cameras, the stills cameras and the B.B.C. camera, though, to be fair to the cameraman, he was not there on holiday. Once the beasts were still enough, their bodies were dragged to high platforms where the tominaas supervised the apportioning of the meat—some to the donor's family, some to the funeral family, some to the government as tax, some to the tominaa in lieu of fees, some as gifts for other services. The German Mactours group, by bringing its own buffalo with whoops and merriment, had earned a portion of carcass.

I know that, if meat is eaten animals must be killed and that the funeral field at Sangalla was no more obscene than a Western slaughter-house, and I dutifully delivered myself of those opinions on celluloid; how 'We like the beefsteak and pork chop but dare not watch the animals die'. At the time I even thought I meant it. Now I would retract. Carnivores in the wild, as far as I know, do not do their deadly work under the curious gaze of a holiday audience.

Under the gaze of hungry cubs, perhaps; but the difference is between light, ambling curiosity and evident need. Eric Crystal saw, among the tourists, evidence of serious interest in the lives of a people who had religious and life rituals that were still full of meaning. I saw another of the faces of *mondo cane*.

The corpse was lifted down from its lodging under the direction of the dead Queen's responsible relative. It had been his task to collect the offerings for slaughter, his decision, presumably, to open the event for so many visitors. He is himself a Christian. On this occasion he was doing right by a relative who died an old believer. The surprise is to discover that some of the most bloodsome Torajanese funerals, though deprived of their former religious meaning no doubt, are the funerals of Christians. Once the coffin was clear of the bamboo house and settled alongside its *tau-tau* effigy, the bamboo supports were rocked from their moorings, the structure collapsed and it was set alight. While the flames were still bright, bearers took up the coffin and the *tau-tau* under its canopy, and set off at a jogtrot for the grave site. A hardy bearer, with a cigarette nearly burning the corner of his mouth, got a foothold in the notched holes in a bamboo ladder and took the coffin aloft, steadied by two skilled companion climbers. After the coffin was stowed, the moment came for the *tau-tau* to be lifted to its gallery. A woman attendant placed a blue and white head cloth round the Queen's head. A visitor offered his baseball cap, which was preferred. For all I know, the effigy of the last Queen of Sangalla still stares down from her bleak eminence looking as if she is about to bat.

It is certain that the view of Toraja religion which I picked up, with Eric Crystal's help on a flying visit, is over-tidy—partly my doing and partly, no doubt, that of the Torajas themselves, who have noted in Muslims and Christians the characteristics of a 'real religion' and wish to show the same clear lines. The presiding Creator God goes by the name of Puang Matua—the Original Lord, the One who was there before all else. Puang Matua is the name taken from the local language by the Christians for their God. There must be incalculable leakage from one God to the Other. According to one Creation Story, delivered by one who is concerned to be accurate and to preserve the tradition, Puang Matua made his first appearance at the parting of the earth and the sky along with six associates, one of whom went missing and five went in search of her. The sound of anger and the upturning of hiding places in the sky—in a word, thunder—comes from these primal searchers. Puang Matua, left behind, lonely as in some accounts the Hebrew God is said to have been, opted to create the world, which he blew out, animals, plants, rocks and all, from the bellows of his forge. Mankind he crafted in gold. Once, so the story goes, this High God was approachable by means of a flight of steps from the earth, and was willing to hear complaints and give advice. But one rash visitor stole a divine fire-flint. Challenged by this Promethean cheek, Puang Matua, in a rage, destroyed the steps, which lie now in the form of a heaped mountain range in the south of the country. In the after-age, communication with Puang Matua is possible only through animal sacrifice, controlled by ritual specialists who speak a language unknown to the people but familiar to God. The will of God is made plain to the community in the debates in the village assembly.

On each of the *Long Search* journeys, it became a habit to take one substantial piece of reading. For Indonesia, the choice was D. M. Low's condensed version of Gibbon's *The Decline and Fall of the Roman Empire*. The director of the film, Malcolm Feuerstein, is a conscientious Jew. During the filming there was a free day to coincide with Jewish New Year, and the director, in yarmulka and prayer shawl, did

he Jewish vigil appropriate to the day. In the evening, we
oined him for a meal and a glass or two of sticky white wine
bought in the local market in celebration. After dinner I
went back to another page or two of Gibbon. He had this to
say about how the Gnostics nearly two thousand years ago
regarded the religious practices of the Jews. It drew a
curious line through the meal, the director's day of prayer,
the animal sacrifice of the Torajas, the incautious rapidity
with which I felt myself having to sum up a particular
people, the danger of superficiality and error. Gibbon
writes: 'They [the Gnostics] asserted it was impossible that
a religion which consisted only of bloody sacrifices and
trifling ceremonies, and whose rewards as well as punish-
ments were of a carnal and temporal nature, could inspire
the love of virtue or restrain the impetuosity of passion.'

In the reduction of a people's tradition to a tidy shape for
export, it is possible that Puang Matua, the Creator, is given
a key position he does not hold in the minds of the people.
The nearer presences are those of the Ancestors and the
Deata spirits, who assembled themselves as the days went by
into the base angles of a triangle: Puang Matua at the top,
Ancestors and Deatas beneath. Of the two, the Deatas seem
to haunt rice fields, rivers, certain plants, certain places.
When seen they are small and yellow and they speak
Torajanese. They belong to no particular family but they
may take up lodging on family property and have to be
placated. In the moments before a shrewdly-aimed lance
was jetted into the side of a sacrificial buffalo at one of the
greatest ceremonies, the Deatas were encouraged to make
themselves scarce for fear of being wounded. They live in
the outside world. They are the regulating spirits of nature.
They remind the human part of creation that there are
other parts which have rights, carry benefits, need care and
attention. They are the ecological enablers and censors, who
protect the people so long as the balance of man with nature

is right and punish the people when the balance is wrong. Their bemused Deata relatives must lie bleeding in all the mine shafts, factories, towns, under all the motorways, in all the car exhausts and jet trails and the polluted oceans of the U.S.A., Japan, South Africa and Europe.

Sometimes the Toraja Deatas can be shrewd obstructors of progress. In early 1975, government engineers started work on a modern bridge over the Sa'adan, the revered river that flows south through Toraja territory, but the foundations would not stay firm. Local opinion knew the reason. The surveyors happened to have chosen a part of the river which a particularly powerful Deata assumed belonged to him. Before further work, the Regency Governor came to the site with an offering of a pig, a chicken and a bamboo funnel of palm wine. A tominaa was called in to watch over the ritual details. The sacrifice was made, the ruffled spirit pacified and the bridge completed without further difficulty. On another occasion the director of the film attended a ceremony in a Toraja brickworks at which a chicken, a supply of betel-nut and tobacco were offered by the owner in fulfilment of a vow made to the Deata spirits and Puang Matua. Part of his work force had gone down with an unexplained ailment. He vowed that, if they recovered, he would make an appropriate sacrifice. They recovered. He sacrificed. An interpretation offered by a Toraja Christian was that, either when the factory was built or when it prospered, no proper ritual clearance was obtained from the resident spirits, no thanks were offered. Rather than persist in their impiety and collect, along with their higher wages, the punishment of the Deatas, the men fell sick from a fear that lay deeper than they could ever explain, the fear of being wrong in the watching eyes of those who were there before.

All living creatures—the rice, the bamboo, the buffalo, man and woman—have ancestors. Properly cherished, ncestors bring prosperity, health, happiness. Neglected, heated, undervalued, they bring sickness and misfortune. The number of prohibitions over which the ancestors stand guard has been put at 7,777, mostly to do with the avoidance of incest, the proper ritual care of the dead and the maintenance of a sharp division between life rituals and death rituals, the tending of the rice and the disposing of corpses, ceremonies (in a telling local expression) of the rising smoke and of the falling smoke. It was at the coronation of a new High Priest of the rice rituals that the Deatas were asked to leave before the buffalo was lanced. Part of the same ceremony was a long chant by the candidate giving his ancestral lineage and summoning ancestral support. He then turned to the buffalo and said he wished he could recite the buffalo's ancestry too, but sadly did not know it. Perhaps the human ancestors know the buffalo ancestors and can supply names. He then listed a number of historic buffalo as possible forebears of the beast who was now to accompany the dead High Priest on his journey south.

To us, to whom every ritual observance was a novelty, it was hard to sense the ritual rarity of the events we saw that day. The usual funeral colour is black; the funeral foods are cassava and corn (certainly not rice); Deata spirits, whose particular habitation is the rice field, do not usually attend funerals; at funerals close relatives usually do not dance. At the funeral of the old High Priest and the instant coronation of his successor all these taboos were deliberately broken. The funeral colour was yellow; rice was offered, cooked and eaten; the Deatas were welcomed except on the slaughterer's knife; the new High Priest danced behind his father's coffin. We were witnesses of what Eric Crystal called a 'rite of reversal'. The High Priest presides at the greatest rice rituals; he is the life priest. His funeral deliberately breaks the rules. There is a further ritual, a B.B.C. ritual associated with filming, that involves a capacious black bag into which the cameraman's assistant plunges his arms, elbow-deep, to change and seal up his reels of film away from the light. Objections were raised during the filming of the funeral. The black bag stayed out of sight till a messenger brought back from the market a length of yellow cloth which was tacked together to make a decent, ritually acceptable overbag under which the black was out of sight.

How, or indeed whether, these 'bloody sacrifices and trifling ceremonies' (to use the prejudging words that Gibbon puts in the mouths of the Gnostics) can 'inspire the love of virtue and restrain the impetuosity of passion' is a question I can only ask and have no knowledge, experience, insight to answer. Of the twenty-three prisoners serving sentences in the jail at Makale, the Toraja capital at the time of our visit, only one was a Toraja traditionalist. This could mean that the lawbreakers are all outsiders and likely to be Muslim or Christian; it could mean that the traditionalists are too quick for the police; or there could be a connection between piety to the ancestors, expressed in tenaciously exact rituals, and avoidance of civil disorder.

The funeral of the old High Priest called Ne Dena and the coronation of his youngest son, Tatto, in his stead, took five days. In preparation Tatto had to build a bamboo gallery on the south wall of the house, a flight of bamboo stairs from the gallery to the courtyard, a ring of spectator booths. He emerges, in translated conversations, as gentle, extremely bright and fiercely traditional. He does not, however, chew the traditional betel-nut out of respect for his fine white teeth. He learned to read and write at a Roman Catholic school but described his Christian religious education, with a piece of mime that needed no translator, as going in one ear and out of the other. His main criticism of the Roman Catholics is that, for them, Mary and Jesus carry sins away whereas a Toraja knows that no one but the sinner can clear away sin. Mary and Jesus are inadmissible as scapegoats. His parting message, after we had been with him for most of the five days, was that we should tell the people of the West that the Torajas are not, as the Muslims and the Christians would have them believe, infidels and animists. They worship a god; they respect the ancestors; they are right with the spirits of nature.

When preparations for the filming were made, Tatto's father was alive and was to have been the film's main spokesman for *The Way of the Ancestors*. He was well on in his nineties, an unchallenged authority on the rice rituals and, on his own admission, knew the taste of human head. Those of us who met him were impressed by his generosity, vigour and calm. For some years, having decided that Tatto was to be his successor, he had been handing on the traditional lore. He alone wore the horned head-dress that had passed through seven generations of his priestly family. The first time it rested on Tatto's head (and was seen to be too small) was at his coronation as new High Priest. Between the preparation and the shooting of the film, old Ne Dena died. I saw him only in a photograph taken by Eric Crystal and considered by the sitter to be not entirely satisfactory, as it omitted his body and legs and only showed his head. Whether he died resting on the outstretched legs and cradled in the arms of his family, we did not ask, but it is possible, since this is the Toraja way.

On the night before the climax of Ne Dena's funeral, Tatto, his mother, and the rest of the family sat knee to knee in the upper room where the body lay. Though it was already in its coffin, it was still ritually no more than 'sick' and on the east/west axis. No one wept, some smoked, there was quiet talk. Who gave the signal for the next move was unclear. A few of the men rose, lifted the coffin to a north-south line and sat down again. Ne Dena was now ritually dead; his soul could start its southwards glide; the time to mourn had come. Women, pulling their wraps over their heads, gathered to lean on the coffin and howl. Tatto's mother, with a sarong folded on her head, sat where she was and covered her eyes. Tatto's smile vanished. When his father was young, he said, there were many great tominaas in Tana Toraja who knew the Ceremonies of the Ancestors and could guide a new priest. Now there are few and their knowledge is incomplete. 'It will be a dark future. I am like a chick whose mother has been caught by an eagle and I am alone. The rope I held on to has broken. The ground has collapsed. Where can I look?'

During the following days, visitors from far afield arrived with pigs, chickens, wine, buffalo, some to pay off old debts, some to set up new ones. All these visitors had to be fed, lodged at night in one of the new booths, received by one of the family, made welcome. Rice for a multitude was cooked in great black pots. A squad of small boys thwacking bamboo rattles rehearsed, perfected, put on yellow sarongs and grass head-bands and gave performances of a slow, jumping dance. Tatto went about his ritual duties. At the start of the day he offered food to the venerable head-dress, the horns of which, so said a long tradition, had emerged from the sea. Rituals later in the day called for a particular ritual technician who was variously described as a transvestite and a hermaphrodite. This role had been given to a young man who had married but had soon shown a deep disinclination to sleeping with his wife. He was now divorced, needed not by his wife but by the rest of society to stand for the two in one, male and female, the ambiguous figure. Why, I asked Tatto, do you need a hermaphrodite in your ceremony? 'So that *we* can kiss', was his answer. Having heard that it is the Toraja way to value singularity —the oddly shaped stone, the curious tree, the person with a useful difference—I was prepared to admire the Toraja for handling human variety more fearlessly and compassionately than my own society can quite manage. But the hermaphrodite did not appear. He did not wish to be ritually useful. He had gone to work in the fields. A quick substitute was found—on the first occasion in a woman who had had a child but whose anatomy was somehow mannish; on later occasions by a flamboyantly male stand-in who descended the ritual ladder on the south face of the house either locked in or avoiding sly love-play with a fellow tominaa. The boisterous derision from the audience was very like that by which the Ugly Sisters in *Cinderella* know they are a pantomime success.

In the seventy years or so that Tatto's father presided at the great Toraja rice rituals, the Ancestors have taken considerable knocks. Christians brought schools, hospitals, administration, new job opportunities, new rice technology, expanded horizons, citizenship of a bigger world. The Way of the Ancestors offered a backward glance, the same economic yield to feed an expanding population, a curb on change, yesterday's solutions to the problems of today. The Toraja Christian who died away from home, among the Muslims and Christians of Macassar let us say, could expect a Christian burial, for Christianity is a worldwide religion and Christians have a worldwide knowledge of the proper thing to do. The Toraja traditionalist, when he leaves home, goes into ceremonial exile. Strangers, even the neighbouring strangers of Macassar, have no idea what to do with him if he dies. His ritual way is not exportable. It is no comfort to him to know that two hundred million of the world's population are in the same plight, have ritual systems that are tied to their own earth, customs that will not travel, 'primal', umbilically-tugging home religions. Nor does it comfort him to know that, growing here and there in the prosperous world, is a fresh concern for the phenomenon of 'the primal', the local, the home-based, the small and the beautiful. All he knows and fears in his extremity, is that some Muslim or Christian, thinking he has no 'religion' worth talking about, will pitch his corpse into the sea and leave his ghost-soul howling for burial. And the Ancestors surely cannot wish that. At a census conducted in 1965, half of the Toraja population claimed to follow the Way of the Ancestors, the Old Way. In 1971 the number had fallen to about a hundred thousand, just over a third. If all the forecasts of the last seventy years had proved true, there would have been none.

On the night before Ne Dena's funeral and the clear start of Tatto's reign as High Priest, the yard to the south of the family house was jammed with people ready—or so it felt to one who was trapped in the middle of them with no way of escape—for trouble or fun, a baton charge or a display of bold magic. Dancing and trancing were promised for later; tongues slit, blood spat, and the wound suddenly healed; knives drawn across arms and legs, a quick leaf-poultice, no visible scar; the ascent, on uninjured feet, of a ladder of sword blades. To create a space where space was needed special police drew brands from the fire that burnt in the yard's centre and swung them, flaming in wide arcs near the powerless feet of the crowd. Visiting officials and their huddling ladies sat on leaf mats in the observation booths and craned to observe. Loud-speakers, hung in the trees, spat vicious static over the assembly and called for quiet. The time had come for the politics.

The speaker was Mr Kila', whose dress was as near as civilian clothes can come to a uniform, and who is in favour with the Governor of Tana Toraja. He works in the political arm of the Way of the Ancestors—called the Foundation of Customary Law. For an hour the crowd heard him chart the ups and downs or, to be more precise, the steady down over seventy years and the recent up in the fortunes of the Ancestors. In 1969, as he reminded them and us, the Indonesian Government recognized the Old Way, *Aluk To Dolo*, as a 'religion' on a par with Christianity and Islam, placing it, for office purposes, as a sub-cult of Hinduism. It is hard to imagine that there had been an outbreak of spirituality in high places or that it made any difference in Jakarta whether the Toraja traditions lived or died. But 'religion', in Government terms, seems to mean 'that which resists communism', and traditional rituals are as likely to do that as sophisticated, international missionary faiths. Hence the seal of approval, the gesture of support, the sudden first aid, to the Ancestors. Hence Mr Kila' 's political energy.

He rides to work in a Government office in Makale on a moped given him by the Governor. On a patch of ground behind his house there is to be the new headquarters of the Way of the Ancestors. Work is beginning on a Book of the History and Rituals of the Toraja, meant to sit alongside the Bible and the Qur'an, which are the Books of outsiders. In August 1976 all primary schools were taken under Government control. The Christians lost their near-monopoly of Toraja education. Soon tominaas with a Book may claim the right to teach Toraja children the Way of the Ancestors, as Christians with a Book have taught the Way of Jesus, and Muslims with a Book have taught the Way of Islam.

Mr Kila' 's experience among the Christians has made a deep mark, though not evidently as deep as that of the Ancestors who lost him for twenty years and have now reclaimed him. He became a Christian at the age of 14, when most of his class-mates were Christian too. His parents were never Christian. His grandfather was a powerful tominaa. Schooled, as they never were, he left Tana Toraja and went to work in Macassar, down the coast. During 1957, as he reminisces, he fell ill. In his dream or his delirium, he met his grandfather sitting on a rock. For a time he kept his distance from the old man for he had opted for Jesus; but the Ancestor beckoned him: 'Why don't you come closer? I'm going to blow on you.' Mr Kila' approached and his grandfather blew a soft breath that spread all through his sick, incompletely Christianized limbs and pervasively restored him. The next day his fever had gone. He 'cut a chicken' (Eric Crystal's colourful rendering of the Toraja phrase for the key action in the ceremony in which a Toraja re-establishes ties with his past) and returned home.

I remember sitting with Mr Kila' and Eric Crystal in a murky, white-washed market café in Makale, eating rice and charred meat. At each mouthful my gut said no. I hoped that absorption in the conversation would draw attention off the amount I was not eating. What, I asked Mr Kila', is the advantage for you of the Ancestral Way over the Way of the Christians? He pointed instructively to his plate, to Eric Crystal's and mine. 'It is my Way. I ate all my rice. Eric ate half. You ate two spoonfuls. It wasn't your Way. But it is mine.' 'He's absolutely right,' I found myself thinking—the first truly 'primal' thought I had had since the search for 'the primal' began—and I put down my spoon. Mr Kila', ill in Macassar and meeting his Ancestor in a dream, knew what he had to do and went home. It was up to me, queasy in a market-place café, to get up and go home too. My own ancestors may be beyond placation. My own Deata spirits may have expired under the concrete. My Puang Matua—if Nietzsche is to be believed—may already be dead.

But at home at least I may start to try to make sense of myself, discover how to live in a city, how to grow a vegetable, how to greet a neighbour, how to heal some of the splits both here inside and in the world that surrounds me. That is my 'primal' endeavour. Mr Kila', if I read him correctly, wants a Central Office, a Holy Book, an assembly of tominaas, the support of the Government, a hand in education, greater investment, an influx of tourists, the restitution of the Ancestors alongside the benefits of modernity. Eric Crystal, if I understand him, wants to see Toraja culture outlast its enemies, to tell the world of its value, and at the same time to keep the world out. I, if I know myself a degree better after the journey to the Torajas, just want to be at home, where I can eat all my dinner, Eric Crystal will eat half of his and Mr Kila' will manage no more than a spoonful. It may not be their Way. But it will be mine.

10

Zulu Zion

The most memorable, intractable, immobilizing conversation I had on the matter of Black Africa was with a Zulu who said, in the course of it, that he had never met any European who had any real understanding of how an African thinks. The speaker was Peter Mkize who has behind him thirty years of generous collaboration with whites. At least, I thought, as the words caught me between the eyes and made me wonder why we did not pack up and leave, the words were spoken and shared. There was that much of a new bond between us, for they tumbled out with the air of not having been spoken before. He at least thought me capable of understanding that I did not understand. And that was a firm start.

South Africa had not been the first choice for the African journey. Ghana was preferred, but there had been a breakdown of understanding between another European film crew and the Ghanaian Government on what could properly be filmed and we inherited the bad feeling. The day before we were due to leave for Ghana permission to film was withdrawn, and the search shifted to South Africa. The great advantage of Ghana over South Africa, for our purposes, is that the Ghanaian Government is black; control of the churches, the universities and the schools is black; hotels are black. Radio and television are black. If drivers lose their way, promises are broken, muddles occur and the fault is not ours, blacks are to blame. In South Africa, control of Government, press, radio and television, education and, ultimately, church affairs, is with the whites. They create the space and the restrictions within which blacks move. The blacks are never to blame. It is not possible, so it seemed to me, to do a Zulu in South Africa the honour of finding him obstructive, nasty and inefficient, for he is not his own master. And each time I admired, thought well of, warmed to an African, I had to stalk my reactions for signs of creeping white condescension. Did I really admire and think well of him, or had South African politics neutered and sent me out into the Zulu reservations incapable of anything sharper than a grin and a nod of appreciation?

Every night in South Africa we returned to a comfortable hotel in Durban—one of the three or four allowed to admit blacks and expensive enough to be out of the range of all but the most privileged. Peter Mkize's room was across the corridor from mine. Once or twice he braved the dining-room to eat with us but usually ate in his bedroom, either to save on his allowance or out of unease. The Zulu room-girls had never before had to tidy up after a Zulu guest and had boisterous glottal Zulu conversations with him about where he worked, where he lived and the whereabouts of his family kraal. Every night in ball-point copper-plate he used to write notes on the doings of the day, underlining the key points in red and adding generous explanatory notes. He was schooled and taught to lay out a coherent English statement in a Lutheran mission school. The skills have been refined through his work for the Johannesburg diocese, his service on one or two Soweto School Boards and in the Johannesburg bank which employs him. He lies, I should guess, in the trap that is known to all the good boys of the world, all those who listened to the teacher, did not make blots and came top in class. He has attracted the jealousy and suspicion of a number of those who did make blots. His work takes him daily into Johannesburg. The Race Laws take him nightly to a house in Soweto. In 1960, feeling no doubt the strain of his straddled city-township life, he started his own cottage industry which occupies him far into the night. He bought a sewing machine and learned how to make a shirt-collar from the stuff of a shirt tail. Word has spread and has brought a clientele and a new placing in the community. In dreams and visions the spirit of his dead mother has revealed to him that his proper destiny is to be a healer. This call he has so far resisted, though it weighs on him increasingly. Shirt-surgery may be the beginning of a response.

Peter Mkize's father left the family kraal and went to work in Johannesburg before Peter could properly remember him. He returned infrequently. His mother never moved, brought up the family, saw to the land, used the money that came through from the town to eke out the rations and set her family up in school and, when Peter became as successful in class as everyone hoped he would be, it did not cross his mind to resist the thought of going to the city. For as long as he can remember, he has been the knot on the rope in a tug-of-war. His father pulled citywards, representing schooling, daylight, rationality, European standards, rewards in cash, the suppression of dreams, the denial of a mindscape that the whites labelled 'primitive'. His mother pulled landwards, representing skills not learned in school, night, sources of knowledge not schematized by usual reason, African standards, bare subsistence, the cultivation of dreams, unapologetic 'primitive' personhood. For most of his life the father-pull has had more muscle than the mother-pull. He is, by African standards, well-off, well-housed and well-regarded by the whites who employ him. His daylight persona, apart from his skin-colour, is impeccably European. Now the mother-pull is drawing him her way. The European verities are not as sturdy as they may once have seemed. If he does not go the way of the whites, his income is threatened. If he does not go the way of black Africa, his nature is threatened. For the whole of the search among the Zulus, I had alongside me a quiet man in whom a grim battle was raging.

His mother died in 1938 and has exerted, since her death, a pull she seems not to have had in life. She draws him back regularly to her graveside, where once I accompanied him. It is in a straggling copse three or four miles off the main road, a three-hour drive from Durban. As we approached, genuine bush telegraph went down the valley ahead of us, ululated from kraal to kraal through an exchange of vigilant and open-throated women, carrying the word that a white had been sighted. There was no curiosity to look at us. The downward path skirted barred and bolted huts and collapsed enclosures. If we had been what we were no doubt thought to be—i.e. police on a man-hunt—no man stayed to be hunted. The grave is by itself in a tattered copse, marked out in breeze-blocks and set about with dusty white plastic flowers all but hidden in weeds.

Return visits by his mother started in the early sixties, occupy his dreams, seem to have him cornered. The first tested case of her advice being offered, taken and brought to a good conclusion concerned a sickly relative. The wife of one of Peter's cousins was long overdue in pregnancy. This was news to Peter himself but known to his mother, and in what he called a 'vision' she appeared to him to rouse him to the danger, diagnose the obstruction and set up a search for the one herbalist in Johannesburg who had the cure. At first he resisted, and he and his wife agreed that, even if the dead woman's warning were true, the problem family were schooled people and unlikely to take notice of night warnings. Only when Peter himself became ill with what sounded very like a severe attack of remorse did he deliver his warning, seek out the herbalist, relay from his mother precise instructions on the making of the mixture and see to it that the medicine was taken. Within a day or two the pregnancy ended, a boy was born and the mother recovered.

This faculty of lying open to the ancestors, letting them settle on the back, unhinge the everyday mind so as to slip through from one world to another with otherwise unchartable information is what makes the traditional Zulu diviner, the *isangoma*. There is said to be a certain delicacy of bone, heightening of temperament, feverishness of sensitivity that marks out one who has the gift of an *isangoma* and many of those who accept that destiny, go through the ancestral drubbing that precedes acceptance, shoulder their past and let it speak through them, are women. Among the signs that the ancestors have laid a claim are turbulent dreams, uncontrollable yawning, sometimes flatulence, sneezing, a fondness for snuff, sickness. It is not thought possible for anyone to resist an ancestral claim once the ancestors make it. When and if Peter Mkize stops resisting and becomes some sort of ancestral ventilation shaft, will he be thought to have broken down or restored himself, lost his senses or come to them? He seems not to be, by temperament, one who can step aside and let the ghosts ride past him. Rather he will let them ride through him. Sometimes they shine out of his eyes. Haunted myself, I paced out the Zulu journey in the company of a haunted man.

Once we sat, backs to the wall of a round, domed, grass hut and saw an *isangoma* at work. Her name was also Mkize. She practises usually in her township near Johannesburg. For money she came up-country to treat a country patient. She had the help of an apprentice who was trying out her vocation to the work of divination and who led the congregational responses. The diviner worked in the centre of the hut. Beside her sat the patient and a woman relative. Round the wall were family and friends. Before her lay her ritual kit: a fly-whisk, black threaded with white beads, with which she should flick at the ancestral weight on her shoulders when it became too heavy; a colourful knobkerrie, patterned in beads; a sjambok, a rhinoceros-hide whip; plates, one set with incense sticks and one with a candle; two drinking vessels—a clay pot full of beer and a sturdy calabash for the medicine brew. She took snuff: some up the nostrils and some she scattered on the ground. She stirred the calabash with a brisk stick until the liquid foamed. This indicated the willingness of the diviner's ancestors and those of the patient to let the cause of the patient's sickness be known.

The diagnosis had the mounting tension of a guessing game. The patient did not parade symptoms, but waited to see whether the ancestors guided the diviner to sense them out unaided. If the symptoms are mis-imagined, the patient has no reason to trust the cure. An *isangoma* is as good as her last diagnosis. On this occasion, the patient and her friends were satisfied. Mrs Mkize diagnosed painful feet (at which the company chorused '*Siyavuma*', 'We agree') that send their pain up to the hip ('*Siyavuma*', 'We agree') and on to the brain ('*Siyavuma*', 'We agree'). The disease was picked up on the way back from the river (the *siyavuma*'s continued). It was laid there by a neglected ancestor. Since the patient's marriage no goat had been sacrificed (*Siyavuma*). For immediate relief of ancestral stress, a calabash must be prepared, a goat sacrificed and two chickens. For long-term relief, the patient is referred to Mr Gcwensa, a herbalist who works in Durban. At one stage, added the diviner, the patient wished to be a Christian. (She agreed.) The ancestors were not pleased. (She understood.) Only now did the diviner solicit approval: 'Do you agree with what I have said?' The patient agreed. 'If you are not satisfied, please say so.' The patient was satisfied. In celebration the diviner and her assistant sang, drummed and danced. The rest of us clapped in time. In a high mood, Mrs Mkize then diagnosed that Peter Mkize had round his neck a slender bead necklace. He agreed. I too agreed before he fished down his shirt for it, for his collar was open and sometimes, as he moved, it showed.

My impulse as a European, in the case of the woman in the hut, would be to keep an eye on the patient's feet, that part of the human machine which carries the ache, and see if the ache went away. If it persisted and grew worse, I would assume that Mrs Mkize's divination had been faulty. If it went away, I would assume that healing was going to happen anyway. It is no part of my training to see an ache as a shared ache, a social ache, an ache administered by overseeing ancestors. I have no faculty to sense out and see the wounds in some airy tissue that binds families together in groups, envelops both me and my living dead. If the ache in the patient's leg is an ancestral warning that it is danger-ous to be isolated, then I am all ache. I shall not, I think, when the next perceptible ache comes, seek out a hut and a fly-whisk, a calabash and a ritual drum. But behind the showmanship and the ritual bedazzlement of the *isangoma*, there is a serious challenge to think again about the meaning of 'health'. Later that evening Peter Mkize wrote up his notes on the events of the day and ended with a footnote: 'N.B. The élite/educated African does not openly admit that he/she believes in the practice of the traditional *isangoma* (diviner) or *inyanga* (herbalist). They in fact become active patients secretly and pretend to know nothing of the existence of the above' (meaning the traditional healers).

Slowly, with great pain and at some risk to his reason, Peter Mkize seems to be drawing into the daylight things that have long been in the dark. In part, it is his particular story, the plight of a banker with the temperament of a healer who can no longer keep urgent parts of his nature in tidy suppression. In part, he is divining a shift in black consciousness against which the details of his particular story have an interest but point beyond themselves. It is a slur on the Zulus, he says, to speak of them as worshipping ancestors. Ancestors are *not* worshipped. They are reverenced and acknowledged, as Christians—of the Catholic sort at any rate—have always reverenced and acknowledged saints. Beyond them lies the Creator God, uMvelingqangi. He is, in his etymology, the one who emerged first. He lies at the back of the Zulu palate and to say his name involves a control of the tongue and the sounding cavity in the roof of the mouth that few Europeans can master. What Europeans cannot master they deny an existence to, and Africans have been taught that, before the missionaries brought his Christian counterpart, there was no Zulu god. With the Christian God came His white-skinned son, Jesus. Here Peter Mkize moves into his own heterodoxy which suggests to me that the time has come to seek other opinions but, as a pointer to mounting ancestral unease in a conscientious Lutheran, they claim attention.

I put to him that, to be a Christian, it is necessary to grant that (in the exact words that passed between us as we sat on a hillside a few yards from his mother's grave) 'Jesus has a particular relationship with God which is even greater than that of your mother. Would you agree with that?' His answer began in a style I was to grow used to: 'Well, I would pretend that that is so, but in reality, Jesus is as removed as God himself.' 'As remote?' I checked, giving him a second chance. 'Yes. Because I do not know God and the person I know better is my mother or my father. And, if I were to communicate with God, I feel there are two stages where I shall be lost . . . because . . . between God and myself is Jesus Christ. He is also a stranger to me . . . I cannot see myself getting lost if I were to ask my mother, whom I regard as an angel, not as an evil spirit or anything of the sort, to convey a message to my God.'

Above the font in the Lutheran church at Mapumulo was a pale, Nordic, white Jesus of a frail beauty which would make even a handsome European feel inadequate and, to an African, must seem to come from the moon. The congrega-

tion for the Sunday service I attended was swollen by mem
bers of a youth conference that was being held at the nearby
theological college. The matrons of the congregation wore
black dresses, black caps and deep white collars, and sa
together—a burgherly array. Their husbands were allowed
more variety but most wore suits. The unaccompanied
hymns dragged themselves listlessly along like wounded
animals. The sermon was extensive. The congregation
queued with the sedate self-absorption that is the traditional
northern-European answer to the question, 'With what
demeanour is it right for a Christian to approach the table
of the Lord and receive wine and bread?' Afterwards, Pete
Mkize rose and lengthened the service by criticizing the
congregation on its wearisome singing, and conducted them
passionately through a rehearsal of hymns he knew they
could do better. On that occasion at least, they proved him
wrong.

The woes of the morning were taken in the afternoon to
the former Rector of Mapumulo Theological College, the
Rev. D. L. Makhathini, and a clutch of students. All the
animation that was not in the singing burst out on the
college lawn. To those of the young who see simply that the
whites brought the Bible and took the land, Jesus, white o
black, would seem to be a lost cause. Among those who stay
with Jesus are those who imagine He cannot be other than
white, a European import, the boss's man; and those who
need Him to be black to believe He is who He says He is. The
Mapumulo students, to a man, saw no reason for Christ to
be white, though, whether out of deference to me, who was
white and solo and clearly had no wish to colonize them
they were prepared to let bygones be bygones. 'But, unfor
tunately, in Africa now, you see,' urged one of them, 'when
we youngsters want to introduce our own indigenou
church, we have' (here a daring thumb flicked toward
Rector Makhathini) 'old-timers here who . . .' What th

old-timers do was lost in a crack of laughter but the word was enough to inspire Rector Makhathini to take the brats and spank them. 'What do you know of our tradition,' he weighed in, 'unless you sit down and learn it from me?' (He flicked an elderly thumb back at the youngsters.) 'I can foresee what is going to happen to these fellows. They become burning here—just like students in universities—burning everything. But by the time they go out there' (indicating the world in which there is a living to make) 'they will be conservative, very conservative. They'll just disappear and you'll never hear of them' (outrage and mirth bubbled up as expected) 'doing anything except collecting money, Mr Chairman, and getting bigger and . . .' It seemed a waste for such an effective provoker to be *ex*-Rector unless Zulu Lutherans have a surplus of energetic and gifted teachers.

But playful argument on a sunny lawn can become cracked skulls and bleeding insides on another day, and the history of Europe is stained with the blood and sweat of one group of Christians fighting to put down another group of Christians in the name of Jesus. Suddenly I felt a revulsion to hearing the Christ of history tolerated further. 'Why not,' I challenged them, 'get rid of Christ? I put it to you quite seriously.' They were not quite sure that they were picking up my shocking drift. 'Why not say, "Look, Jesus has done many mighty things, but He has caused a lot of trouble. Let's start again with another name. Let's not have it associated with Europe at all." Why not? I mean, why not get rid of Him?'

To hear a black radical repudiate Christ as white cannot be unusual. To hear a white European urge the repudiation of Christ, even in argumentative play, raises the missionary spectre in reverse. First the whites bring the Bible. We, the blacks, take their word for it and make it our Word. Now, because Europe has ceased to be so sure of itself, it is spawning a breed of anti-missionaries who once again dislodge our certainties by the corrosive limpness of their doubts. Words in answer seemed not to come readily to any of the boys. They left 'the old-timer' to pull the discussion through. 'There is no problem about Christ,' said Rector Makhathini, 'if we would understand that He reveals Himself to the people to appear like the people. If He reveals Himself in China, He is Chinese. If we would understand Him as one of us, yes, I would agree that He is black, because I think black, I am black.' To hear in measured certainty that 'there is no problem about Christ' raises the question, 'Then where is the problem and why have Christ and the problem become so entangled in the history of the decline and fall of Christian Europe?' But that may be a question to delay until, as some white Christians who know Africa have predicted, black Christians reach the shores of pagan Europe bringing the Faith.

The South African journey only skirted the main Christian denominations, touched the Roman Catholics not at all. The thinking behind these omissions, reasonable enough when the options are so various, was that the Orthodox Christians of Romania, the Roman Catholic Christians of Western Europe and the Protestant Christians of Indianapolis had all had their say, not to mention the pervasive Methodism and Protestant moulding of the searcher, and that the search in Africa should largely bypass the regular African Christians and go for a moodier property called 'African-ness', the underpinning of a whole continent. Wiser to a slight degree after the event, I wonder if African-ness shows up anywhere so well as among convinced African Christians. I learned more about respect for the ancestors, spiritual healing, the social nature of sin, the integrity and dimensions of the family, Zulu personhood, evil spirits, the validity of dreams, the aliveness of the land, from Rector Makhathini than from any African traditionalist.

Peter told me how in the crisis of an illness, when he was given up for dead, he soared in spirit over a grass plain 'like a golf course', all fresh and dewy in the morning, to a set of mighty brass gates at which he was prepared to enter had it not been for his grandmother who took and spun him out through the air, told him he had reported for eternity too soon and sent him tingling back to earth with a slap on the behind. As he was recovering, his grandmother's handmark showed dark on his skin, scaled over, stayed long enough to remind him for the rest of this life how near he had been to the next. 'I am convinced, by God's providence and ways, that our living dead are somewhere, not disconnected from our interests but still with us. Somehow.' Had he not, I asked him, given up much of his Zulu past by being a Christian? 'This is what I am expected to have done,' he replied, unrepentant. How would he react, I wondered, to someone who called his dream-lore, his care of his ancestors, his resistance to change, 'primitive'? 'Yeah,' he nodded, 'they have said it. They have said it sounds "primitive". And I always interpret "primitive" as "pure". I think if somebody would like to be really himself, he should be a little "primitive". I think it is a beautiful term meaning you are still very original, you are still down to nature and that's where the dreams belong. You can be very highly cultured and yet still primitive. That is where nationhood belongs. And I see now among Africans people who say, "We don't want to be primitive. We want to be civilized." So you begin to float and you don't know where you belong; whereas to be primitive to me is to be genuine, to be pure, to be yourself, to be as your people were in the general layout of things.'

At least when my own family 'floated' from the rigours of farm-labouring, of being rented out as farm-hands and serving-girls, to the mining villages and factory towns of South Yorkshire, they floated household by household. With Wesleyan cement, the main unit held. The industrial revolution for the floating Zulu offers no such inevitable possibility. If money is to be made, father must work in town. If land is to be held, mother must stay in the country. After ten years of satisfactory service to one employer, or fifteen years of satisfactory service in more jobs than one, an African can apply for a house in a township. While he waits to qualify (when his marriage is fresh and his family young) he may see his wife as rarely as once a year. With this chill information, we went to a town-and-country wedding.

The ceremonies, the animal slaughter, the plighting of troths, the competitive dancing, the praising of the ancestors, the hymn-singing and the beer-drinking took place in the husband's family kraal, a spacious cluster of huts with a cattle-pen at the centre and an interrupted palisade on the outside. The kraal lay on a slope, and the main approach was from the valley. Cheerful ladies in their best European dresses and chapel-going felt hats, and wearing extensive white aprons, axed their way through hefty limbs of meat and stocked an array of large black cooking pots that sat on outdoor fire-grates ranged round an open-sided cooking hut. The older men, among them a representative of the local chief, sat under a tree and drank beer. The groom's brother led in one of the cattle and tethered it to a stake. The bride's advance party arrived: her father wearing the skin and feathered head-dress of a Zulu warrior and carrying a shield and spear, and a group of her girl friends, mostly in plain European dresses and cardigans. With the bride's girls as witnesses and a group of the groom's supporters as counter-chorus, the tethered beast was sacrificed while the bride's party chanted the Zulu equivalent of 'Let our sister's cow sleep', and the groom's party fought back with 'Let the beast wake up'. The bride's girls pierced its stomach. The cow, after juddering and flailing through the knife-work, slept.

At about this time the groom, who had been indistinguishable among his friends in a sweat-shirt and slacks, emerged from the main hut in a neat brown suit, white collar, sober tie and carrying a shapely dark-brown trilby. Across the fields the bride's party was sighted, and appropriate traditional action was taken to receive her: the gateway of the kraal was blocked in preparation for a merry war in which the bridal party would advance and be repelled, the groom's party would surround and absorb the bride, the bride's party would fight to take her back again. The depletion of one group and the enlargement of another by even so little as one person involves struggle and readjustment, resistance and acceptance by everyone involved, ancestors included.

It would be, we had been warned, a muted wedding. A week before, the groom's eldest sister had died in hospital in Durban. One opinion was that the wedding should be postponed; the other, which prevailed, was that with scattered guests and the groom on leave from his city boss, it was better to go ahead. But the chief's representative decreed that, for decency's sake, the groom's people should not dance.

Down at the gate and through the high corn stalks, the bride's party and the bride appeared at last. Her family are Zionists, they belong to one of South Africa's three thousand five hundred independent, pentecostal, extra-orthodox, Christian healing sects, and the women wore white Zionist uniforms and head cloths. The slender bride wore a white European wedding-dress with veil and orange blossom. With a shrilling of what looked like police whistles that hung from the necks of the senior Zionist matrons of honour, and the baying of basso bamboo funnels, the bridal party, the bride included, advanced on the gate, curving bodies down to the earth and treading out the rhythm of a euphonious loud chant. When the pressure on the gates was felt to express the right strong purpose, they were released and the bridal dancers entered. No sooner were they through than a dancing phalanx of the groom's people set up an independent rhythm and sang the first few rounds of the counterblast, announcing that the side to which the bride was coming had its own strong character. No sooner was the groom's rhythm established than the chief's representative was up from his tree stump and rounding on them for lack of respect for the dead. Subdued, they sauntered away leaving the bride's Zionist dancers in a one-sided dance contest.

But the pressure to dance became overwhelming. The groom's group sauntered back together again and set up a fury of dancing that no chief's representative could stop. And, to keep him in his place and out of the line of battle, a group of formidable aunts of the groom left their cooking and pinned him to his tree-stump with the why and wherefore of the need to dance. There is a classic statement by an experienced witness of the ways of Africans, to the effect that they do not argue out, pray out, preach out, think out their religion. They dance it out. The battling dancers edged nearer to each other, withdrew, edged nearer. Once they were clustered and still maintaining their different rhythms but intermingled, the bride was claimed by her husband and, when the groups parted, the bride and groom stood together, she in her orange blossom, he in his wedding suit, surrounded by the triumphant dancers while the depleted side withdrew. But the girl's family needed extra assurance that the groom's family meant to stand by her and they reassembled their forces behind a hut and mounted a rescue attempt. If the groom's family dropped their dancing guard, the bride's side would claim her back again. The challenge was beaten off in a swirl of dust. The groom's side had put its foot down.

The marriage itself was a customary union, witnessed by

the chief's man who held both bride and groom by the hand as promises were exchanged. The groom will break no customary law if he later takes another wife. A Zionist preacher, in his white linen coat and looking like a nicely turned out dispensing chemist, preached a short sermon, clutching his Bible in his right hand. The bride's father beat his spear on his shield, strutted before the assembly and sang out the praise-names of his family and ancestors. At one moment in his praise-singing he stood and wept. At another, when the matters he was touching on may have concerned her, the bride's mother left the bride's side and danced in the space made by her husband, one arm clutching her handbag, the other carving the air with her umbrella as if it were a cutlass. A close-harmony group of Zionist boys put their heads together the better to hear each other and sang a mellifluous hymn. Through all this the dusty bride and groom stood side by side near the cattle-pen. That night Peter Mkize summarized the day in his duty notes: 'This was a mixed marriage of Western concept and tradition: the bride being Christian—Apostolic Church in Zion—and the groom an atheist, who lives in the present and belongs to the past.'

There was a graphic dissonance about the events of the day—the wedding-dress, the sacrificed beast, the groom's neat tie, his father-in-law's loin-cloth—assembled in a floating acknowledgement that no one seemed quite to know who he or she was supposed to be. At the same time and on a different axis came the dancing. Somehow, in the dancing, the union was grounded. It is hard to imagine a vestry chat in more familiar Christian circumstances that could better demonstrate how dangerous, unsettling and raw it can be for both sides when a girl from one tight group splits away and seeks out the group of her husband. A day or two after the wedding the groom, his leave ended, was due back at work in Durban. If his wife was to have in-law troubles, she would have them by herself.

African townships are a concession by the South African Government to the need for Africans to enter the cities to work and to leave the cities with somewhere nearby to live once work is ended. Kwa Mashu township is a landscape of grey boxes without electricity and with a pumped water supply in the back garden. Before Kwa Mashu came into existence in 1958, most of the inhabitants lived in a lean-to shanty-town called Cato Manor. Kwa Mashu is about fifteen miles from Durban, and access to the city, except for the small minority that can afford a car, is by bus and train. In 1965, on the line between Kwa Mashu and Durban, a train mounted one of the intervening platforms killing fifteen people. In these days of hurtling machinery, fifteen people is a modest toll compared with the five hundred and seventy-seven killed in the Tenerife air disaster and the forty-two who died at Moorgate Underground station in London as the train ran itself into a concrete stop-wall. But most international commuters have at least some hours of their day when they can feel they are not at the mercy of the utterly alien, whether in the form of other people's vagaries or the whims of metal fatigue. The township African has no such let-up. His right to a house depends on his claim on a job. His claim on a job depends on the goodwill of an employer. His right to move from his house to his job depends on having the right government documentation. When a train mounts a platform and carves an arbitrary way through a handful of startled people who have scarcely time to wonder, 'Why me?', it is not surprising that the event should assume mythic proportions and dramatize the pervasive African experience of uncontrol. Against this background the upsurge of 'independent' Christianity, all the phenomena of what is often called 'Zionism', start to shake down and make sense.

To pinpoint the Zion of African Zionism demands more

than a knack with maps. Zion City near Chicago, Illinois, is the home base of what has been called an 'apocalyptic healing movement', that formed under the leadership of a late-nineteenth-century missioner called John Alexander Dowie and took root in Africa. Zion is also that part of Jerusalem that is favoured of the Lord. It is also an enclosure in the mind which keeps the evil, the alien, the godless at bay, and guarantees the integrity of the person. It is a gathering within gates of those who submit themselves to the cleansing of the Holy Spirit and renew that cleansing through the mediation of the Zionist healing group.

Mrs Grace Tshabalala is an inhabitant of Zion. Every day, as she has for the last thirty years, she takes the bus from Kwa Mashu to Durban where she cleans for an appreciative European family. Our first meeting, which she approached with wide eyes even wider, took place in a Durban hotel where we shared a tray of tea and I encouraged her, in spite of her fears, to make a parcel of the uneaten cream buns and take them home for her grandchildren. Later I learned that the family had worried when she did not arrive home on the usual bus. Both town and township have lurking dangers which not even the assurance of Zion can quite will away. As a widow she has no automatic right to stay in the township but she lives with her son and his family. He is now minister of the Zionist congregation that his father built up. She, when she was a minister's wife, shared presidential power. Now she is a Zionist dowager, a power behind the scenes, though she is careful to defer to her son whenever he is present. During the day, he works as a messenger boy for a firm in Durban.

Thursdays are Grace Tshabalala's ladies' days. For over twenty-five years she has pioneered an ecumenical movement among Zionist women, drawing them together the better to bear each other's burdens, preach the Gospel, encourage the young to avoid beer and tobacco and the flesh of unclean beasts, trinketry, dancing and cinema. She uses the buses that ply the Kwa Mashu–Durban circuit as mobile pulpits and preaches to the trapped if not the converted. She is winningly unsolemn about her bus ministry. When she sings, they often like it. When she asks them to give up alcohol, they often shout her down. 'Do you always win in the end?' I asked her. 'I always win sometimes,' she retorted succinctly.

The one Thursday meeting I attended took place in the area to the front of the Tshabalalas' house on a sweltering afternoon. About sixty Zionist ladies glowed under multi-coloured umbrellas. Their predominant clothing was white, styled usually to the dream specifications that had been given to the founder of their group or to the 'prophet' who vetted and cleansed them for Zion. Some had stitched to their garments cloth emblems: a cross, a star, a triangle, the names of their congregations. Some wore stoles or capes of a darker hue. All wore white hats, most of them starched and resembling those of nurses or New England Puritans or Dutch country women. They had removed their shoes and piled them near the gate in deference to the business of the afternoon, as Moses removed his shoes to approach the Burning Bush. They carried their staves, scrubbed white sticks, in the shape sometimes of a snake-trapper, though some bore a simple wooden cross. The Zulu name for these is 'weapon'. They mark out the Zionist warrior. They ward off danger. The grant of a stick by the congregation means acceptance into Zion. Each stick is a Zionist identity.

The meeting fell into three parts. First prayer, loud and extempore, sometimes for one, sometimes for the whole congregation. Those moved to speak spoke. If, as I sensed, they were thought to have spoken too long, a hymn-swell rose to bear their words away and the mouthing speaker eventually subsided. After prayer and preaching and the recollection of God's Word, the service turned in on those who were in need of healing. One by one the sick, the troubled, the insecure, stood forward and ten or so of the sisterhood circled round them, pulling down on them with their hands, stroking off the malaise with prayer and pressure. In a case where the ailment had infested deep, the patient had her stomach pummelled, screwed up her face, held her hat on, bracing herself against the buffeting. Throughout, the congregation and the healers prayed and sang. A collection was taken. My two-rand note was raised in the air and received a round of applause. When the healing had subsided, the women took their ministry to the rest of the township. Bearing their staves and swaying to the rhythm of their hymn, they processed two by two down the dirt road on the way to visit the sick, work on the doubters within Zion, show the unredeemed outside Zion that, afloat as they may feel themselves to be, Zion, at least, stays firm.

While Grace Tshabalala's son is chief minister of their church, the chief prophet is a leather-faced, thick-wristed man called Mtambo. He had lawless beginnings and in early days was leader of a gang of *tsotsis*, township hood-lums. When he married, his tearaway tendencies took the form of fierce drinking. His wife, in the meantime, became involved with the Zionists and, through their endeavours, as it seemed, his sick child was healed. Mtambo's first contact with the Zionists was suffering the racket of a heal-ing service in the house next door, and beating the wall to shut them up. He came face to face with them when he invaded a Zionist meeting to reclaim his errant wife. Doubt that she would follow him if he ordered her to come away, fear of losing face, hesitation before the possibility that Zionists may have had a hand in the recovery of his child, kept him in the room. Soon Zion brought him to his knees. At the end of a process that, in traditional society, could well have turned him out a healer, he emerged a 'prophet'.

The Holy Spirit, channelled through his fingertips, his pores, his dreams, seeks out devils, corners and expels sickness, explores the stresses in the walls of Zion and shores them up with healing motion. The prophet works in the dangerous extremities; the minister holds the centre. At a Zionist service on the following Sunday it was possible to watch and admire the dynamic interplay between Minister Tshabalala and Prophet Mtambo, in a ritual journey that started with Bible reading and prayer, moved through a period of risk and torment, and ended with a prolonged, satisfied, slow dance.

Minister Tshabalala stood behind the lectern on the platform wearing a surplice and parson's collar, and carrying in his right hand a brass-topped staff, heavy with responsibility. Mtambo and his adjutant prophets stayed down in the body of the hall among the congregation. The minister led the worship, signalled the shape of the service, the time for praying, singing, healing, dancing. The prophet made no administrative decisions, but during the time for healing broke the ministerial control and let the Spirit in. The Spirit, that afternoon, buffeted three main candidates. One was a girl of about 17 who wanted a Zionist staff but was having dealings with traditional Zulu medicine. All invading substances—whether country remedies or sophisticated antibiotics—are forbidden to Zionists. She failed the test. The next was a girl possessed with a depressed spirit. She feared no one would marry her. She was tempted to kill herself. The ring of prophets, men and women, took it in turn to try to dislodge the ailment. They treated her carefully, sometimes coaxing, sometimes seeming to bully. A new access of the Holy Spirit made itself felt in a sudden infection of leaps and cries that caught the prophetic band and rattled it. During the link passages, while the last candidate withdrew and the next stepped forward, the minister led the worshippers in a sequence of deep-harmony

'Amens'. The last skirmish was with a young man who was thought to be the victim of an ill-wisher. At the approach of the prophet, the young man's alien occupant propelled his body from side to side of the prophetic circle in attempts to break free. At last, with the prophet's stretched hand cupping the forehead and face, the jerking limbs became still. Calm restored, the entire company took up their staves and circled the room in a snaking line, swaying in time to an expansive hymn with a restful rhythm. The existence of disharmonious forces had been marked; their power had been tested; they had been kept at bay.

It seemed to matter extremely to any Zulu I met to be 'at home', to feel 'at home'. Grace Tshabalala was not 'at home' in that hotel in Durban, but Zion helped her through. Nor was Peter Mkize, though his papers were absolutely in order. Rector Makhathini's daughter, a nurse in a Lutheran hospital, described how patients fear they will never recover because they are not 'at home'. Relatives smuggle in home medicines. Patients spend a weekend at home, slaughter a goat, take traditional health cures, come back feeling better. The most 'at home' African to come my way—or rather, I went his for he lives well up-country and does not move much—was a herbalist, philosopher and herder of lightning. (He distracts sky storms from the dwellings and crops of his patients.) His name is Laduma Madela and he has had something of an international reputation since Dr Katesa Schlosser discovered and published a book of his drawings of the Zulu god, of the god's wayward younger brother who let disease, death and deformity into the world, of the Lizard, that did for the Zulus what the Serpent did for the Judaeo-Christians.

Because of flooding, we reached him by helicopter. He stood beside a broad field wearing a boilersuit and a fur hat, and blowing an old army bugle to see us safely down. He took us to his prosperous kraal, showed us his drawings, nodded to the hillside forest where he had seen God, became impatient at my slowness to understand that the god you can see can never be God, but simply his image. He knows the language of animals and birds and sang us the song of the mourning dove. He seemed entirely 'at home' and devotes his energies to enquiries into why even 'at home' there should be instability, disease, unhappiness, decay. But very few, not merely Zulus but few people anywhere, have Madela's singularity, his touch of genius, the encouragement he has been offered by people outside to stay where he is and become a celebrity. 'Home' for many black South Africans I should guess (for I respect Peter Mkize's feeling that no European can know how an African thinks) would seem to be more a hope than a fixture. It cannot be in the city where the money is, because of the pass laws. It cannot safely be in the township because the township is not safe. It cannot, with the back turned on the city, be up-country in the kraal, for the pull of the city is too great and the returns from the land too small.

There is a patch of ground about eighteen miles from Durban called Paradise. It is a wooded hillock at the centre of a small estate called Ekuphakameni, 'the place that is lifted up'. Here in a modest mausoleum a Zulu prophet, Isaiah Shembe, lies buried. He was born in 1870 and died in 1935. His followers now number, it is claimed, a quarter of a million. Like Moses he spent time alone on a mountain and received, in some incalculable sense, his orders. Like the psalmist, he wrote hymns for his people. When he had much impressed a small gathering of Roman Catholic priests and they asked him why he did not join them he answered, in words recalling Jesus, 'I was a Roman Catholic before you were born'. Like Jesus, it is said of him that he rose from the dead. Though he never claimed divinity, such claims were made for him that his son and successor, Johannes Galilee Shembe, had to issue denials. His first brush with Christianity was when he joined the Wesleyans. Because their rite of baptism seemed to him inadequate, he moved to the Native Baptists. Breaking from the Baptists, he founded his own church, the Church of the Nazarites. Before he became a Christian he had an awesome reputation as a healer. His authority grew to such an extent that he was buried as Zulu royalty. He had, say some, others say he still has, the power to regenerate Zulu society. He is called a Zulu Messiah.

Messiah is a debatable word, but an element in it has always been that of political leader, unseater of the powers that be. Isaiah Shembe was very particular about anti-white agitation among his followers, claiming that since the whites brought the Gospel, it would be mere Godlessness to fight against them. Isaiah Shembe died, remember, in 1935. These words are being written many deaths later. I took with me to Ekuphakameni the feeling of tension, of pressure on the bones where the neck runs into the head, that had seemed impossible to shake off throughout the South African journey. Was Jesus, when He preached His Gospel, talking about self-cultivation and changing the world by changing myself? Or was He talking, as Messiah, about the removal of injustices by social and political action? Or have His words the divine privilege of ambiguity and can they seem to support conflicting causes?

Peter Mkize and I took our shoes off by the white stone that stands at the gates of Ekuphakameni and joined the barefoot crowds on the path down to the rising ground called Paradise. It was the Sabbath, i.e. Saturday. The Nazarites mostly wore simple white smocks. Many carried round their necks, like icons, small framed photographs of Isaiah Shembe. The leader's seat was empty (J. G. Shembe died in 1976). Possible successors were his two sons, though his brother, Amos K. Shembe, was 'acting bishop' and, to judge by the dreams he reported in his sermon (visitations in support of him by his father and his brother), he meant to succeed. The Shembe hymns have a trailing grandeur and harmonious density that raise the question of how Isaiah noted them down and taught them to his followers for, until late in life, he did not write. Peter Mkize described them as 'the most authentic Zulu sound I have ever heard'. At one point in the service a traditional 'praise-singer' sang out the praise-names of Isaiah Shembe, his forebears, his son, Johannes Galilee, and those of the Zulu royal kings. When the acting bishop invoked Shembe, the worshippers responded with a surge of 'Amen—Thou art Holy'.

With what privilege and in what isolation I sat on my special chair to the left of Amos Shembe's table, with its table-cloth and bowl of artificial flowers, near Isaiah Shembe's throne and a stone's throw from his resting place! The Nazarites sat on the floor, sang hymns and intoned 'Amens'. Though we were extremely conspicuous, no one chose to look at us. Gently, with no abrasion, we were kept at bay. They must have wondered at the indefatigable notes that Peter Mkize took down in his notebook. Just before the collection was taken (why at that point, no one explained), we were asked to leave. The drift of one of the Shembe hymns that Peter Mkize had recorded faithfully in his notebook was:

'I am tired; I am going to that everlasting land where I will lack nothing. There we will live in joy. No sorrow, no tears. The widow's tears will be wiped away. The orphan shall be comforted. In that everlasting land.'

11

TAIWAN

A Question of Balance

ECHO—of things Chinese is an English-language magazine published in Taipei. It carries fine photography, a rundown of what's on in Taipei, and substantial accounts of things Chinese for those who are not Chinese but would like to draw a little nearer: T'ai Chi Exercises, the Occult Science of Geomancy, Puppets, Ch'ing Ming—the sweeping of the ancestors' graves, the Ten Courts of Hell, the Lonely Ghosts Festival, Acupuncture, the Eight Immortals, Fortune Telling, Dragons, Opera, the Earth God, Acrobats. The editor is Linda Wu, the Art Director is Huang Yung-Sung and the Associate Art Director is Yao Meng-Chia. (After a time the names trip off the tongue as nimbly as Smith or Johnson.) They were my good companions for the whole of the search for as much of China as we were allowed to penetrate. We were confined to Taiwan. Red China would not let us in.

The magazine headquarters is in a back street in Taipei, capital of Taiwan and, now, of the exiled Nationalist Government of China. On a filing cabinet in the editorial office rests a fine wood carving of Confucius, who, being not just Confucius but a Confucianist also (i.e. a scholar and civil servant), lets his voluminous sleeves tumble over and obscure his hands. Trailing sleeves are presumably as fit as hands to waft government papers from one department to another and he has no intention of raising a pick and shovel.

On the office wall hangs a hefty plaque that carries the diagram of interlocking Yin and Yang, the T'ai Chi, the Great Ultimate. No other design that I can think of carries so much so elegantly and is so satisfying to doodle.

The design itself, I gather, is not ancient and is thought to have appeared at some time during the twelfth to the sixteenth centuries A.D. The insight it captures, however, is ancient and distinctly Chinese. In the beginning, as a

Chinese Book of Genesis might go, there was undifferentiated potentiality, a field of possibilities but no separation into things. Linda Wu, thinking to help, called it 'chaos', yet understanding can easily take a step backwards at the use of a slanted word. 'Chaos', as commonly used by speakers of English, means disorder, mess, what results when the grip is loosened: in classroom, kitchen, farmyard or filing cabinet. 'Chaos', if used by a Chinese to describe the primordial state of things, has to mean latent order, latent balance, of an undivided majesty that none of the later balancing acts can rival. Out of this undifferentiated potential, a drop forms, the first lurch towards polarization. Within the drop, there is a movement. This movement is the birth of the Yang. It is followed by a complementary settling, the birth of the Yin. From the Yang and the Yin all the myriad things that bear their separate labels are generated. Rocking from Yin to Yang, time moves and involves the myriad objects in the process of change.

Yin and Yang originally referred to the two sides of a hill: the Yang was sunny, the Yin in shadow. By extension, Yang represents light, heat, dryness, summer, action, the masculine; Yin represents dark, cold, moisture, winter, repose, the feminine. All processes, the shapes of all movements, involve a pull by the Yang on the Yin, the Yin on the Yang. There is no Yang without Yin, no Yin without Yang. Summer is summer by comparison with winter. The valley is the valley by reference to the mountain. On a sweltering night, you kick off the bedclothes in a search for the cold. On a wintry night, you pile on the bedclothes in a search for the warmth. Cold, warmth, winter, summer, wet, dry, masculine, feminine, are neither good nor bad. Those Judaeo-Christian absolutes—Evil and Good—do not rest in the scales of Yin and Yang. If they find a place anywhere in the Chinese account of things, it may be possible to say that a balance of Yin and Yang is good; prolonged imbalance, anything that would impede the constant swaying of Yin to Yang and back again, is evil. It is also doomed. For, just as Yin is at its height, there appears in it a grain of Yang, represented in the diagram by the tadpole-eye; and just as Yang is at its height, there appears in it a grain of Yin. Winter is born at the height of summer; summer, at the height of winter. In the 'eye' too is a complete interplay of Yin and Yang, each with its eye that encloses in itself a further eye and a further eye, and onwards and onwards. Where we, in a Western tradition, would unthinkingly speak of 'Creation', the Chinese, on the evidence of the Great Ultimate and Yin and Yang, are more likely to think 'Generation'.

I wish, in retrospect, that I had had the wit to start the

search for the religions of China by asking what big bold Western assumptions I should shed before I turned to look at anything Chinese. I could then have saved time spent looking for Chinese equivalents of Western shapes. Good and Evil as God-given Absolutes, I should need to discard. With them, any idea of the Creator God, either in One Person or in Three. There appears to be no Chinese equivalent of the Fall. Or rather, when a group of philosophers put forward the notion that mankind was born evil, their opinion was thought to be unsound. If the language of heresy has any place in the unwinding of Yin and Yang, they were heretics. Since the days of Mencius, expositor of Confucius in the third century B.C., Chinese orthodoxy has been that man is born good, or at least perfectible, a momentous investment for China's future. Many of my questions were theological questions; they concerned that area in which those in the West who would claim to be involved in 'religion' are most expert. Very soon it became clear that dogmatic theology, a whole range of God-questions and the quest to reach a wording for Divine Truths, is not a Chinese pastime.

What, then, is the Religion of China or is even that an inapposite question? Linda Wu's sleekest answer was that the religion of China is being Chinese. At a meal of rare delicacy, she said that the religion of China was eating. I should not, now, discount either of those replies as flippant. When she felt it appropriate to give an answer to suit the solemnity of the question, she answered that China has Three Religions—the *San Chiou*—Confucianism, Buddhism and Taoism. The West likes a good 'ism' and 'Three -Isms' seems a good answer, though again, they are not to be seen as equivalent -isms, each with its Founder, its Holy Book, its Deity. And outside the Three Religions is a whole undergrowth of traditional popular belief and practice, in which anyone with too set an idea of what a religion should be

Torajanese village market

would probably lose track of himself: parallel sentences
written on the doorposts of houses, gate-fortresses for spirit
armies set on the boundaries of villages, the habit of bowing,
setting alight special paper money in a celestial bank trans-
action, resorting to oracles. The Chinese are rated a
practical people: hard-working, thrifty, materialistic and
not specially 'religious'. Another way of phrasing that is that
we, white devils and Western barbarians that we are, define
'religion' in a way that makes us unable to see it in China.

Filming began at 10 a.m. on Monday, 21 March 1977.
The exact time was chosen in consultation with a fortune-
teller. It happened also to be about the time that we would
wish to begin, so there was no embarrassing tug between
what seemed sensible and what would turn out to be for-
tunate. Linda, Old Huang and Baby Yao (the names were
Linda's suggestion and mark the fact that, though all are
somewhere in their early thirties, Huang was a little older
and Yao a little younger) saw the fortune-teller on the
morning of Saturday, 19 March. He was one of a row of
consultants in small, open-fronted shops alongside one of the
finest and oldest temples in Tainan, the ancient capital of
the Taiwan island. He spoke Taiwanese. Linda speaks
Cantonese, Mandarin and English. Old Huang speaks
Mandarin and Hakka, the language, as different as Welsh
is from English, of the 'Guest People' who were driven from
the north of China southwards and preserved their old
traditions among their new neighbours. Huang is Hakka.
Baby Yao speaks Taiwanese and Mandarin. In the fortune-
shop I spoke to Linda, she to Baby Yao, Baby Yao to the
fortune-teller and back again. There must have been
enormous slopping of buckets as the words passed to and
fro. The fortune-teller asked my exact time of birth. He did
not ask the place, as would have been usual for an astrology
reading, but perhaps, on his particular charts, 'England'
was precise enough. He scanned the columns of Chinese

characters in various almanacs, and produced the propitious time: 10 a.m. the following Monday. With careful brush-strokes he wrote his prescription and a message of good luck on two slips of red paper, and asked that they be attached to our machinery. These reassuring auspicious banners fluttered from the camera and the tape-recorder at least for the first day or two. The only complaint about the ten o'clock start was from that section of us that left the hotel a little late for the hour-and-a-half's drive to the first film location. The driver took his deadline so seriously, and drove, it was felt, so dangerously, that the passengers forced him to slow down, preferring possible ill-fortune to certain death.

March 21 also happened to be the birthday of the T'u-ti Kung, the Earth God, the community guardian. Shortly after 10 a.m. we approached a tree, on a small hill, by a river. Under the tree was an area a few feet across, set out with flagstones. Treewards a low wall curved up to make a stone backing for the stone table on which offerings to the T'u-ti Kung could be placed. At the opposite side of the area, and towards the river, was a large pot for incense-sticks. Anyone who faces the tree and bows his respects to the T'u-ti Kung turns to the incense-pot and bows his respects to the T'u-ti Kung's greatly superior superior, the Jade Emperor.

Throughout the day a trickle of men, women and children, old and young, brought their incense-sticks, chicken, ham, tins of salmon, bottles of wine, kettles of tea and offered them to the Earth God, pouring out the liquor in delicate cups, setting the food on and round the stone table. Mothers and fathers led their families through small ceremonies of bowing, burning incense, setting 'god-money' alight, addressing a few words of greeting and petition to the god on his birthday. Once the offering had been made and presumably accepted, the food was retrieved and carried away in baskets or on the carriers of bicycles. The four of us stood in a respectful line before the tree shrine, put palms together and bowed low. Whether by accident or design, the moment was marked by a shocking cannonade of fireworks just behind us. From the look on the face of the man who had lit them (for the shock put a messy end to the bow) he was minding his own and the god's business and had no wish to involve us. Chinese at their shrines and in their temples seem to go about their duties with a pious self-absorption and a practised knack of excluding from their ears and their sightlines disturbances that would break up most imaginable church services.

The T'u-ti Kung has his shrine and his area, very much as a policeman may have his station and his beat. He deals with mean spirits and malign, unseen outsiders as a policeman traps cat-burglars. He patrols and sees to the welfare of the earth. He holds his appointment from his spiritual superiors and is answerable to them and to the community he has been appointed to serve. If the people in his area have any complaint about him, if the crops fail, if a drought lasts uncomfortably long, if a river floods beyond reason, the community can complain to the local civil administration to have the T'u-ti Kung reprimanded or replaced. According to Linda, he may be sentenced to a whipping. The spirit of a dead and respected village elder may be appointed T'u-ti Kung to another community. It is not traditional Chinese administrative practice to let a man serve the state too near home.

Though the T'u-ti Kung is a local official with limited jurisdiction, he belongs to a vast celestial bureaucracy. The Jade Emperor presides. Deities rise to eminence and fall from favour. Their hauteur and prickliness need constant placation and sacrifice. Their wilfulness may (who knows?) be secretly resented by some farmer struggling to make ends meet, but who knows that without their support his petitions will never be heard at court, will never even get as far as the ante-chamber. I have heard China described by a sympathetic Westerner, in a phrase I would have no right to invent, but, once heard, is not forgotten, as 'the oldest police state in the world'. Within such a state it is to be expected that the people will secure what liberties they can—by placation, bribery, keeping the top of their head rather than their traceable face towards the official, celestial or earthly, from whom they wish to extract a favour. It is not to be expected that a god will be personally friendly. Nor are most other bureaucrats, though out of office hours they may crave to be. But there are ways of averting their ire, winning their support and rousing them to action. And these are skills in which the Chinese have had long practice.

Hsi Kang is a small town about half an hour's drive from the ancient capital, Tainan. In recent years the community has prospered. Now a part of that prosperity is being ploughed back into the community temple of Ching An Kung. Plans were made in 1969. Work began in 1970. It is due to be finished in 1982 at a cost of around £750,000 or $1,500,000. Such extravagance may pain any extant earthly bureaucracy, but the heavenly bureacracy accept their spacious new quarters and have taken a hand, through mediums, seances and oracles, in the planning. The temple has a presiding deity but it belongs to no sect, Buddhist or Taoist. It is served by no regular priesthood though Buddhists and Taoists may be invited in for special ceremonies. It is a community expression of community confidence and community gratitude. Someone somewhere has been kind to them and has to be thanked. Not all assets are visible assets.

When our gang of four trod our way through the scaffolding, past the newly laid cement, past displaced gods, the temple was part worship-house, part workshop. Rows of apprentices under a master carpenter sculpted, if they were beginners, exquisite little butterflies; if they were more advanced, characters from Chinese romances, traditional worthies, heroes of the people. Stonemasons in an outside workshed were chiselling out the twisting dragon columns that will guard the doors. So it must have been in the great cathedrals of Europe at the time of their construction. High on a wall a solitary painter was adding red, blue and gold to gigantic reliefs of the gods of Prosperity, Posterity and Longevity, those three assertions by the Chinese of what they wish for themselves: Wealth, Offspring and a Ripe Old Age.

When a pilgrim bus was sighted, bringing yet another energetic influx of admirers, worshippers, gawpers, loud welcoming music was punched through an over-extended public address system and kept up its racket until the last pilgrim had stepped back over the threshold and the bus driver was blowing his horn to round up stragglers. Then the sound was turned off and the apprentices could once again hear themselves hammer. Here and there in areas of the temple not over-run by the builders, statues of gods presided sitting on long platforms as if they were holding court. High on a wall opposite one echelon of deities was a television set in full working order. Linda explained the logic of it. Traditional Chinese opera is performed, in the first place, for the entertainment of the gods and only secondly for the people. When a new means of entertainment comes to supplement the opera, that too should be offered to the gods. The set was a gift from a member of the community. The acceptance of a free television set has been known to cost an aspiring politician his career. It is evidently no such threat to a god, or to his benefactor.

Two main altar areas were in use at the time I saw Hsi Kang: a large platform of gods and generous incense-pot near the main door of the temple, and a small rear chapel in which a seance was taking place. There a Master of

Ceremonies guided a Master of Magic and a Medium on a dive down to the Courts of Hell to find out, on behalf of an afflicted family, in what way they were displeasing a grandfather, recently dead. The Master of Magic, blowing a horn and wearing a general's head-dress from ancient days, led the charge. The Medium, in the voice of an infernal courtier, spoke in his trance the wishes of the Lords of Hell. Two men, in trance or near it and each gripping two legs of a small rough chair, swung over at the appropriate moment and traced out Chinese characters on a table-top. The Master of Ceremonies interpreted the characters. In this way the dead man spoke a piece of his mind.

Given that the events were highly mysterious, there was no attempt at mystification, no darkened room, no solemn wail of the Chinese for 'Is there anybody there?' When the writing was over, the chair-bearers lit up their cigarettes and chatted. The Medium, in trance and in communication with Hell while his feet touched the ground, unplugged himself with a large leap into the air and backwards, wiped his face with a towel and put on his shirt. Bystanders took it all in and, when it was over, drifted away. The word 'Hell', by the way, which slipped past, dragging Judaeo-Christianity with it, needs to be sinicized. At death, one of a person's three superior souls (he is usually thought to have ten altogether) has to undergo purgatory before rebirth. This purgatory has ten courts ruled by ten lords and their bureaucracies. Distraught scampering about with the labels 'Taoist', 'Confucianist' and 'Buddhist', in the hope of being able to attach them somewhere, is not to be recommended. The Buddhists evidently supplied much that the Chinese hold about life after death but the Taoists, representing a movement of mighty native Chinese opposition to an invading missionary religion from India, took the Buddhist graphs of after-life and rebirth and made them theirs. A likely Confucian reaction might be that, until we learn to achieve order and sense in this life, it is inadvisable to waste time worrying about the next.

At the main altar, supplicants sought help in a less strenuous way—by means of oracle blocks. These, which come in pairs, are painted red and are made of wood in the shape of a crescent moon. They can be held, flat surface to flat surface, to make a shape somewhat resembling a small bulging red banana. Separated, they have a flat side (Yang) and a rounded side (Yin). The supplicant first pays proper respect to the god with offerings of incense, perhaps of food and god-money. Then he seeks the advice of the god by posing an interior question to which a yes or no answer would make sense.

Holding the question in mind, the questioner rocks the blocks in his hand and throws them to the floor. Two Yangs or two Yins downwards and the answer is not yes: in the first case the god is said to be angry; in the second he is said to be rocking with laughter. One Yang, one Yin face upwards and the answer is yes. Beside some altars are oracle-sticks in a container that resembles a large umbrella stand. The sticks are numbered and, if the god gives a yes with the blocks, the supplicant may, by bouncing the sticks or letting them fall loosely through the fingers, detach one of them. The number on the stick refers to a rack of oracle-verses that are usually ranged on a nearby wall. So long as at each stage the god gives a yes, the supplicant may proceed to the end. On the one occasion I carried the process through, the words of the oracle slip were so stirring and appropriate that I have no intention of making them public. Does this mean then that I have lost my senses or gone Chinese? I think not. To use the blocks acknowledges the presence of a puzzle. To delay respectfully at each throw holds back precipitate action. If, say, your question is too sudden, too passionate, too ill-considered and the god appears to support your mood by giving a yes to your question, it may strike you as an unusually moody and destructive thing for a god to do. So you may go on to ask him or her: 'Are you trying to make me take that course of action so that I make a fool of myself?' To which a 'yes' could be a strong aid to a quietening and the scrutiny of motives. This limited word in support of oracle blocks goes no further than a plea not to scoff too soon. Linda, though, speaks of 'efficacious temples', the power of one god to produce results which another cannot, particular advice which, when taken, has led through danger and to a good outcome. Here she speaks as an insider.

Most of the people's gods were once people but none of the people would wish to be gods. That, as far as I can sense it out, is the popular Chinese consensus. A good life is one lived in reasonable comfort, well into old age. Then the ten or so souls can dispose themselves as is proper. Some can return to the earth; one will stay by the coffin; one will inhabit the ancestor tablet on the family altar; one will go through its purgation and await a rebirth when the time is ripe. With sons and grandsons left behind, the dispersing members are assured that they will be remembered, their graves swept, their hunger assuaged with regular offerings. But calamities happen, people die young, fishermen are lost at sea, speeding cars swing off mountain roads, unused energy, incomplete lives, are catapulted into the air. And it is somewhere in this suddenness, this lack of fulfilment, that it is said you find god-material.

The goddess Ma-Tsu has the title Queen of Heaven. She was raised to this rank by the Emperor in 1685, largely for her help in sea battles. She is known and much revered in the sea-board provinces of southern China and in Taiwan, though she would be unknown, I gather, elsewhere. In Tainan, the old Taiwanese capital, she has a great temple; or, to be just as exact, a great palace. Dragons fight for a pearl on the tiled roof, embodying the lightness and vigour of heaven. Swallow-tails trail upwards from the gable-ends, indicating that this is a lordly house. The forecourts are open to the sky and rise in tiers. The goddess herself sits like an empress, surrounded by a retinue, under cover on the furthest and highest platform. She is guarded by two fierce tamed demons: one, a dark-bluish colour, with his hand shielding his brow, goes by the name of 'Eyes that see a thousand miles': the other, rich red, is 'Ears that hear with the wind'. She sits in perpetual audience. But her origins were humble.

About nine hundred years ago she was a fisherman's unmarried daughter of great piety and power against evil. She lived on an island off the coast of Fukien. One night, in Linda Wu's version of her story, she dreamed that her father and her two brothers were in a storm at sea. Using her special powers she went to their rescue and seized a brother in each hand and held her father in her teeth. At that moment her mother came into her room and spoke to her. She opened her mouth to answer, still in dream, and let her father fall into the sea. To her mother's bewilderment she set about mourning her father. In a day or two her brothers returned fatherless, describing a miraculous rescue and their father's sudden lapse backwards. Ma-Tsu died at the age of twenty-one. Unmarried, she had a particular reason for resentment, for causing trouble to those who were left behind. Being who she was, she used her powers for generous purposes. Her bracing intervention was felt first in local crises, then in national emergencies. Her rank in the hierarchy kept pace with her effectiveness.

As ruler of a household, she is generous. She, in the best Chinese tradition, is a follower of 'the Three Religions'. One wing of her palace is given over to the Buddha. There, on an altar, sits Gautama himself, encased in gold leaf. Alongside him sit the Arhats, the Buddha's Worthies, eighteen of them. Popular Taoist deities are her courtiers. To the rear of the palace, in what would be the private living-quarters, is Ma-Tsu's family altar. The inscribed ancestor tablets of her mother, her father, her brothers, rest on a long table indicating that she takes seriously the message of the sage Confucius, on the need for respect within families, within communities, within the state. The same small room is set about with card-tables and chairs. It is a meeting place for the older men of the quarter. They play chequers, draw tea from a generous tea-pot or watch television. Children slide down the marble banisters that skirt the steps that descend, level by level, from the height of Ma-Tsu's throne to the level of the first court and the front gate, where new arrivals pay their respects to the Jade Emperor and acknowledge the power of the house they are entering by lighting their incense-sticks and leaving them smouldering in an ornate cauldron-like incense-pot. On the walls, as the visitor passes and ascends, are painted panels, telling legendary stories. Not once but three times the wall tells, in different forms, the story of the meeting of the sage Confucius with the Old Man, Lao Tse. If the search for China had not begun in a newspaper office in Taipei before a wall design of Yin and Yang, it could have started here in Ma-Tsu's Temple in Tainan before a wall-painting of the meeting of Confucius and Lao Tse, for here too Yang meets Yin.

Whether Lao Tse was just one old man or the composite of all old men who thought as he thought, is of interest to those for whom it is of interest. But Lao Tse lives. Confucius, or to give him the name he had before the Jesuits latinized him, Khung Fu Tse, Master Khung, belongs more certainly to history and is said to have been Lao Tse's younger contemporary. They lived well over two thousand years ago at a time when a society was splitting at the seams and they stared at chaos: not the chaos of unexpressed potential, the gestating womb, but the other face of chaos— the collapse of loyalties, the arbitrary whims of war-lords, disorderly greed, fear that runs across-country like a plague. As doctors, they gave prescriptions. As prescriptions, one is Yang, the other Yin. Master Khung recommended the smack of firm government, respect between ruler and ruled, elder and younger, parents and children, living and dead. Much has been done in his name that he might disclaim; the creation of tortuous bureaucracy, dogs in office expecting to be obeyed, the enslavement of lower ranks by higher ranks, the facelessness of the system. But these are the vices of his virtues. His virtues are the Yang virtues of security and order. He did not found a cult but propounded an ethic. He was concerned with this world, not the next, and with the part of this world that men can by their powers of restraint, intervention and management, do something to control. The people have made a god of him. As a god he appears in the wall-paintings in Ma-Tsu's temple. Not far away, in Tainan, he has his own temple, the altars set out with his ancestor tablets and those of his disciples. Once a year, scholars gather to perform a liturgy in his honour. But his real memorial, I suppose, would be the Chinese civil service, the Imperial state machine as it was before first Chiang Kai Shek, then Mao, broke it.

Lao Tse too can be seen as a breaker of machines, though the power, grandeur and opacity of his great work, the *Tao Te Ching*, the Way and its Power, can carry a variety of interpretations. All of them, if Confucius's way is Yang, are Yin: not more government, but less; not bigger plans, but smaller; not twisting nature's arm and making her labour, but respecting her power and letting her lead. 'Actionless action' becomes an ideal; not supine inaction, but action that follows the grain of things, that respects the Tao, the Way. Consider, he might seem to say, not the lilies of the field, but the water. It moves where it can; it seeks out low places; if one way is blocked, it finds another; if most ways are blocked, it forms a lake; if it reaches a cliff-edge, it cascades in a waterfall. It does not argue. It skirts and accommodates. There is more than one way of running a course. Yet the power of water will wear away mountains, tunnel through rock, carry off livestock, jeopardize cities, tear out a route for itself if too much impeded, swallow up men and, when it can tumble no longer, yield up its force to the sea. Lao Tse too has become a god: for the Chinese people in general; for those in what goes by the name of the Taoist Religion; and for nameless individuals in growing numbers in wealthy societies who ask at what price the wealth is created, whether the machines run the men or the men the machines, and how to draw back into oneself some of the power that some jack-in-office has siphoned away.

Once, in Taiwan, did I see a Taoist priest spectacularly in action. He was master of ceremonies at the funeral of an old woman. It was a forty-nine-day event, must have cost £30,000 ($60,000) at least and took place at the dead woman's small family house. A marquee, open at one side, housed the Taoist altar which consisted of a mountain of trestle tables fronted by richly embroidered hanging cloths. Along the side walls were representations of the Ten Courts of Hell in which migrant souls, overseen by the Lords of Hell and their officers, suffered appropriate purgatory. The back wall, the wall against which an emperor would sit if this were his palace, did what it could, in embroidery and graphics, to represent the Tao, the Ultimate, and it did so in the form of a Taoist Trinity, the Three Pure Ones. They are not gods or even God, but a shock to anyone reared westwards and hitherto trying to shed all Christian expectations. For this Taoist Trinity, which existed, as far as anyone knows, before the Chinese heard of the Father, the Son and the Holy Ghost, seems to trace out three aspects of a familiar triangle: Ultimate Origin, Ultimate Expression, Ultimate Harmony; or the Absolute, the Presentation of the Absolute, the Power of the Absolute. The Ultimate Expression, the Presentation of the Absolute, takes the familiar form of Lao Tse himself. The dead woman's family could have called in a Buddhist priest to carry through the funeral rites and they would have gone along similar lines; but they opted for the Taoist alternative, the authentic Chinese-thing.

The Taoist Church, as sectarian Taoism is sometimes called, was not founded by Lao Tse in the sense that there is some continuous presence of Church Taoist action from the supposed time of Lao Tse's death to the present day. Church Taoism seems to have arisen during and after the second century A.D.; though, in the sense that Lao Tse may be an Ultimate Expression of the Tao, he is not to be confined to his own lifetime and is traceable into and through a great number of distinguished incarnations. In the usual scholarly accounts, Church Taoism arose as a home-grown Chinese response to foreign, successful, en-croaching missionary Buddhism. Without Buddhism to fight against and learn from, it is possible that Taoism in the form of an institutional religion would never have taken shape. In the course of a patient attempt to help me through these Taoist thickets, the great China scholar, Dr Joseph Needham of Cambridge, suggested a comparison with what might have happened in England if the local Druids had put up organized resistance to St Augustine or to the Celtic missionaries, pirating the shape of the liturgy, learning from their opponents' skill in church government, taking over a husk of Christian theology so as to preserve for the future something authentically British.

The part of the forty-nine-day funeral spread at which we were present was the day or two before the coffin left the house, and the day of the great procession to the grave-site. As we arrived, narrowly escaping collision with a boy balancing himself and three or four enormous wreaths on a motor-bike, the Taoist marquee was in position alongside the front of the house. The priest was parcelling out and arranging his liturgical props, very like a travelling show-man, and behind the house a squad of cooks were cutting up meat and vegetables and feeding them to great black cauldrons over open fires in anticipation of feeding a multitude. The main events of these days, in brief, were the support of the soul through its purgation, its release from imprisonment, its restoration to the upper world where it can rest before its journey to a pleasurable place, to which the family back on earth will have sent on ahead a spirit mansion with spirit furniture, spirit flowers in the garden, a spirit television set, a spirit car, a spirit telephone. This, in exquisite paper modelling and needing the strength of four men to control and lift, was carried down the path to the house ahead of us, placed in its own tented show-place where visitors could inspect it as, in the English tradition, visitors to a wedding inspect the presents and the wedding cake. After a few days it would be 'transformed' for use in the spirit-world by being burnt to ashes.

The words, 'restoring', 'healing', 'completing', 'rounding', 'balancing' thread their way through most descriptions of what the rituals of a Taoist priest are meant to achieve. A death is a breach in nature, an imbalance, a sudden upsurge of Yin. The Taoist, by his understanding of the workings of Yin and Yang and his training in appropriate rituals, is called in to heal the breach and restore the balance. Ordination of a Taoist priest is usually from father to son or father to adopted son. The Taoist priest to whom I owe most of what little I understand of Taoist rituals (for enormous secrecy and clannishness surrounds them to the extent of making them seem, to some eyes, shady), is a Dutch scholar, Dr K. M. Schipper, who teaches at the Sorbonne. He was adopted by a Taoist master on Taiwan and ordained in 1964. It does not often cross my mind to single out one person through whom insights into this situation or that were obtained, for there are usually other sources that would do just as well. But, when the *Encyclopaedia Britannica* article on Taoism calls Schipper's ordination 'the most significant event in the past several centuries of Taoist history', and says of him, 'His systematic, first-hand researches into Taoist practices may very well revolutionize scholarly knowledge of the religion, which will thus acquire an unforeseen historical extension, in the West, and into the future', the case is special.

The Taoist priest stood with his acolytes on stools surrounding a small table. In an earthen pot over a charcoal stove they were concocting an elixir of immortality. This would be applied to paper effigies of the dead woman and of a number of other dead family members whom the costly ritual was meant to benefit. The priest wore elaborate court robes, for he held down a job in the celestial administration. On his head he wore a black Taoist biretta crowned by a flame-shaped pin set with a pearl. This indicated the spirit of the priest tending upwards. He wore wooden shoes that lifted him five or six inches above the ground and nearer Heaven. He made ritual passes over the elixir with a live (Yang) cockerel and a live (Yin) duck. The medication was then fed to the effigies, not, in crude terms, to raise the dead and achieve immortality that way, but to restore them to Yin-Yang harmony and fit them for the rough passage that lay ahead of them. A bubbling elixir might make a very satisfactory Taoist emblem. In the pursuit of immortality, the elixir, what the West might call 'the philosopher's stone', the Taoists were China's pioneer alchemists, proto-experimental scientists.

For the next ritual, the priest vested himself for his descent from heaven with 'a writ of pardon'. On his back he bore an embroidered emblem of the universe. His descent was a dance, spinning, tracing out figures-of-eight on the ground, holding aloft the precious folded paper. This, like all the other rituals, was accompanied by an energetic small orchestra, inveterate cigarette smokers all, who wedged their smokes in the corner of their mouths, drummed, fiddled, possibly (for their skill with their instruments and their cigarettes was remarkable) blew.

In the meantime the acolytes had divested themselves to reveal black track-suits. They were now the runners who would accompany the writ to hell. One carried a paper horse; another a paper rider; others a paper phoenix (Yin), a paper dragon (Yang). Under the eye of the priest, who now became a ring-master, they circled the area before the altar, then ran, then turned cascading somersaults, still holding their paper charges. Finally one by one they stood on a chair on a table and spun themselves off in a twirling flick down to the earth—a dramatic, ritual, circus analogy for the start of an infernal journey. Energized by so much circling action, the paper horse was set on the earth, the paper rider was made to mount. The writ of pardon was securely wedged in his belt. The Yin phoenix and the Yang dragon flanked him. Paper money, spirit currency, was piled at his feet, for use on the journey, to pay infernal lodging-house keepers and to bribe, if necessary, infernal officials. After a check that nothing had been left undone, a lighted match was applied to horse, rider, writ and all. And the next stage of putting things to rights had begun.

All day the members of the dead woman's family, down to the smallest children, went about in over-garments of sackcloth. They also wore sacking bonnets that overhung at the front with flaps to hide the face, though these were not designed to be too efficient. When the journey to hell was in progress, they sat in rows like the audience at a show. When the effigies of the departed needed medicament, the men held the effigies. When the story took a new turn, the women clustered round the coffin in its small bare room and wailed 'don't go away'. At other times they served the funeral guests with the food that was constantly coming to the boil round at the back. No one but them was expected to look solemn. During those parts of the ritual—which were many—that took a clowning turn, they too laughed.

Once it was known that the writ of pardon was on its way, the time came for the priest to lead his charge on hell. It was well on in the evening. Outside the lit funeral area, the railway embankment, the fields and the neighbouring houses were in the dark. The priest, in elaborate comic cross-talk with a straight-man, described in an allowable boast how he would handle any night-walking spirit that might try to trip him up. In the meantime two paper towers, four or so feet high, were held upright by crouching members of the family in front of the altar-table at which the priest was preparing himself. While they waited and made the towers tremble in anticipation, the priest took a trident, a bright metal fork on a wooden shaft, treated it with a necessary preparatory ritual and came round to the tower for the attack.

At that moment, out of the dark, there burst into the en-closure four men, each at the end of two long poles that trapped between them a sturdy and empty wooden chair with five fluttering pennants at its back. The men scythed their way through the assembly, which scattered and watched from a safe distance. They were under the spell of one of the Plague Gods, the Wang Yeh, from a nearby temple. The Taoist priest, though he respects the gods of the people, has his own place in the celestial bureaucracy, is even (in that sense) something of a god himself, and he is well capable of carrying out the ritual for the release of a trapped soul from hell without help. If, on the other hand, one of the local Wang Yeh insists on coming to help, he is not snubbed.

At first the bucking chariot reared, charged and back-stepped like a bull suddenly loose in a crowded street, and the people reacted appropriately. Then it swung its porters round and made a series of runs on an old man in the crowd. Soon the old man allowed himself to be drawn to his feet. He moved from the huddle of people and trotted alongside the god's chariot. On his arm was tied a red band. He was a medium, a 'divining lad'.

In the meantime the priest had completed the rituals leading up to the assault and came round to face the trembling paper fortress. The Plague God swerved behind him and the trotting medium kept alongside. With music from the tireless band braying defiance, the priest thrust his trident through the paper walls and sliced them, on all four sides, from top to bottom. No sooner was entry effected than the charioteers charged forward and (the likeness to a bull recurs), savaged the remains of the fortress as if they were battling through demons to reach a dungeon. His trident stowed, the priest sped in again with a blue parasol which he opened and spread over the wreck of lath and tissue paper. The emerging souls, blinking back into the light again, needed some such hood to shade them. With elegant rapidity the priest twirled the parasol away from the ruins and towards the room in which the corpse lay. Close family in their sackcloth crowded after. Leaving the rescued spirits in the care, once again, of their relatives, the priest emerged, shut the door tight and beat the earth round about with sparking rush-matting which he twirled like a drum-major and threw over the altar. As a last warning to any demon that had decided to lurk, he let off a kite's tail or two of fire-crackers.

It is a text-book cliché in university schools of literature, to trace the origin of drama to a ritual and a religious root. But what satisfies the examiners does not necessarily course in the bloodstream, make the hair stand on end, prove itself on the pulse. That night I saw the Harrowing of Hell, the gates broken down, the burning galleries mastered, the locks orced and the dead brought to life again. And it was all chieved with a few sheets of tissue paper, a lath frame, a pot or two of glue, a trident, a chair on poles and a parasol, ielded by one visible protagonist, with five helpers and a horus of auxiliaries. When the souls were safely stowed, the ivining lad, as if he were still running back up the slope om the underworld, threw himself down at a table and, rumming with his fists, told out the sights he had seen. The words of this gasping messenger ended an incomparable play.

A day or so later, Linda Wu, Old Huang and Baby Yao ummoned us to a war-council. Baby Yao, in particular, was evere. He thought there was a danger that we were giving oo much coverage to what he called the 'shamanistic' parts f Chinese religion, the mediumism, the trance-walking, the nimistic undergrowth, to the neglect of the subtle, the cholarly, the civilized. Since Yao, the gentlest of com- anions, rarely spoke except to share his pleasure and offer upport, we took his words to heart.

A ritual celebration of Yin and Yang takes place daily, vithout the aid of any plague-god, medium or entrance- nent, in the public parks of Taipei, Tainan and no doubt f many another Chinese city. Early risers gather singly, or n groups, for their T'ai Chi Chuan, the T'ai Chi Exercises. Vith more enthusiasm, I feel, than they had for seances, Linda, Huang and Yao arranged for us to watch their T'ai Chi master at work. The first impression, as the exercises volve, is of slowness. The effect is particularly striking on lm. That plane of vision in which the master moves seems o go in slow motion. The eye also expects the background nen and women with brief-cases and shopping baskets, on heir way to work or to the market, to move in slow motion oo. But they keep the rate of strike appropriate to busy eople. Only he holds time back.

He begins by seeming to surrender his limbs to the pull f the earth. Nothing is shaped. All is potential. Slowly his

right leg lifts; he settles the foot; Yang has been born. Wit[h]
his weight carried over to rest on the Yang, the Yin [is]
released; his left foot eases and grounds itself sure. Th[e]
balance returns to the centre, releasing the next flow [of]
Yang, and so, on and on, slowly evolving, till the pendulu[m]
motion settles to rest and all effort drains down to the eart[h].
To practise T'ai Chi Chuan is to mirror, trace out, enac[t]
embody, as the Chinese might say, nothing less than th[e]
movement of the universe.

During the days we spent in Taiwan, the year edged i[ts]
way out of the Yin of late winter and towards the Yang [of]
the summer. The great festival that marks the tilt of th[e]
balance is Ch'ing Ming, the Spring Festival, the time [of]
eating spring rolls and sweeping the ancestors' graves. Eve[n]
with some notion of expandable time, it is hard, in retro[-]
spect, to believe that I am recalling from now on the event[s]
of one day. In the morning we joined Mr. Lin in hi[s]
compound. Mr Lin is a Hakka. He farms and make[s]
umbrellas. The Lin compound is a simple fortress-enclosur[e]
for about sixty Lin families. The two highest buildings ar[e]
the square gate-house, from which the spirit guardians kee[p]
a look-out, and the family shrine. At one end of this large[,]
pillared room is the altar, on which twenty generations [of]
Lin ancestor tablets rest. Beside the altar, painted on th[e]
wall, are parallel sentences extolling the virtues of famil[y]
piety. The day began with Mr Lin, his wife and two son[s]
paying their respects at the shrine, and seeming to a[ll]
appearances to be going on a picnic, taking their provision[s]
chicken, rice-wine, beer with them. The sites of the famil[y]
graves were two miles or so from the compound on a hillsid[e].

The siting of graves and houses involves the science [of]
geomancy, the tracing out of currents of 'wind and wate[r]'
that make a place happy. It was the geomancers of old wh[o]
perfected the magnetic compass to aid their work. It wa[s]
poets of a geomantic turn of mind who spoke of drago[n]

lying curled in the earth, happy when their subtle coils are respected, vengeful when they are disturbed. There's the story of a large dragon curled in a hillside in Taipei. A multi-storey international hotel was cut into his back. In the same year the Nationalists lost their seat at the United Nations. A geomancer might see a connection.

The Lin graves were parcelled out for cleaning among the branches of the clan. Mr Lin, as the eldest son of his generation, had particular responsibilities. With an adze and rake, he cleared away a rich year's-worth of vegetation from each grave. Once a grave was cleared a burst of fire-crackers announced the start of the filial ceremonies, the offering of food and wine to the dead, the standing in a family row and bowing with incense-sticks. A small stone, like a mossy milestone, was the mark of the local T'u-ti Kung. A few rice cakes were offered there. Along the brow of the hill a row of small children watched the entertainment. They were 'grave-children', young goatherds whose flocks graze nearby. Sweets were left on the graves to encourage them to keep their animals clear. Particular care was taken to make an offering to the hungry ghosts. For every contented spirit that enjoys generations of respect from its family, there are many lonely ghosts without food, attention, respect; and, neglected, they can become resentful. Small amounts of spirit money are set alight and transferred to their account. Small offerings of food are left to absorb their malice. Once I too suffered their displeasure, though, for anyone not attuned to the presence of vengeful spirits, there would be other explanations.

We were driving along a mountain road in central Taiwan. Along the narrow verges and in the branches of small roadside trees, we noticed what seemed to be litter, small paper tokens. We noticed too that on each hairpin bend or when the grass verge shrank to nothing, the amount of litter increased. By this time we were used to the sight of spirit money, silver for the ancestors and gold for the gods, but we were slow to recognize its use here as a form of comprehensive insurance. Near the skeleton of any wrecked car must linger the raging ghosts of the people who died in it. Down in the ravine, hidden by trees, there must be at least one or two wrecked cars. A handful of money might distract the ghosts, leaving the driver to curb just the machinery and his urge to snip a minute or two off his travelling time. Luckily, when our driver dozed and we came off the road, we were travelling in the rock-side lane. Had we been coming rather than going, our ghosts too would probably have joined the pack and have needed Mr Lin's pious attentions. As the side of the car grazed the rockface, the lorry behind us threw out a handful of ghost-money and overtook. The landscape was very like that in which as a child I pictured the Good Samaritan giving a helping hand. Eventually, and before night drew in, a lorry bearing a small crane pulled alongside and for the equivalent of £5 ($10) in regular currency hoisted us off the rock and back on the road.

By the late morning of Ch'ing Ming, duty done to ancestors, T'u-ti Kung and hungry ghosts, we were back in the Lin compound where (the better the day, the better the deed) other turning-points in the Lin calendar were being marked. A Lin bride was preparing to leave home and go to join her husband's family. Outside the house, a large lorry was piled high with her dowry, which included a television set, a large refrigerator and a motor-cycle. The bride and groom emerged, she in white with a head-dress and orange blossom, he in a grey suit and white gloves. A small band accompanied them across the compound and to the family shrine playing, as they went in to pay their respects, a sprightly pavane and, as they came out, a funereal rendering of 'Here comes the bride'. As the door of their taxi was closing, an aunt threw at the bride's feet a pair of fine dead hens, meant perhaps to encourage the same prodigality in child-bearing (especially of sons) as that shown by a broody hen.

Whilst the marriage car was being waved through the turreted gate, another branch of the family was setting up chairs and round tables in the shrine hall to celebrate one month of life for the first son of a new generation. Before that, his birth was not fully acknowledged. Having survived a month, he was thought likely to live and his father could start to be proud of him. Rice, meat, vegetables were cooked, as at the funeral, in outdoor cauldrons, and about fifty people, all Lins, sat down to eat. The youngest Lin of all, dangled and admired, wore a white knitted bonnet to which were stitched three small gold discs. The middle one bore the T'ai Chi, the emblem of Yin and Yang.

In the afternoon, the opera came to town. The opera stage was a scaffolding construction hung with a painted backcloth that obscured the actors' tiring-room. The backcloth carried gigantic garish paintings of the gods of Prosperity, Posterity and Long Life. Next to the stage was a low muddy river. Across the river was one of the more ornate town temples. The town was a couple of miles down the road from the Lin compound. At the chance of a crowd, stallholders set up their charcoal grills and skewered spicy fish pieces across the flames. Small gambling games collected their small crowds. Among the children, ice-cream and fruit drinks came second favourite to pig's blood soup, the solid part lifted to the mouth with chop-sticks. In prospect was a matinée performance of a ritual preamble—the dance of the Eight Immortals or a Parade of the Gods whose grander likenesses filled the backcloth—followed by an evening performance of one of the traditional Taiwan Opera stories. But before an actor could set foot on the stage, the right audience had to be present, and the right audience, for a civic entertainment, is the full assembly of the civic gods.

A tractor pulling a trailer, and a small open lorry, carrying a five-piece band and a clutch of community leaders, went in procession to invite the local T'u-ti Kungs, the Earth Gods, to come to their own opera. As they stopped at each tree shrine and dismounted, the band led the way. The civic delegation followed, one of them with a canopy to shield the god should he consent to go with them. With affecting gravity, a spokesman stepped forward with his smouldering incense-sticks, bowed towards the tree and, in classical Chinese, offered the community invitation. The band played throughout. Celebration fire-crackers were let off. The god did not refuse and, with the canopy held aloft, the contented company took their guest to his carriage. A turn or two on the tractor's starting handle and the slow-speed motorcade, without outriders and police sirens but in simple majesty, trundled down the road to the next shrine and the next and finally to the opera-field.

There was, to one way of thinking, a plangent absurdity about the events of that afternoon: invisible gods under an empty canopy serenaded by old men playing ancient instruments on their way to a seat at the opera. And if time is money, and money is prosperity, and prosperity is one of the great Chinese aspirations, there must be many Chinese board-rooms that would never spend time placating a T'u-ti Kung and would never leave him an empty chair; for the T'u-ti Kung is rural, sometimes obstructive, frequently slow. At the same time and behind the quaintness I had a sense of something quite different going on. Here was a community saying, in its own way, 'Until you're right with the earth, nothing can prosper and there's nothing to celebrate.'

12

CALIFORNIA
West meets East

A distinction has been drawn (not by me, though I steal, use and am glad of it) between *California* and *Californialand*. California, goes the thinking, is a locality, the T-junction in the far west of the U.S.A. where the covered wagons reached the sea, home of orange juice, the Stanford University Linear Accelerator, Hollywood, foot-long pine cones in the Redwood Forests, the Los Angeles smog. Californialand is a commonwealth of ideas, a cluster of needs, but enough Californialanders live in California to explain how the two names come to be so similar. Californialand is held in by no state boundaries. Its inhabitants carry no particular passports, though in the main they start by knowing something about city life, something about opulence, something about mobility, something about the rights of man, which effectively confines them to what has hitherto been called 'the free world', 'the developed world'. In general they know that they are sure of their next meal, that they can move if they are too uncomfortable where they are, that they have a variety of inalienable rights. There are Californialand pockets throughout the U.S.A., Canada, in England, on the continent of Europe and, no doubt, elsewhere. We happened to pitch our search for Californialand in California.

The Californialand bird is not best recognized by its plumage. Beneath a shaggy Wyatt Earp look may beat the tyrannical heart of a movie mogul. A collar and tie may hide a determined meditator, transpersonal therapand and organic food enthusiast. There is possibly a touch more denim among Californialanders than among the rest of the population, but it is worn, I should guess, less for style than for durability. If I go on to suggest just one or two indicators by which it may be possible to sniff out a Californialander, it should be understood that these can be no more accurate than licked fingers stuck in the air to find out the changes in the wind. For Californialand is, by its nature, a landscape of the spirit. One sharp observer, writing in 1973, called it 'a state of confusion, mixed with a raw hunger for transcendence'. Four years later the state of confusion is mine, and the immediate raw hunger is for some way of nailing down what it is I think I am looking for.

I should say, for a start, that Californialanders know and speak the language of Yin and Yang. If the predominant culture is Yang—pushy, mechanized, exploitive—Californialand is Yin. Californialanders quote Lao Tse, often without knowing it. Lao Tse speaks reverently of the Spirit of the Valley and the Eternal Feminine. Californialand men are not scared of their own femininity or of the masculinity of their wives. They would wish to go with the grain of their own wood. They nurse, these Californialanders, if not a nostalgia, then certainly a fascination with those times in history when people have had to live with the sharp and immediate consequences of their actions. As one of their number put it: 'People who must live with the consequences of their acts are, by definition, spiritual people. That's why primitive peoples are all spiritual peoples—because they cannot escape the consequences of what they do.' Californialanders would wish to be spiritual people too. But their spirituality is not fed to them through dogma and a fervour of believing. They need to experience it—on the pulse, through the surface of the skin, from head to foot. They may

CALIFORNIA: West meets East

not reject machinery but they understand the power of machinery to distance people from each other and it is the distance that they reject. It is important to be in touch—as totally in touch as possible. Thus, to use a telephone to stay in touch when there is no nearer alternative is seen as sensible. To use a telephone to keep the touching down to a minimum is a symptom of our current malaise.

They distrust all manner of 'media': the entrepreneur who steps between the craftsman and his buyer, the manager who separates the work force from the intentions of the firm, the politician who stands between the people and the destiny of the nation, the film-maker, television 'anchor man', the news reporter who ferries impressions between sets of people who are otherwise utterly out of touch with each other, thus wasting the time that could be devoted to those with whom they *are* in touch. Elsewhere in the world, for instance, the arrival of a film crew can create alarm, curiosity, rejection. Only in California (at points where it starts to impinge on Californialand) did I see signs of a knowing hostility. Television, as was evident, had been there before; had looked, distorted, inflated, belittled, caricatured, shown hostility. Now, no doubt bitten more than once, they turned the tables. We were not welcome.

Wherever they are in their spiritual quest, few Californialanders have been there very long. That is the nature of making a journey. The whole-hearted organic gardener of today may have been the whole-hearted peace-marcher of yesterday, the whole-hearted flower-child of the day before, the whole-hearted trekker to India of the day before that. The transiency of Californialand can be seen either as lack of substance, instability, rootlessness (the common view of the majority who have a deep wish not to be transient); or as zest for life, divine discontent, acceptance of life as it really is—transient. Transients may also one day decide to settle down.

Californialanders are deeply concerned about the future, not simply their own future but that of the planet. It is Californialanders in many guises who speak of the need to conserve resources, respect the earth, leave future generations with the hope of some future. At the same time they reject what their parents and grandparents may have accepted—the anaesthetic use of 'tomorrow' by all manner of insurance companies, whether those who propose pensions or those who preach paradise, to sweeten the bitterness of today. Californialand professes to deal in the 'now', the quality of life as lived moment by moment, and in working out how to harness the 'now' and ride on its back. Perhaps that last sentence has stumbled on the most useful way of throwing a loose net over what Californialand, as I have been using the term, may be. It is a commonwealth of the means by which the generations of those who have been thrown off-balance by the expansion of the cities, the growth of machinery, the belittlement of man and the plunder of the earth, try to draw themselves upright again.

I feel through all those generalizations as if I had been hanging, in my suit, on a hanger in a wardrobe, and am glad to be off the hook. Yet it seemed that some generalization was necessary, that the territory needed to be mapped out a bit. For there is no predominant Californian orthodoxy. Simply by way of comparison: it would be perverse to confine a survey of Christianity to the Copts of Egypt or a survey of Muslims to the handful who live in Romania. Egypt is Muslim; Romania is Christian. Their orthodoxy speaks for itself.

But in California there is no such certainty. There are well-established Christian communities, a well-established Zen community, a newer and growing series of Tibetan Buddhist foundations, the Sikhs, the Sufis, the Theosophists. There are wave upon wave of new cults, many claiming to be simply restatements of the Hidden Truth that has been with us all along, others crashing in with the force of Divine Revelation. There is whatever may be the fractured spirituality of an opulent society at the height of its technological accomplishment in the second half of the twentieth century. There are, in the University of Stanford and at Mount Palomar, scientific establishments that may be mapping out the shape of things to come. And now there are the concerns of ecology, the use of the word 'appropriate' to describe desirable technology, the use of the word 'small' to describe what is beautiful and the sudden intertwining on the free air of all those words that spring from the root word 'whole' and seem not till now to have known they are interrelated: wholesome, holistic, healthy, holy. Areas of search in California lie as thick and various as the pasted handbills that plague every lamp-post, telegraph pole and spare bit of wall round the university campus at Berkeley—all of them urgent, all of them dear to the heart of someone or other, and all of them, in the case of the handbills, with a life expectancy of twenty minutes before they are buried beneath the next wave of stickers. If the journey to the San Francisco Bay area has any shape and the shape ever manages to skirt matters of real consequence, it is thanks very largely, in the early stages, to strong words and clear direction from one particular adviser.

Theodore Roszak has poised himself very carefully to be able to do what he has done. He has a regular job teaching, lives in a proper house in Berkeley with his wife and family, has neighbours he may not know all that well and, to that extent, belongs to what he might agree to call 'the prevailing culture'. But, on another plane, he is an isolate, an outsider. His first book, or certainly the one that brought him to prominence, was *The Making of a Counter Culture* and the label 'counter culture' has been an alliterative albatross round his neck ever since. He followed it up with *Where the Wasteland Ends* and *Unfinished Animal*. Sometimes reading

Roszak, but not when we speak, I have wanted to cry out: 'Now come on. You rhapsodize.' At other times: 'No. That's how it is.' Without him I think the search in California would have been devoted entirely to Science and the Scientists or to some of the more rabid outcropping among the new religions, or to cults and disciplines that formerly belonged to the East and are now moving West. With his help, we picked out I think a more unusual and less beaten path: a series of meetings with remarkable women and men who are, in a great variety of ways, living out their portion of the Californialand complexity.

Apart from the Zen Centre, to which I was connected with a trailing filament throughout the time in California, the only formal 'religious' group I to any extent came to know was a section of the Sikh Community of San Francisco. The 3HO North Regional Headquarters for the U.S. Sikhs is a corner house on Waller Street. The 3 H's of the 3 H Organization are Healthy, Happy and Holy. They are snappier slogans than would perhaps have occurred to the founders of Sikhism, but they serve to show the neighbours that American Sikhs have not ceased to be American. They also make a bold claim. But then, the name Singh, which every male Sikh attaches to himself, means 'Lion' and it is the goal of Sikhism to generate warrior saints.

The mentor and president of the Waller Street Ashram is Sat Santokh Singh. If, like a tree, you could slice his trunk and count his rings, you would have a calendar of many of the movements which idealistic, disaffected, American young people have supported over the last twenty years or so. He was born a Jewish boy in New York, studied Nuclear Engineering and changed to Philosophy in the hope of help with the pressing question 'What is the Good?' He left philosophy unhelped. In the early sixties he was active in the Peace Movement and the movements for Civil Rights. When psychedelics rather than politics seemed the way ahead, he experimented with drugs and found himself working alongside one of the most famous Rock and Roll Bands of the time. His aim, as he sees it, was to be a frontiersman. His difficulty was to find a frontier. The turning point seems to have come when he stopped seeking and allowed himself to be sought. He had enjoyed all he wanted to enjoy, and had done all he wanted to do, and knew there was no way forward without a spiritual discipline and a teacher. He met his teacher, yogi Bhajan Ji, at a gathering a few months later in New Mexico. Yogi Bhajan is a Sikh and a teacher of yoga. Sat Santokh began with yoga (this was in 1970). In 1971 he became a full Sikh minister. When we met, he was also a teacher of yoga. Now his beard bristles, his white turban comes well down on his brow; he carries a small comb, the bracelet and the token sword, and wears the garments that mark him out a Sikh. Of his past he would seem to have made a clean, white sweep.

Sat Santokh is clear about the appeal of Sikhism for someone of his temperament. Sikhism began as a movement to unite East and West, to bring together, in the first place, Muslims and Hindus in India five centuries ago and by implication to override all sectarian barriers. Three members of the Waller Street Ashram sat on the floor and sang to a guitar after a yoga class. The drift of their song was:

It doesn't really matter what colour you are—
A tree and then a stream and the brightest star—
Because we all come from one Creator . . .
It doesn't really matter to what religion you belong,
How short your hair is or even how long,
Because . . .
It doesn't really matter how you call his name,
Allah, Jehovah, Sat Nam—it's all the same.
Because . . .

It doesn't matter if you love me or if you hate me—
  that's fine.
God's love is infinite and it surrounds us all the time.
Because . . .

As well as the Sikh message, there is the Sikh discipline.
This is not that of the Christians or the Muslims or the
Buddhists. The song does not say: 'It doesn't really matter
if you practise or not . . .' for the Sikhs of Waller Street have
a strong shape to their day. By 4.30 a.m. they are expected
to have shaken off dull sloth and readied themselves for
work. From 4.30 to 7 a.m. they do their first practice: yoga,
prayers, chanting, breathing. After breakfast they go out to
their other practice—work. It is a Sikh obligation to make
ends meet by their own hard labour, not to withdraw from
the world, to be a household, to have children, to share what
they have with others. There were about fifteen Waller
Street Sikhs when I met them. They were running a house-
painting firm. Some taught yoga. Of the four invitations
that came my way for a Hallowe'en party, one came from
Waller Street.

Once, when Sat Santokh went home to New York, his
grandfather asked him why he needed to become a Sikh,
why he could not stay with the Judaism he was born to. His
answer was that among the Jews he had not met a teacher.
His grandfather discounted such an argument. Judaism is
rich in teachers. But not, said Sat Santokh, for *me*. Quite
why Eastern religions and Eastern disciplines have such an
appeal in parts of the West was a recurrent question on the
California journey. Is it easier to shed your old identity if
your new identity has travelled a long way to meet you? Or
is one area of the globe more productive of sublime ideas
than another and do we happen to have been born in the
wrong area? It seems unlikely. Theodore Roszak's view is
that, though the West is as rich in its spiritual traditions as

256

anywhere, what most Westerners know of them is an impoverishment: a matter of church on Sundays, certain ethical notions and a requirement to *believe* in a series of credal propositions that may once have had life in them but seem to have life no longer. What is the place of experience? The Buddha marked out the action-field for the climb to Buddhahood as the 'fathom length of your own body'. The Everest peaks of the religious classics of India speak of a state in which the little self opens itself up to the Bigger Self and knows (not just believes, but *knows*) that the two Selves are identical. Time spent in the West defending claims to be carrying the whole of the Truth is time lost to the spiritual work, practice and experience of trying to find out who I am. God is what he is. Who then am I? This is the great Californialand question.

Certainly I am a myriad more processes and potentialities than I know myself to be. Some of them show up on the dials and in the sound signals of biofeedback machinery. Dr Kenneth Pelletier spent his early years training in medical school to diagnose and calibrate illnesses and is now interested to diagnose and calibrate health, if such is at all a possibility and as far as electronic instruments will take him. His own path took him first to Zen meditation and now he works with various Tibetan techniques. He does not overrate what his biofeedback machinery can do. Nor does he underrate it.

Seen from one point of view 'biofeedback' is happening to us all the time without machinery. Usually, for instance, when we blush, we know we are blushing. But there are other reactions that are less obvious: variations in body waves, skin and muscle tension. Each produces a measurable amount of electricity and all of them tell a story. The machinery, by taking these measurements, allows us to observe in ourselves what would otherwise be hidden. It is not a treatment or a medicine; it does not in any way change your situation. It reflects your situation and, from there, by paying attention, you can perhaps help yourself. It is the electronic equivalent of that friend to whom you turn when you see someone who twitches or sniffles or grinds his teeth, and say: 'If you ever notice me doing that, please tell me'. The machine tells you and has been used to help patients with a great variety of problems: insomnia, heart disease, hypertension, migraine. Since it can also trace the journey of the brain from its usual state of agitation (beta waves) to a state of meditative alertness (alpha waves), to a state in which the brain seems able to hold one image still and direct the attention to different parts of it without losing grip on the whole (theta waves), biofeedback has been called 'electric zen', and the sound emitted by the machinery as the mind starts its descent an 'electronic mantra'. Kenneth Pelletier is wide awake to the moment at which claims for the machinery must stop and further work needs teaching or rather, he went on to say, a teacher.

As he hesitated after 'teaching', and I repeated the word and hesitated myself, and he, with the smile of one who had not intended to be quite so specific, changed the word to 'teacher', he more or less invited a discussion I more and more needed. Do you need a teacher if you are to venture into the areas where the instruments do not follow you? By teacher, I mean a person living now and standing by as surely as a swimming teacher stands by with the learner's chin resting on his hand, knowing when to move into deep water, when to take his own feet off the bottom, when to let go. There are some words by one of the Orthodox fathers to the effect that anyone who has no teacher must search for one 'in tears' till the right one is found. And, from a Hindu source, I think, comes the thought that, when the pupil is ready, the teacher appears. All very unsettling when you have been brought up in a Protestant tradition that preaches individuality, individual responsibility, a closer walk with

God, with Bible reading to light the way, but no guru.

My question to Kenneth Pelletier was: 'Do you need a teacher?' His first answer was: 'I think perhaps at a certain stage of meditation, you do.' Knowing I had, as far as I know, no one teacher and recalling the Orthodox words about tears and searching, I pushed the conversation over the bump and on. But very soon Kenneth Pelletier brought it back again, to great effect. He quoted a cardiologist from India whom he had heard speak of the general misunderstanding of gurudom. It is not, he had said, a title bestowed once and for ever. It is a temporary ascription. Whenever a person wakes up to a higher aspect of himself, the guru is present and the wakener, the guru, may be another person, a thing, an experience, a sickness, a jolt, any one or any thing that comes with a reminder that, puffed up as we already are, there is more to us than we know: and that knowing it, we will gain our proper modest size.

Gay Gaer Luce, like Kenneth Pelletier, owes much to the arrival in California of the waves of Tibetan Buddhists. Like him, she works to augment health rather than to patch up the ravages of sickness. Like the Sikhs, though no Sikh herself, she identifies what is healthy with what is holy. 'I think,' she says, 'there is no such thing as health without some spiritual development.' And, taking as one what most of the rest of the world take to be two and separate, she sets herself to work. She ran, when I met her, a number of groups under the label 'Sage': older people who choose to disbelieve what the prevailing culture tells them—that to be old is to be finished—and lay themselves open to the next new beginning, whatever it happens to be. At the start of a 'Sage' weekly meeting a group of about fifteen people, including Gay Luce and one or two helpers, 'occupied' their rented room. It was in a Berkeley hotel, was large and faceless and belonged to no one.

Within ten or so minutes it was hung around with merry

wall-drapes and a small gallery-ful of energetic 'two-minute paintings'. These, done by another Sage group on large drawing sheets, represent what members could achieve in two minutes with colour, paint-brush and a little fearlessness. The rest of the afternoon unfolded in this transfigured room. We stood in a circle and held hands. With no forward planning that I could see, a few locked hands began to rock backwards and forwards. Soon the whole circle was swinging its arms forward and back, a little further and for a little longer and to more bracing effect than anyone might have anticipated. Loosened and, even for those who had met before, newly acquainted, we sat on cushions on the floor and tried palming—rubbing the palms of the hands vigorously together till they felt raw and warm, then bowing the head to cup the palms over the eyes. After each exercise, anyone who saw a reason to comment, ask a question or even lodge a complaint, did so. We tried a long walking meditation, a deliberate deceleration of everything that is conditioned to thunder forward to its destination, head in the future, feet in the past, middle off-balance and nowhere. We sat in pairs and massaged each other's tight shoulders, tense necks, curvaceous backs. Two women, kindly but firmly, silenced a retired doctor who had plans for the group that not all the group liked but had so far lacked the courage to say so.

Without too much labelling, Gay Luce takes her games from any likely source—the meditations from the religious traditions, the argumentation from the rationalist, post-Protestant air we breath, and some of the escapades from her own research into the needs and fears of children. Her earliest work was with the young. She then discovered that the snarl-ups of childhood did not suddenly dissolve with growing up, and that exactly the same fears haunted the elderly—fear of being taken over, fear of being left alone, fear of trying and failing, fear of not being allowed to try and, more urgently in the elderly though doubtless the root of much evil throughout the whole of a life-span, fear of dying. The Sage groups talk about dying, says Gay Luce, 'a lot. It is a subject that's not too far away.' How, I asked her, would you help someone in mortal terror? It would not, she thought, be in the shape of a piece of advice, as it might be a pill, that would work on the organism without help from the patient. It might be in a form of some meditation. All our lives we are schooled in the terror of dying as if death were some unthinkable obscenity that should not be there, whereas dying is wholly a part of living. The end of each meeting, each journey, each time-span, each step, each breath and the start of the next has been through the process of dying. Once anyone starts to 'experience' himself or herself in this way—as living and dying moment by moment—the one great death may not be so great or so dead or so lonely. May not.

A day or two later I met one of the members of Sage by chance in the street. He was not sure, he thought, when the time came, whether he would be able to resist medicines and pills and go in for his dying in the full-blooded way that Sage sometimes talked of it; or whether he might skulk and be medicated and quake with the rest. But the truly remarkable thing to me is that we should be standing in a street in Berkeley and having that particular conversation at all: treating death as a matter with options—death resisted, death denied, death experienced, death accepted, death as a life-fact in a safe universe. He recommended to me a book on the powers of the mind, picked up his shopping bag and took his spry leave.

If death shall have no dominion, there would seem no reason to put up with the imposture of many other less awesome tyrants—such as the garage mechanic, the chain store operator, the battery-chick farmer, the whole breed of interveners who flourish in a society which specializes in specialists and in which the rest of the population seem to have surrendered so many of their powers. The spiritual dimension of do-it-yourself has rarely, as far as I know, been explored and the majority of those who do it themselves may well do so to save money rather than to gain merit. But a few do it themselves with a sense of mission, an alertness to the possible consequences for their own health and that of society generally.

The young man who ran the Briar Patch Co-operative Auto Shop refused to be drawn on spirituality. He gave statistics. The shop was opened in spring 1973 in Palo Alto, and seventeen hundred people bring their cars there for servicing. Twenty per cent of them come in and mend their own cars, either unaided or with the help of one of the mechanics. The rest accept servicing as they would from a normal garage, but, since all the members are stockholders, they are expected to attend the Annual General Meeting of the company, and they may even find themselves being elected directors. Not everyone may wish to enmesh himself to that extent in the welfare of his car, but if, as one Briar Patch member put it, 'cars stand at the neurosis-point of American society', the point at which self-determination ends and the otherness of machinery takes over, then the Briar Patch Auto Shop may be one small way of pushing the take-over point further out, and winning a fraction more space to manoeuvre in.

The mysteries of wholesale and retail are likewise pierced at the Briar Patch Co-operative Market, Inc. A family joins for ten dollars and pays not less than five dollars a month until a hundred dollars have been invested. There is a direct charge of fifty cents a week to cover running costs. Each family member over eighteen years of age has to put in four hours' work every six weeks—stocking the shelves, cleaning, manning the membership desk, working the till, though during the time I was there members leaving the store with their shopping mostly totted up their own items and worked the till themselves. After a day's take, it is usual to find a small margin of overpaying—anxiety not to underpay and cheat themselves perhaps. The food is sold at cost with one or two per cent added for spoilage. Small committees choose which brands of goods their store shall stock. They go for quality, cheapness, considerations of ecology and limit the choice to one or two, thus cutting out ad-man frenzy. For both the Auto Shop and the Grocery Store there is felt to be a right size—big enough to keep itself afloat and give the right service, small enough to feel like an organism and not an assembly line. The Grocery Store had settled at about a membership of five hundred and fifty households. Another store then opened to take in the surplus and, as interest has grown, a third is planned.

The Briar Patch question is: How do you live, with some degree of dignity and joy, in the nooks and crannies of a society in which such considerations are not priorities? But there are more radical and more Taoist questions, such as: How do you live, with some degree of dignity and joy, when the cities and the drains collapse, the milkman no longer brings the milk, the petrol pump coughs up its last drop of juice and dies? And further, even more radical and Taoist questions such as: Is it possible that dignity, joy, health and spiritual growth may actually increase if central government crumbles a bit, central services slacken, central efficiency goes off in a spasm of yawns? This is not a question to address to the great cities—London, Tokyo, Chicago, New York—for their high scaffolding supports millions of wobbling people and the answer to anyone who preached the shaking of the foundations could only be one of panic and rage. But it produces a warm glow in a sunny climate, where there is a stretch of earth to take the seedlings, a back garden to house a goat, and emergency support systems for the experiment that goes wrong.

That is, on reflection, a truly Puritan trick: to suggest, because California is wealthy, free-wheeling, blessed with a good climate and a quantity of citizens who seem to enjoy themselves, that their Californialand experiments in ecology are somehow suspect, playful, of no direct use to those of us who are elsewhere and not smiling. I will start again. California, with its wealth, its climate, its acres of land and a serious concern among a section of its population for matters of wholesomeness and health, is the natural site for experiments in simpler living, better relations with the earth, wiser use of available resources.

In the early seventies, citizens of Palo Alto launched a scheme called Ecology Action. It started modestly with the recycling of glass and metal, and continued modestly with allotments, bee-keeping, goat-keeping, the spread, through the Ecology Action Community Centre, of ecologically sound advice. Yet if, with bio-dynamic/French intensive gardening methods, it can be shown that a family can grow its own vegetables in a twentieth the space that is commonly used, Ecology Action may turn out to be building Noah's Ark.

There is a house in Berkeley, alongside a railway track and singled out from its neighbours by the vigour and spruceness of its vegetables. It is run by the Farallones Institute, an educational and research organization begun in 1974 to look into 'environmentally sound' building and design, 'low technology' solutions to energy problems, the use and re-use of all resources. A swarm of schoolchildren were shown a glassed-in section of a hive of bees, simple structures to trap and use the heat of the sun, devices to receive and recycle human waste and feed it back fresh to the garden.

Out at Occidental the Farallones Institute has its country quarters, an acreage of garden and a small experimental settlement of thrifty new-age house designs. A duty guide showed us round, answered questions, stuck to his brief—ecology, solar energy, gardening methods—a display of low flying, no aerobatics, no hint that growing plants and conserving the sun may be as consciously 'religious' as going on pilgrimage or sitting and counting your breaths. To all appearances he was selling certain techniques; and perhaps he had found that his down-to-earth audiences listened best when he talked of the energy crisis, the exhaustion of the planet, the bleak prospect before us. But I do not believe that, for instance, that particular boy was digging his garden just out of fear for his future. His past would not suggest it. He had stopped being a law student, had lived in a Tibetan Buddhist Community, now practised za-zen. If, as Zen Master Yamada Mumon had instructed in Japan, sitting in Zen leads you to know that 'the flower is I and the moon is I', then rearing a plant and tending the earth can become self-cultivation. This may not be appropriate matter for a Farallones report on ecology. But then, I ask myself, why not?

Up in the forest beyond Sacramento, Gary Snyder, beat poet, original Dharma bum, has built himself a house, part Japanese farmhouse, part wigwam, in which to settle down. The end of the road, like the end of that other road, the *Tao Te Ching*, is a place where 'the next place might be so near at hand that one could hear the cocks crowing in it, the dogs barking; but the people would grow old and die without ever having been there'. He moved there in 1970. He is not, as far as I could tell, there to prove anything: that you can support a family on so many acres; that friends seen across a log fire through smoke that curls up and out through a hole in the roof look better than when they are clutching their sinuses in the desiccated air of a centrally-heated urban rabbit-hutch; that children grow straighter in the neighbourhood of ponderosa pine. 'We are not doing this,' he said, 'to survive. We are doing it because it's beautiful.'

Further back down the road he studied Amerindian oral literature, Far Eastern Languages and Forestry. He spent six years in a Zen monastery in Japan. His wife is Japanese. There is a photograph of his Japanese Zen master on a small house altar on which, at the time I saw it, was a small stone and a bird's feather. The altar, he explained, is the place for things you want to keep and can't think how to store. His intention, now, is to stay put.

'There are things you learn by staying in one place,' he said, 'that you can learn no other way.' 'Like what,' I asked? 'Like that tree,' (he was chopping wood at the time with great swings of a hefty axe and I was sitting alongside avoiding the chips). 'Like that tree as a person, as an individual.' He singled out a tree that to a day-tripper like myself seemed like any other tree. 'I can identify it as ponderosa pine as all these other trees are ponderosa pine.' (The sweep of an arm took in a dark surround of pine trunks.) 'That is to know it as species. But, if you stay in one place, you can come to see each tree, each rock, each wild flower as an individual entity. You can't do that by travelling through a landscape.' About three hundred feet north of the wooden house was a tree scarred by a lightning burn. 'I stayed still long enough for lightning to come to me.'

If Gary Snyder has a lesson to teach (and it is certainly not delivered with any sort of didactic frenzy) it would seem to be the primacy of learning as a style of living, learning from everything: the insect community near his house, American Indian skill in collaborating with the forest, a system of home-made hydraulics to pump up and ferry a water supply, a part-time job as Chairman of Governor Jerry Brown's Arts Council, local community politics, Zen solutions to one or two tough riddles, books used as a sensible man's tool kit, the children, the children's cat, the neighbours. It is not quite a political platform, or a religious stance, or a piece of exemplary social engineering. But somewhere—in, around and through it—there feels to be the shadow of a possibility: the possibility of living healthily in a tribe, without too much direction from far-off, generalizing and ignorant central governments, and without mercantile manipulation. Once those forests housed a population of people that lived in a rough balance with a population of plants, a population of plants that lived in a rough balance with a population of insects and animals. The needs of any one did not throttle the others. But as grey squirrels come after red, so do grey people, and they turn out to be better predators than either plants or animals, not just in the forests of California but universally. If Christ is with us, as on God's promise He is said to be, or if the Buddha looks round the world with his Eye of Compassion, the world that Christ lives in and that the Buddha sees is a world out of balance, off its rocker. Perhaps irretrievably so.

These and related matters were chewed over in a campfire conversation with Gary Snyder and with one of his near neighbours—Raymond Dassmann, a scientist who used to work for the United Nations. 'Future Primitive' is a phrase not invented but used by Raymond Dassmann to describe, as he sees it, a coming necessity. As the Earth's resources shrink and its population explodes, there must be some check on human grandiosity. If disaster comes, the check will come, willy-nilly, from outside. If wisdom comes to even the smallest degree, the check may come from inside and may turn aside disaster. 'Future Primitive' means not a return to cave-man technology (bows and arrows, and buffalo etched on the ceiling) but the restoration, with all the know-how at our finger-tips, of some of the ecological balance that spells out health, survival, herding our power, knowing our place.

'There is a phrase,' said Gary Snyder, 'current in the occidental world—"self-interest". The component of that which is not thought out so closely is "What is the self?" If you define your "self" in the smallest possible way, your "self"-interest is just for today. If you define your "self" just to include your family, your children, then your "self"-interest goes one generation ahead. If you define your "self" to mean human beings, your "self"-interest embraces a thousand years. If you say mammals, vertebrates, multicellular creatures, entities with existence, you embrace the cosmos.'

You pick up the highway not very far from Gary Snyder's forest community. To the enormous satisfaction of all of us who like to move from one place to another fast, it elbows the forest to one side and carries a multiplicity of carriageways to and from Sacramento, to and from San Francisco. In the car park of a hotel in Sacramento styled to recall The Wild West, is a plaque which reads: 'The Ladies of the Evening. To commemorate that ubiquitous segment of society who have been unacknowledged; who, though obscure, made an essential contribution to the settlement of the West.' There is the West. There is the myth of how the West was won. There is the other myth of how the West was lost, when the Indians were tricked and defeated, the buffalo decimated, the forest plundered.

By 'myth' I do not mean 'lie'; but rather one of the masks that are used by the Truth when it condescends to sit down in a chair and have its portrait painted. The whole Truth never sits down. If I were Tarzan, I would swing through the trees and meet Jane. If I were a gypsy I would wrap a hedgehog in clay and roast it in a wood fire. If I were the Mahatma Gandhi, I would so confine my intake of food to the fresh, the vegetable and the unvinous that my predator teeth would lose their cunning. But I am none of those and am woefully compromised. Somewhere on the tarmac or in the air is the plane that will ferry me back to London, scattering caustic waste into the cloud banks. I am not proposing to walk from Sacramento to San Francisco either.

As I flick the switch before sitting down to pen these pieties, I expect the light to come on. As I pull the lavatory chain, I expect the water flow to remove the waste. And it has not slipped my mind that the subsidy on which I circumnavigate the globe comes from a television company. If I snarled into the camera lens, 'Switch off your machinery, viewers. Don't look at me. You don't know me. You don't know whether I mean what I say; whether I've been where I say I've been. And, even if I am all you think I am, what can that matter to you? For you are not present to me.'—if I said just that, then looked and said no more, I should be recalled home in disgrace, if not strapped to my seat and sedated. Who pulls the strings when I dance? Could I ever (this is the great puppet myth) chew through the strings and break free? If I did, would I fold up—or stand up and walk?

The journey to San Francisco turned bitter to the taste with a bitterness not of wormwood and herb-o'-grace but with the bitterness of foul breath and a slow puncture. I was tired of holiness, holistics, health, the small self, the big self, the Long Search, the Thin Search, changing planes, pretending this or that might be 'where it's at', when I had a decreasing grip on 'where I was at'. I know that Theodore Roszak, Kenneth Pelletier, Gay Luce and Sage do not rush; nor the Sikhs nor Gary Snyder nor Ecology Action. They rather conspicuously stay where they are. But I was rushing when I saw them and, as can happen when two trains are side by side and one moves and there is a moment when it is not clear whether we or they are standing still, one or other of us is *certainly* moving and it may as well be they.

With thoughts like these scraping across the spirit in time to the windscreen wipers, I was taken on a rainy night to meet Jacob Needleman. We sat in a deserted Japanese restaurant where we had the alternatives of sitting on our legs, feeling Japanese and getting cramp, or trailing our legs in an under-table pit and accepting defeat. We talked about

Californialand—for he was the one who had called it 'a state of confusion, mixed with a raw hunger for transcendence'— and there was no doubt a fair amount of high level discourse. (He is, for sure, Professor of Philosophy at San Francisco State University, wrote *The New Religions* and *A Sense of Cosmos*, edited and contributed to compilations called *Sacred Tradition and Present Need* and *On the Way to Self Knowledge*, is general editor of the Penguin Metaphysical Library, was poised, when we met, to direct a 'Program for the Study of New Religious Movements in America' at the Graduate Theological Union in Berkeley.) But my gratitude is not to the professor, the pundit, the one who knew, but to the man who sat opposite me, let his doubts chase each other across his face, broke into sudden smiles and sudden waves of sweat and DID NOT KNOW, simply DID NOT KNOW. And what is more, he KNEW THAT HE DID NOT KNOW. If I was some sort of mole scrabbling my way through submerged territory I could not see and could not predict from, meeting him was like bursting into another gallery where another mole, better informed no doubt, with more general muscle and longer claws, was scrabbling too. If, when I had burst into his gallery, he had been sitting there facing me, cross-legged and serene, ready to answer my questions, I think I should have ducked back to my own gallery preferring mud in the mouth to a discourse on digging. The real spiritual guide, he was to say at a later meeting, does not answer questions or offer solutions; he takes the questions and deepens them; he deepens the search. In other words, the guide must be digging too.

Not to know the answer was a nightmare in school and the answer came after the question, bringing with it, on a good day, self-esteem and a pat on the head from the teacher. And must I now accept that there are some questions that do not have those sorts of answers? And, what is more, that the questions that do not have answers are the only questions that are finally worth asking? How can teacher ever be pleased if no one produces the answer? Might it not lead to despair? A battlement of fearful conditioning has to be broken down before these become thinkable thoughts. The religious establishments of the world have not grown plump preaching that they do not have the answer; though ironically, it seems to have been the religious traditions that, somewhere inside them, have carried these unanswered questions and kept them unanswered. When is a human being most alive? When he is hugging an answer or asking a question? That is the question.

Jacob Needleman, as far as I heard him, never spoke ill of a search or a searcher. The once I saw him nearly angry was at the story I told of a Hindu teacher by the side of the Ganges whose general advice to the Western young who came to see him was: Go home; look for the truth in your own tradition. The guru himself had gone home. He had been a professor in the engineering department of an American University. 'Gurus,' said Needleman, 'are too quick to reject and decide.' How does he know what they need till he knows them? How can they look till they know what they need? The moment to come thundering down on somebody's hopes, if anyone has the penetration of spirit to do so safely and know what he is doing, is when the searching stops, an answer is produced and a new religion sets up shop.

The puzzle that seemed to have Jacob Needleman and me firmly in its grip whenever we met, was how endlessly puzzled we were. I had been looking at, and he lived among, taught, had written a book about, people very like ourselves who know they are not all they could be, want to see changes but cannot see quite how to get them to happen. Religion, by definition, comes from a source that none of us ever created. If the aim of religion is to create a new mind (I said 'if'), no mind can create a religion. The best that a mind seems able to do is to gather a few insights, collect a few fragments, give them a name, call them holistic and sniff them. In their own day and using different fragments the Children of Israel raked up their earrings and tried to make a religion—solid, well-made, satisfactory, something to lean against, something to pray to, something that did not talk back. But the Golden Calf was the ultimate blasphemy, not just somewhat less satisfactory than God, but an utter denial of God, a scandalous parody, an idol.

So where do we run? To the temples and churches? But they proffer answers as solid as gold. To make something new? But it seems to be not in our power to 'make'. Do we stay as we are? Perhaps we do. But then, how do we change? A long silence follows, me down my mole-hole, Needleman down his mole-hole, you, perhaps, down yours. If you don't break the silence, I shan't.

How Needleman put it was this: 'In other words, it's in weakness there's strength. If we can stay weak and keep open, keep moving around and come to the point where we just give up and know that what we are doing, where we are going is hopeless, really hopeless, and not grab on to something else and try to build a structure out of it, then we reach a state which in the traditions of the West is called Despair. Another word for Despair in this sense is Deep Openness. When you're in Despair, when you come to the end of the rope, only then can help come.' Talk of Despair and the ends of ropes can sound a bit alarming, and perhaps there are other less desolate wordages. But it should be possible, between being born once and being born a second time, to think of a rope as a life-line.

And if, when I return to California, I find that Jacob Needleman has 'grabbed on to something else', and 'tried to build a structure' or started to climb up his rope, it will not alter the fact that at a certain moment, when I needed one, he stood in as my guru.

13

Loose Ends

Those who wished to be friendly, wished to acknowledge that I had been away somewhere but needed to make quite clear that they thought the whole *Long Search* endeavour a trifle quaint, used to ask me, 'Well, did you find it?' If I had said, 'Yes', and thrown them back against the wall with a blast of high-voltage evangelism, they would no doubt have fought me off, but at least they would have gone away thinking that the search had been successful. But to return not noticeably changed, and without having cast a vote for one or other of the candidates for the Best Religion of the Age Award, seemed to indicate failure. For those who think along these dramatic lines, I am happy to let it be thought that we failed. For any who are still as puzzled and engaged as I am, there are just one or two things I feel I can say.

No doubt the noisiest and best-aired onslaughts on religion have been from those who attack it from outside. They have first to decide what they think it is—which is no mean feat—and then they can set to. Religion, in its time, has been attacked as an enemy of the people, an enemy of the ruling classes, an excuse for repressive policies, an incitement to revolt, an opiate and a dangerous stimulant. Its enemies, if they were to set out their trenches to coincide with their opinions, could happily shoot each other down in a war in which supposedly they are fighting on the same side. But the attacks on religion from motley outsiders are mere scattered fire compared with the deadly accuracy, effectiveness and persistence of attacks from within. It is these which, as far as I can see, foil all attempts to say that all the religions and all the religious are for ever and ever this or that.

The voice of the teacher of religion who attacks the complacency of religion, its tendency to ossify, to turn up with the answer, has a venerable history. There may be earlier such accounts, but one of the ancient Hindu Vedas tells ironically of the boy, aged twenty-four, fresh from seminary and his pious teachers, 'greatly conceited, thinking himself well-read, arrogant', who returns to his father knowing the answers and finds himself suddenly facing the questions: 'Since you are now so greatly conceited, think yourself well-read and arrogant, did you ask for that instruction by which the unhearable becomes heard, the unperceivable becomes perceived, the unknowable becomes known?' 'How, Venerable Sir, can there be such teaching?' And once again he is learning. Among more recent and conspicuous enemies of religion would seem to be Jesus Christ, who hammered away at the pious of His own tradition: 'But woe unto you, scribes and Pharisees, hypocrites! for ye shut up the Kingdom of Heaven against men; for ye neither go in yourselves, neither suffer ye them that are entering to go in.' (St Matthew 23); the Buddha, whose teaching roused the Brahmins; the Prophet Muhammad, whose clean sweep of the idols in the Ka'aba no doubt offended the religious susceptibilities of those who went there for support; the hymnodist Kabir, who mocked the pieties of both Hindus and Muslims: 'There is nothing but water at the holy bathing places; and I know that they are useless for I have bathed in them . . . If God be within the mosque, then to whom does this world belong?'

In the course of *The Long Search* I met figures who spoke to the same effect. Brother Guy in Leeds sympathized with the anger if not with the action of one who daubed in tar on the wall of a fine new cathedral the words 'Christ was born in a stable'. Yamada Mumon-roshi in Japan quoted from a Zen source: 'If you meet the Buddha in the road, kill him'.

Bishop Justinian in Romania wrote: 'The Christians made a great mistake when they transformed Jesus into a religion'. The Venerable Anandamaitreya in Sri Lanka was one of many who compared Buddhism with a raft ('Use it to cross the river. Once over, do not carry it on your back') or a thorn ('Self is a thorn in the flesh. Buddhism is another thorn with which to dig it out. When the self is out, throw both thorns away'). The history of the great idol-smashers is that they have been universally idolized. Yet their first word seems to have been one of radical criticism. And, whenever a religion needs to slough a skin, renew itself, an appeal appears possible, within the tradition itself, to an idol-dissolving source.

When, as often happened, someone suggested that all the Great Religions say the same thing, I have never known how to respond. (Perhaps all the Great Religions say the same thing in the sense that all mountaineers climb mountains. But that does not mean that all the ascents are the same, though it is perfectly true that all ascents are about going up.) I should feel on safer ground with the suggestion that all the Great Religions *attack* the same thing, though they seem to go about it in a medley of ways.

The mountaineering parallel, once set up, recurred again and again on the making of *The Long Search*. It seemed to help me to see unity where unity existed, variety where variety existed, and to respect even when I could not quite follow. One of the last pieces of celluloid to be tacked in place at the end of three years was a series of alarming shots of a climber turning a hazardous bend on a high mountain, sometimes clinging, sometimes swinging out into space. Against the pictures came these words: 'Perhaps each of what we call "the religious traditions" offers, among other things, a climbing kit. The kit won't be the same because the climbing hazards won't be the same. It doesn't quite make sense to worship your axe and your ropes and your irons, though it's hard to imagine getting very far without them. The climb occupies all your energy, all your will, all your skill. And the very idea of leaning across and shouting abuse to another climber—whether you have in mind a religion or mountains—seems to me contemptible and dangerous and silly. Somewhere on the rock-face too there may be a hint of an answer to the question: "Which religion is best?" Which would be parallel to the question: "Which mountaineering kit is best?" A mountaineer would presumably answer: "Show me your mountain and I'll show you your kit." '

When the last image of the last midget climber had shrunk to the size of a tackle-draped fly on a slippery wall and the mountain had faded, I appeared alone in a room with which I was quite familiar, though now I scarcely recognized it. Two powerful lamps hit out from one corner, a microphone gleamed on a chrome mounting, a cameraman took a light-reading somewhere above my right eyebrow, a director's patient assistant, index-finger on button of stop-watch, looked up and said, 'Have you a comb? Your hair's sticking up,' and facing the lens that throughout had stood in for an absent audience I aped solitude and said (and meant): 'Heady stuff, this. Though having climbed so far, I may as well continue. I have a feeling that, if all the impressive people I've met all over the world were ushered into this room, there would be respect and harmony between them. And probably silence. Of course, I dare say I could fill it a hundred times over with other people— whom their enemies call bigots. The noise of the argument would be deafening and they'd probably end up machine-gunning each other. But I have an idea, amounting to a certainty, that the silence of the small group would eventually drown the noise of the large one.'

But the substance of *The Long Search* is whatever is there when the camera, the lamps, the support system have gone, when it is inappropriate to make public pronouncements for no one is listening. That line of Blaise Pascal which roosted with me twenty years ago has never gone away: 'I have often said that the sole cause of man's unhappiness is that he does not know how to stay quietly in his room.' Well, here I am—in my room. Now what happens?

I do not wish to make the whole of *The Long Search* seem to be a journey towards Jacob Needleman in San Francisco (for who knows what nonsense he may be up to when he is not talking enormous sense to me?), but it so happens that we had one day a long conversation during which we did seem to be pushing at something quite sharp and nervy. I had asked him a question about change. If, as seems the case, we are under constant pressure from Teachers and Teachings to change, to be born again, to realize our Buddha-nature, to be made alive in Christ, to crack the small self and understand our identity with the large Self, what is the first step to take, the basic beginner's move? At first we sparred. 'In order to have any kind of exchange on this subject,' he said, 'I'd want to know from you what you hit against in life, what makes you want to change. Just change for the sake of change? No. You want to be happy? It's not that really. There are many things being offered to make you happy in some sense. In response to your question, I think the first step I feel being urged on me by the Great Teachings is to look into myself and see what it is about myself that I wish to understand; to look, to observe, to study myself as an unknown entity, something that I have never seen before. Now this is the step that is missing very often in religions both old and new. They start a little too high. They start with us as though we already know what we want, as though we're ready to make our commitments. But we are not. We are much below that. A real practical mysticism that could really work change would, I feel, have to start with the work of studying myself as I am. That is the rung of the ladder that is left out.' Still on the level of creeds and commitments, I persisted: 'What should I do? Should I sit? What's the action?' To which he answered: 'Could you do it now, now while we are talking?' 'Why not?' I, countered, still talking but the words dribbling away: 'I mean, if there is some technique . . .' He broke in sharply: 'I am not asking you *off* camera. I am asking you *on* camera. Now. As I am talking to you. Could you do it? Could you see what you are—now?' 'You mean to say,' I shifted, 'it's not just a technical matter?' 'It's not a technical matter. It's not a question of sitting in a lotus posture or being in church or having a guru. There is something right now preventing us from knowing who we are.'

At this point in the filming the camera ran out of film, and from being who we are talking about who we are, we became who we are waiting for the magazine to be reloaded and clicked against the camera lens. We began again with what seemed like the same question: 'Let's say that somebody says to you, "Fine. I understand that change and growth has to be gradual, in one cell, one person at a time. But what do I have to do to set about making myself available for change?" What would you say to that person?' He hesitated. 'I am not going to answer you the way I did before because that was before and I don't feel the same thing in your question.' (Pause.) 'To be available for change, you have to make room, I think. This is what you get if you read or approach the Great Teachings in a state of need rather than a state of curiosity. In a state of need you are not just interested in getting information; you are willing to set something aside, to give something up. Nothing cliché here. It is not the sacrifice of your home or your family or anything like that. But, if you ask that question of, let's call them the "Great Teachings", whatever they are, they may answer you: "What are you willing to give up for it? What are you willing to pay for this change?"

And then you are on the spot because you see that you don't have anything to give up maybe.

'That question, when it comes back to you, is a measure of your sincerity. It's a measure of your seriousness. And perhaps you see that you are not all that serious: "I just wanted to know what you were thinking, Buddha. I didn't want you actually to do anything to me." And the Buddha will say, perhaps, "Well, all right. That's fine. Goodbye." So the question that comes back to us is: "How serious are you? What do you really want?" Now can we answer that?' At this moment I still wanted in some sense to volunteer, to claim seriousness, to say I *do* know what I want, really want, for the language of not knowing is painful. But Needleman left no space. 'Can we answer that? I think we cannot. I think we are left speechless with that. Now—can a Teaching exist and speak to us in that state of total speechlessness where we are not exactly just curious, nor do we know what we want?' Here he did leave a gap but I had no impulse to try and fill it. 'What I think we come back to if we ask your question [which was, you remember, What do I have to do to change?] is "Who are you?" "Who's asking?" The moment that *that* question is asked, you get into a real relationship with the Teaching, because you see your lack. You have a need (even if it is not the need you thought you had, which was for the Great Truth), you have a need to be in contact with yourself at this moment, and you see that you haven't been in contact with yourself. At that point you are in a real relationship because you are empty, not in contact, wish to be in contact, wish to be more situated in yourself, wish to have what they call Presence, Being. You wish to *be*. In *that* state you can hear the language, hear the symbols, feel the presence of the Teacher in a very different way from when you started. And I think, you know, it's along these lines that real exchange takes place; not with giving creeds, giving doctrines, giving pamphlets. There is not enough time in life to read pamphlets. You have to have the relationship with the Teacher ... and the Teaching.'

It is now a year since I walked into my kitchen for the last shot of the last *Long Search* film and made a pot of tea which no one drank, for the verities of filming rather than the verities of tea-making mean that the same shot has to be repeated again and again till it looks as though it has never been done before. It is a year since I said, more than once, 'It's pretty easy to put a title like *Loose Ends* at the start of the last film of a long series. It's not so easy an hour later to come to those ends and leave them loose when your fingers and everybody else's fingers are itching to see them tied into a neat bow.' The films themselves were tied into a neat bow and can be spun backwards and forwards, looped on an editing machine, so that Jacob Needleman, Linda Wu, Bishop Justinian, Peter Mkize, the Pope, Yamada Mumon-roshi, Dr. Zahira Abdin and I hop up and down stairs, through doors, along corridors with the purposeful agility of crazed acrobats; and, played at high speed, our voices and our bits of wisdom have the stridency of the chatter of chipmunks. We were once there doing it. Now we are here watching it. And when we have stopped watching it we shall still be here, though by that time 'here' may well be somewhere else.

The Long Search has radically rearranged my ignorance. Specifically it has rearranged my ignorance of what is and what is not a matter of religion. Though the large majority of those who left their mark on me were religious in that they professed and practised some nameable Faith, nothing in their behaviour suggested that there is, or ever could be, a secular area and a religious area, and that it would benefit me to move from one to the other as fast as possible. Yamada Mumon-roshi was as immediate shuffling off through his garden in his carpet slippers as he was preaching Buddhism.

Dr Abdin was not noticeably more engaged talking about Allah than she was tending a girl with rheumatic heart disease. Bishop Justinian was as attentive and composed sitting with a shy bus driver and letting him talk as he was, crowned, frail and awesome at the Liturgy. The Little Brothers of Jesus were as domestic about their Mass as about their meal times. The small ceremony with which Mr Lin on his Taiwanese farm handed us warm, fresh face towels was little different from the small ceremony with which he brought a present for an earth-god.

Some people seem to run a finger along every part of their day as others now and then run their finger along a banister. There seems to be an unbroken connection, an interdependency, a self-acceptance, a penetration, a repose, a stillness, a jubilance, a wakefulness that I can only experience in flickers for my attention moves off sideways, slides into words, images, persistencies, adhesiveness, idolatry.

Perhaps if I stopped talking. . . .

Film Acknowledgements

The Long Search series, in thirteen parts, was made by the B.B.C. TV Documentary Department for transmission on B.B.C. 2. I should like to thank Sir Huw Wheldon, then Managing Director, B.B.C. TV; Aubrey Singer, then Controller of B.B.C. 2; his predecessor, Robin Scott; and the Head of Documentary Programmes, Richard Cawston —all of whom stood by it through rough times.

Peter Montagnon produced the whole series and directed *330 Million Gods*, *Footprint of the Buddha*, *The Land of the Disappearing Buddha* and *Loose Ends*. Mischa Scorer was associate producer and directed *Protestant Spirit U.S.A.*, *There is no god but God*, *Rome, Leeds and the Desert* and *Zulu Zion*. Jonathan Stedall was associate producer and directed *The Romanian Solution*, *A Question of Balance* and *West meets East*. Malcolm Feuerstein was production assistant and directed *The Way of the Ancestors*. Brian Lewis directed *The Chosen People*. They pulled while I pushed, usually in the same direction.

Glorious camera work came from John Else in eight of the films, John McGlashen in three, Philip Bonham Carter and Jim Peirson in one each. Their assistants were Paul Godfrey, Tony Bragg, Pat Turley, Nigel Meakin, Warwick Stratton, Paul Houlston and Martin Patmore. Film sound was recorded with skill and much-tried but never-exhausted patience by Malcolm Webberley (assisted by John Hills-Harrop), Ron Brown and John Hore. There was a small battalion of lighting assistants, one for most of the journeys: Les Colwell, Joe Ryan, Des O'Brien, David Gorringe, Terry Black, John D. Taylor, Edwin Applegate, Ken Aylett, John Barrott.

David Thomas, the Chief Film Editor, cut nine of the thirteen films and—such was his appetite for work and his devotion to the whole project—regretted he could not cut all thirteen. He (and we all) had the cheerful support of Roland Armstrong. Alan Bradley (assisted by Phil Stillman) cut two of the remainder; John Needham (assisted by Ardan Fisher) and Mike Appelt (assisted by Christine Garner), one each. Mike Billing, Alan Dykes, Alan Abel and Ron Edmunds gave the films their final dub. Caroline Mackersey beavered away tirelessly and to great effect both at home and abroad as Research Assistant. Barbara Cannell and Vanessa Hardwicke, under the title of Producers' Assistants, were time-keepers, peace-keepers, continuity-girls and forward-planners wherever we went.

The Editorial Consultant was Professor Ninian Smart, and all the films drew on the knowledge and enthusiasm of many advisers, chief of whom were: Professor Shivesh Thakur, Pandit Vishnu dev Narayan, Professor Martin E. Marty, the Venerable Walpola Rahula, Dr Nandasena Ratnapala, Bishop B. Christopher Butler, Dr David Kerr, Dr Yahya Raef, Dr Nicholas Zernov, Dr Louis Jacobs, Father L. Gafton, Rabbi Dr Pinchas Peli, Dr Eric Crystal, Dr Harold Turner, Mr Peter Palinggi, Dr Carmen Blacker, Mr Trevor Leggett, Mr Michael Pye, Bishop Bengt Sundkler, Dr J. P. Kiernan, Dr Joseph Needham, Dr K. M. Schipper, Professor Theodore Roszak and Mr John Davy.

The opening title sequence was designed by Alan Jeapes and the *Long Search* theme music that began each episode and threaded its way through the tea-making that ended film 13, was composed and conducted by Carl Davis.

These, gratefully acknowledged, are just some of the people to whom *The Long Search* owes its existence.